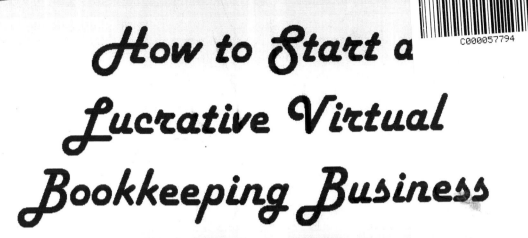

How to Start a Lucrative Virtual Bookkeeping Business

A Step-By-Step Guide to Working Less, And Making More in the Bookkeeping Industry

By E.T. Barton
and
Robin E. Davis

The Creators of the
OneHourBookkeeper.com

Other Products by E.T. Barton, Robin E. Davis or the
OneHourBookkeeper.com website:

THE ONE HOUR BOOKKEEPING METHOD:

How To Do Your Books In One Hour Or Less

HOW TO START A LUCRATIVE

VIRTUAL BOOKKEEPING BUSINESS:

A Step-by-Step Guide to Working Less and Making More

in the Bookkeeping Industry

HOW TO DO A YEAR'S WORTH

OF BOOKKEEPING IN ONE DAY

A Step-by-Step Guide for Small Businesses

10 WAYS TO SAVE MONEY ON

BOOKKEEPING & ACCOUNTING

DIARY OF A BAD, BAD BOOKKEEPER

A Cautionary Embezzlement Tale

for Small Business Owners Everywhere

To Get Your Free Copy of
**"The One Hour Bookkeeper's
Top 10 Strategies for Getting Bookkeeping Clients"**
Go to:

http://onehourbookkeeper.com/wp-content/uploads/2010/06/Top-10-Strategies-for-Attracting-Bookkeeping-Clients.pdf

Also, for your free Printable Bonuses (or to print/see this Book in Color) go to:

http://onehourbookkeeper.com/our-ebooks/thank-you-for-your-preorder/

and enter the password: bookkeepersrule.

We Would Like to Give a Special Thanks to the Business Professionals Who Contributed to this eBook, including:

Tina Gosnold, CB
Set Free Bookkeeping
Owner – Certified Bookkeeper
SetFreeBookkeeping.com

Lily E. Chambers, CPS, CQU
Owner and Operator at **The Virtual Office Goddess, LLC.**
Co-owner and Teacher at **The Academy of Virtual Education**
And Publisher of **The Virtual Evolution**
VirtualOfficeGoddess.com
AOVE.org/bookkeeping.html
TVEmagazine.com

Ross P. Allan Chapman
Ross P. Allan Chapman Bookkeeping
Owner
RossChapman.Name

Jason Rosen
Rosen Professional Services
Owner
www.RosPro.com

Elena Oppedisano
Checks & Balances Bookkeeping Services
Owner
ChecksAndBalancesLLC.com

Linda A. Hunt
SUMSOLUTIONS
Founder
www.SumSolutions.com

CP Morey, CPA
AuditMyBooks - Automated Detection of Errors & Fraud for Small Business
Vice President of Products
Accounting Systems
AuditMyBooks.com

Table of Contents

INTRODUCTION

Why Write a Book About Starting a Virtual Bookkeeping Business?

Believe it or not, the idea for this book was born in a bookkeeping forum. When I was surfing the bookkeeping groups on LinkedIn and socializing with all the like-minded professionals, I realized a lot of the same questions were being asked over and over again. Questions like – *Why did you go into business for yourself? How did you get clients? How much do you charge? What programs do you use? How do you get your clients to agree to become virtual clients*...and so on? Thus, after weeks of seeing these same questions again and again, the idea for this book was born.

My name is E.T. Barton and I am a firm believer in the concept, "Why make someone else rich when you can make yourself rich?" That's why I went into business for myself...

Okay, I'm lying. That's *not* why I went into business for myself. I went into business for myself because my last boss was a jerk with a capital J. He insulted me and put me down every day of the three months that I worked for him before I ran for the hills. The boss before that was no prize either. He was in his 80's and did not believe in equal pay for the sexes. He paid me a third of what he paid all the male associates, and then actually dared to come to me and start a conversation with "those poor sales guys – they hardly make any money at all." When I pointed out his hypocrisy, he got flustered and stuttered something inane about the men needing to support their families. And he had me there...I had no family at that time. But still, before I started working for him, he had two full-time bookkeepers. After a couple months with me, I had created systems to make the whole company run more smoothly, and condensed both positions into a single part-time bookkeeping job. Considering how much money I saved him, he should have paid me double.

The boss before him was the worst of all. He was an Israeli man who believed a good employee was a scared employee. Most of his workday was spent getting in everyone's personal space and "talking" in a very loud voice. He was an inconsiderate bully who would only leave everyone alone if I served him coffee in his office every hour, on the hour. Since it was the only way for anyone to get their jobs done, I did it – and I shall forever maintain that his coffee was served "untampered-with." ☺ When I quit, I took great pleasure in telling him where he could stick his job.

Therefore, to say that I started my business simply because I was tired of making everyone else rich instead of myself is only a small part of the impetus that got me out of my rut. The true impetus was a string of bad bosses, the birth of my first child, and the desire to live a life with less stress. The benefit was making more money, working less, only having to serve myself coffee and working for a boss I actually liked – ME! The fact that I never had to be spoken to like an employee again, that I got to avoid office politics, and that I could come and go as I pleased was merely icing on my cupcakes.

A WHOLE NEW LIFE

If you're reading this book, then obviously you're interested in striking out on your own in the bookkeeping world. Maybe you have some experience and are looking for ideas to expand your business; maybe you're brand new to running your own company. Either way, the one thing you can count on when you start your own business is this: **you are about to get a whole new life**. Forget the 9-to-5. Forget being treated like crap. Forget being micro-managed and stressed as a result. From now on, no one tells you what to do with your days except you. Sounds freeing, doesn't it? *It is and it isn't.*

But, you've picked up the right book.

You see, this book is not just about how to start your own bookkeeping business. It's about changing your lifestyle. It's about forgetting everything you were ever taught about working hard and making money. It's about creating a new life, a new job...and then *running it into the ground.* ☺

Just kidding on that last part.

E.T., can't you be serious for even one minute?

Oh. Hey, Mom. What are you doing here?

I'm here to keep you in check. Bookkeeping is not just fun and games; it's a serious business, and I want to make sure you convey that to our readers.

(If I could roll my eyes, this is where I would do so! ☺) Still...no one said bookkeeping has to be boring!

That's my mom, by the way.   Robin E. Davis...Bookkeeper Extraordinaire. She's been in bookkeeping since the days that accountants used abacuses.

Hey, watch it. You're not too old to ground you know! And besides...the plural of abacus is abaci.

Actually, the plural of abacus is...*never mind*. Let's just get on with today's lesson, shall we? So once more...from the beginning.

"Hi. I'm E.T. Barton, and I blog with my *Mommy*...Robin E. Davis, Bookkeeper Extraordinaire."

Together, we make up the Bookkeeping Blog:
www.OneHourBookkeeper.com

Now to get back to what I was saying, here are some of the benefits you can look forward to when you strike out on your own:

- **Less Stress and Office Drama**: There will be no one but you in your office. When you visit other offices, you don't have to stay. You can leave when someone upsets you. And the only bickering you're going to experience is whatever drama is happening in your favorite soap operas, or on your favorite daytime talk shows. (Well, actually...you may still see office politics, but you'll be blissfully out of the storm.)

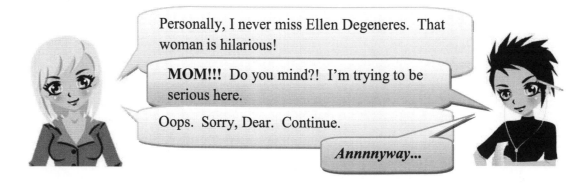

> Personally, I never miss Ellen Degeneres. That woman is hilarious!
>
> **MOM!!!** Do you mind?! I'm trying to be serious here.
>
> Oops. Sorry, Dear. Continue.
>
> *Annnnyway...*

- **More Money**: Whether or not making more money is your goal, becoming a small business owner comes hand-in-hand with a higher income, even if you charge the same hourly rate as working for someone else. The simple reason is that you will only be paying your income taxes at the end of the year, and with all the benefits of being a business owner (aka, business deductions like mileage, your home office, part of your utilities, your computer, etc.), you will get to keep more of that money than ever before.

- **More Me-Time**: Whether or not you want "Me-Time," you're about to get it. Even if you have a family, they will continue their daily obligations while you build this business. That means you'll hopefully be working from a quiet home. You'll get to sleep in when you want, then approach your business feeling relaxed and well-rested. You can do your work anytime of the day or night, and even better, you can work during the time of day you are most productive.

You can also decide how long or short your workday will be. If you want to work a 10 or 12-hour day and take the next day or two off, you can!

Personally, I do my best work from 10 **AM** on.

...While my mind is sharpest after 10 **PM** and sluggish in the mornings. Thus, I do most of my work after my family has gone to bed.

When is your mind sharpest? Because whenever your mind is sharpest, that's when you should do the majority of your work.

- **More Time for Your Family and Friends**: The best part about being your own business owner is that *you* schedule your time. No longer will you have to miss out on your kids growing up, or the fun activities going on in their lives. You can have lunch with your husband on a Wednesday or go shopping with your friends on a Monday morning. You never have to miss an important event ever again because you get to work when you want to work.

Your Goal Should Be – "Make More BUT Work Less"

I can guess what you're thinking...*"This is all good and well, but I just want to make more money. I want security. I want to be happy."*

And if you're *not* thinking that – you should be. Especially the part about happiness.

Like I said before, this book is not just about making money. It's about designing a lifestyle. It's about designing *your* lifestyle. And guess what the biggest obstacle to building your new life is going to be... It's *NOT* going to be "how do I get customers." It's *NOT* going to be "how do I get paid."

The biggest obstacle you will face is yourself...your own belief that you should be working the 9-to-5 for a full 40 hours a week. The biggest obstacle will be that sometimes you'll feel lazy, or like you're not working hard enough. Sometimes, you may even feel like your partner is working harder than you and you're not pulling your own weight. This obstacle will be the biggest stress in your life, and it will make you consider quitting – I guarantee it.

If you're going to be successful in this business, you're going to have to readjust your thinking. You're going to have to ditch the whole 9-to-5 idea and cling-like-saran-wrap to your new goal.

"What is my new goal?" you ask. Easy...it's four-fold.

- Your new goal is to: ***<u>Make More Money But Work Less</u>***
- Your new goal is to: ***<u>Live the Life You've Always Dreamed of</u>***
- Your new goal is to: ***<u>Work to Live – NOT Live to Work</u>***
- Your new goal is to: ***<u>Be the Person You Were Meant to Be – Not who Someone Else Wants You to be</u>***

And when I say someone else, I don't just mean your boss...I mean anyone in your life who wants you to be someone you're not.

...Including the spouse you adore, a disapproving parent who can't envision income beyond a "regular paycheck," or that still small inner voice that says maybe you should just find a job instead of finding a new client.

When you can master these four simple concepts and ingrain them into your psyche, then you'll be able to do this business for a very long time. But if you can't turn these concepts into your life's mantra, then this book will be a waste of your time. Sure, you will gain clients and make money, but the guilt of not doing the 9-to-5 and working 40 hours a week every week will soon drive you back into someone else's employ. Or, if that doesn't make you quit your own business, then a crisis in confidence might. In fact, in my opinion, you should schedule your work for four days a week and take 3-day weekends every weekend.

Thus, having said that and believing you're still with me...let's get on with your new lifestyle.

Chapter 1

Step 1: Getting Into the Independent Bookkeeper's Mindset

SPOTLIGHT ON A BOOKKEEPING BUSINESS – Set Free Bookkeeping

When it came to launching my bookkeeping business, I have been my own worst enemy. Lack of confidence and fear of failure were paralyzing forces for many years.

Rather than finding clients, I was side-tracked with a myriad of excuses and side projects disguised as preparations for my business.

Being prepared is great, but I had to be real with myself. I was procrastinating because I was afraid. Everything came down to one question. "Are you going to do this or not?"

You are not going to know everything beforehand. You are not going to be absolutely 100% prepared for everything. You just need to jump in with both feet and handle the issues as they arise. Ignore your fear. Pretend to be confident and forget that you are not.

The confidence came with my first client, a business owner who had fallen behind with his bookkeeping. I was contracted to do catch-up data entry. I discovered several errors in the way he was accounting for things. I knew different ways of processing his data that cut several steps, making the work easier and faster. Upon completion, I pointed out the errors, letting him know that I did not want to make changes without his consent. I showed him the faster and easier ways of processing. Knowing the average monthly hours required, I was able to offer a flat monthly fee for my ongoing services, so he would never get behind or have to think of bookkeeping again. He accepted my offer. Wow! I was really able to help!

You know what they say, "Just do it!"

Set Free Bookkeeping
(Seattle Area)
Tina Gosnold, CB
Owner – Certified Bookkeeper
SetFreeBookkeeping.com
LinkedIn: Linkedin.com/in/tinagosnoldcb
Twitter: Twitter.com/tinagosnoldcb
Facebook: Facebook.com/SetFreeBookkeeping

If you already know – without a doubt – that you want to be an Independent Bookkeeper or a Virtual Bookkeeper, and your friends and family are 100% behind you, then skip this chapter and go to Chapter 2. This chapter deals with a day in the life of an Independent Bookkeeper, the doubts you may have about opening your own business, and getting your friends and family to support your decision. It's all about the logic in being your own business owner, the changes you can expect, and scripts you can utilize. Thus, if you have no doubts or blockades to changing your life, then this chapter will be of no use to you whatsoever. But, if you aren't quite there yet, or those you love are against you striking out on your own, then this chapter will hopefully change all that. It is the one good deed I can do to hopefully make an impact in someone's life. So, if you need a little bit more convincing or help, read on. If not...see you in Chapter 2.

ARE YOU REALLY READY?

The hardest decision you will ever make regarding your career is the day you decide to start your own business. You will probably spend countless hours and sleepless nights debating if this is the right decision. You'll think about the boss you have right now and whether you could or should hang in there any longer. You'll think about the bosses you've had in the past, and everything you loved and hated about those jobs. You'll remember the office politics and the romantic dramas, the windowless offices and how much you missed being out in the sun. You may even daydream of the days you worked the no-brainer jobs, where you didn't have to think at all, you just worked. You'll long for independence as much as you fear it.

Next, you'll think about your family, whether you're single, married, or have kids. If you're single, you'll worry what your brothers, sister, or parents might say. After all, they're probably going to think you're crazy for "risking everything" to start your own business. If you're married, you'll worry about the strain having your own business might put on your marriage and finances. If you have kids, you'll worry about all the things you'll miss with them, like soccer games and school plays. You'll wonder if they'll hate you for not being around. Maybe you'll lose their college funds or your nest egg. After all, you're not just risking your future; you're risking your family's future as well. And then you'll think, *"Maybe working for someone else is better. It's safer and easier. Everyone will be happier, including me."*

The truth is, **every doubt going through your head is *complete bullshit*!**

That's right...I said ***bullshit!*** But before you put this book aside, be aware, that is the strongest language I use in this entire book and I do it for a reason. I'm doing it because I want you to realize that the F.E.A.R. you're feeling (while natural) stands for False Evidence Appearing Real. That's right, I'm saying your fears are based on a lie.

As much as I love being an American, and would _never_ wish to be anything but American, I have serious doubts about what our culture teaches us from the day we enter kindergarten. Every day of our lives, we learn that having a degree is absolutely mandatory to be successful; that only the most brilliant minds become rich and powerful; that businesses are ran by fearless people who have all their ducks in a row before they start. We are taught that we are meant to do one job for the rest of our lives, and it's our responsibility to find out what that one job is. We learn that a person needs to have thousands – and even hundreds of thousands – of dollars in the bank before we can make a leap into the world of running our own business. And if we don't have those ducks in a row (...or eggs in a basket), then we're better off working for someone else for the rest of our lives. By doing so, we'll one day retire with a pension, a pretty gold watch, and *hopefully* a handful of social security checks.

Are you irritated yet? If you are, *good*. My intention is to shake up your thinking – to get your mind out of your own head. Because the truth is, the more you think about starting your own business, the more you'll talk yourself out of it.

Yes – we're in a recession.

Yes – businesses are closing all over this country and people are getting laid off left and right.

Yes – the current national unemployment rate is 10.2% at the time of this book's publication (*Source: U.S. Bureau of Labor Statistics - Updated April 21, 2010*), which is the highest unemployment rate in the last 20 years.

Of course, these are all valid excuses for staying at the job you've been at for...however long you've been there. But none of these *excuses* are valid *reasons* for **not** starting your own Virtual Bookkeeping Business.

Here are the real facts – why you NEED to open your own business:

With 10.2% of people unemployed, competition for any job is fiercer than ever before – including bookkeeping. BUT with the recession, business owners are looking to save money in any area they can possibly save (thus the layoffs – they're getting rid of the people who aren't helping create profits). Hiring a part-time independent bookkeeper who can do the work quickly will actually save them more money than paying a full-time data entry associate minimum wage – especially if that independent bookkeeper can do the books virtually, without having to supply a computer or utilize any of the business's overhead.

According to the SBA Office of Advocacy's "Frequently Asked Questions" report, there were 29.6 million businesses in the United States in 2008, approximately 21.7 million of which were small businesses without employees (in 2007). Furthermore, when you subtract the number of closed businesses from the number of new businesses, approximately 30,000 new businesses were added to the 29.6 million tally in 2008 – that's 30,000 more businesses opening than closing. This means that while people may be getting laid off, new companies are starting every single day...*and they're going to need bookkeepers*.

They're going to need YOU!

So now that the fear of no available bookkeeping jobs has been put to rest, or that no one will need your services, let's put some other fears to rest.

- **Money**: "*I probably won't make enough money to support myself for at least two years – the average time it takes a small business to become profitable.*"...You will make *more money* running your own bookkeeping business than you will working for someone else.

In fact, you can actually make double or triple your current salary, especially since all of the money you receive will be <u>untaxed at the time you receive it</u>. Then, at the end of the year, you get to file as "Self Employed," thus taking all of the deductions that come with it

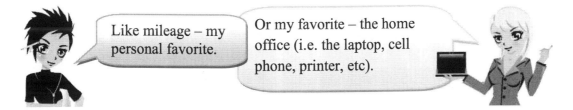

Like mileage – my personal favorite.

Or my favorite – the home office (i.e. the laptop, cell phone, printer, etc).

More than likely, when you file your taxes, you will have to pay very little for the first couple years (especially if you're married), and your new business will get a refund of all the taxes your spouse paid during the year. As far as making a profit right away...this is a service business. That means you will have very little expenses, and most of the money you make will be sheer profit. Plus, if you get tons of clients and hire an assistant at the rate you are making now, you will make even more money for doing nothing but training someone else.

- **Time**: *"If I'm running my own business, I won't have a lot of time for family or friends because I'll be working 80 hour weeks."*...Wrong again. Consider this: if you're making more money per hour, you can work less hours and make the same amount of money you would make working for someone else. Thus, instead of doing 40 hours a week making $15 an hour, you can charge $30 an hour and work 20 hours and actually make *more money*. For the former, your take home pay would be about $420 a week after you pay 30% in taxes. For the latter, your pay would be $600 even, and all of your business deductions will help you keep a lot more of that money every week. Thus, time will become something to fill instead of something you don't have enough of, and you will be able to spend as much time as you want doing whatever you like to do, with whomever you want to spend it.

- **Security**: *"If I start my own business and fail, I won't be able to get my old job back. I'll be unemployed, and it will be even harder to find a new job."*...Think about this: how much do you really like your current job if you're thinking about striking out on your own? Do you really want to spend the rest of your life working for the person you're working for and sitting in the office you sit in every day? Even if your answer is yes, some part of you is longing for more, otherwise you wouldn't have picked up this book. Here's a real fact – bookkeeping jobs are a dime a dozen. You can find them everywhere because every business needs bookkeeping. If you love your boss now, make them a client. If you don't love your boss...**Bounce** *(*which is Gen X slang for "Quit Now! You can do better!"). You see, you can always find a new person to boss you around later, because another truth is, when you put "Business Owner" on your resume, you become a more desirable employee than any other applicants; you have an understanding of what it takes to run a business. The only true risk you make starting your own bookkeeping business is the money you spend to get your office equipment and advertise, as well as your current job position.

- **Lack of Education**: *"Nobody will hire me...I don't have a degree in accounting."* Here's the thing – people that get degrees in accounting...go on to become *accountants*. Bookkeepers are usually created when they begin an office job, and the boss pushes the work onto their desk with a *"you can handle this, right?"* type of introduction. This has a double-edged sword effect. On the bookkeeper's side, they get a basic understanding of bookkeeping, but they lack the confidence that they're actually doing the right steps, which can be carried over to any other type of business (unless they trained under someone else). On the business owner's side, they believe any idiot off the street can do bookkeeping. Thus, business owners will come to believe that "A Bookkeeping Education = A Very Expensive Bookkeeper." My point here is – small business owners (aka, your ideal clients) will most likely *NOT* bother asking if you have a degree. The fact that you run your own business is often enough to make them believe that you know what you're doing. If you want to get more education, feel free...but most likely, if you know how to use QuickBooks, you already know everything you need to know in order to run a large variety of businesses. And sadly, another truth is that any extended education you get is going to be more about accounting principles (like depreciation, amortization, fiscal statements, taxes, etc.) and less about data entry, which is what you would be doing on a daily basis. It would be far better for you if you would just pass that work on to the business's accountant and let the accountant deal with the IRS.

- **What Will People Think**: *"What if I fail? People will know and they will make fun of me for it. They will never support me in this, and I'm going to need support."*...What if you don't fail? What if you become super successful? What if you make more money then you've ever made before but work less? What if you end up living the ideal lifestyle and they began to *envy you*? And what if they end up being proud of you because you were able to build up something from nothing? There's really nothing I can say that will get you over this fear. Kicking this fear to the curb is all about turning those negatives into positives, and it's something you'll have to work out by yourself. But, if you're worried what your friends and family will think, or that they won't support you, then read the section later in this chapter entitled "Convincing Your Friends and Family that this Really <u>is</u> the Best Decision for You." In it, I go over many of the objections they may have, as well as what you can say to sway them to your side.

A DAY IN THE LIFE OF AN INDEPENDENT BOOKKEEPER

If you're thinking this is going to be the hardest job you've ever had, you may be right, or you may not. No matter what services you offer, your day as a Small Business Owner will definitely be different then when you work at one company for one boss. For starters, you get to say when and where you work. For another, you will probably be doing the majority of your work outside the usual 9-to-5. (*That is largely because you will need the 9-to-5 period to meet with clients, make phone calls, advertise, etc.*) And finally – my favorite – you will no longer have to accept being treated like crap just because a Business Owner wants to be a jerk. *You don't need that Business Owner anymore; you can drop them and find a new client.* <u>You deserve better.</u>

You'll begin your day by rolling out of bed and stumbling for your coffee pot. (Or tea, or cocoa, or a fruit smoothie – whatever your "Wake Up Juice" is...for now, let's just say your poison is coffee.) You will stand there, bleary-eyed and weary, watching the dark brown liquid drip into the glass carafe while your mind wonders to the day ahead of you. *Should I go back to bed? Should I take a shower? Should I turn on my TV and wait until my mind is fully awake before I turn on my computer and get to work? Do I have a client I have to meet this morning? Or should I just "Eat the Frog" so to speak* (...a really good book about procrastination, by the way...) *and get to work?*

As you pull the coffee pot from its heating plate and pour the liquid life into your "Office Goddess" mug (or "Office Stud" for guys), you will think about your friends and family and what's on their agenda today. *Will I have time to meet up with them later for drinks (or soccer)? What time will dinner be; will I make it? How mad will they be if I blow them off because I'm going to be tired* – again?

As you stir your cream and sugar with your spoon, you will think about the exact height of the pile of paperwork on your desk that still needs to be entered, and all the business owners who are expecting you to call them "sometime today." *Should I do that data entry before heading out, or just leave it for tonight? When exactly is that paperwork due again? Was it Thursday or Friday?*

And then you'll inhale the thick, full scent of your coffee and like a snap of the fingers – you're awake.

"Definitely shower first," you'll decide. And you'll head to your bathroom, coffee in hand, to turn the water on and let it warm up.

While you're showering, you'll think of all the "Office Politics *Crapola*" that goes with whichever business owner you're supposed to talk to (or meet with) that day. You'll think of the last conversation you two had, and whether their business is floating or flailing. *(Of course, you're not worried about your business...you're a service business that brings in more money than you spend, so you're business is golden.)*

And then you'll think longingly of your TV again? *Maybe I should just catch the 'Price Is Right' before I get to work...or maybe I should finish that book I was reading last night. Or how about I just call my clients today and say I'm sick. I can always do my work tomorrow. Or this weekend; I don't really have any plans this weekend.*

But then you'll remember you did that last week, and you really need to "catch up" this week.

You see, as crazy as this may sound, the truth is, you have a weakness. I don't know what you're weakness is – whether it's books, television, or playing games on Facebook until your eyes cross – but as an Independent Bookkeeper, that weakness will be constantly there, at the back of your mind, calling you away from what you *should* be doing. But I do know this – the best thing you can do is: *get the hell out of your house as fast as you can, and then decide what to do that day while you're driving down the road with your head hanging out the window like an ecstatic puppy.* In fact, you may even want to make it a ritual to keep the coffee out of the house so that you have an excuse to swing by Starbucks where you can check your email while sipping your cup of way-too-expensive Joe.

Anyway, the rest of your day will be spent driving from one customer to another, doing data entry, and dealing with everyone else's "emergencies." Your first client will yell at you for not paying a bill (*a bill he happened to tell you **not** to pay – not that he remembers it that way*), and you'll get angry and frustrated and long to tell him where to *Stick it...*But then you'll bite your tongue, put your head down and get back to work so you can get out of there as fast as you possibly can. Your cell phone will be ringing off the hook with calls from other clients and their vendors (or employees or customers) as you do your data entry, and you'll find yourself returning their calls while you drive to the next location. One of those messages will be from your accountant, who will tell you very calmly that "Client Deadbeat" called *them* to complain about you and to try and get the accountant to "fire" you (not that they could or would), and you'll have to explain that "Client Deadbeat" is just a bitter pain-in-the-keester who owes you money, but doesn't want to pay. Since they don't want to pay, they want to make sure they never have to see you again.

Of course, the accountant will understand and reiterate that they were just "letting you know."

You'll go through the drive-thru for your usual "Spare Tire to Go" Burger and "Right to the Hips" Fries, along with an extra-large "Jolt of Sugary Caffeine" Coke. You'll quickly scarf this all down whenever you come to a stoplight, and then finish off the rest in the next client's parking lot. The trash will go into the backseat with the other discarded wrappers, and you'll remind yourself that you'll clean your car out "this weekend."

At the next client's office, the client will accuse you of not doing your job right because there's no money in their bank account. You'll calmly remind them that you're job is to pay who they tell you to pay, and that the only thing you have to do with the bank account is to reflect the balance back to them and print checks; they're the ones that sign the checks, even when you advise them against it. They'll drop the subject but be huffy about it, which will make you uncomfortable. Still, you'll put your head down and work as fast as you can to get the heck out of there. When the owner's out of the office, you'll check your email covertly, trying to send off quick responses to other client's who didn't get you immediately on the phone, or reminders to those clients who haven't paid you yet. You'll also shoot off quick texts (while the checks, invoices and company reports are printing) to those who text you because they "can't wait." You'll end up working late, just to make sure you get everything done, and then you'll head home – oddly worn out – where you'll have to listen to your family's problems while you covertly massage the stress knots out of your neck.

But on the bright side – you'll never get stuck in traffic.

Now before you email me screaming how wrong I am and how you love bookkeeping so this could never happen *to you*, keep in mind...*this is the worst case scenario*. I am defining the most horrific day possible that you will have so that you won't be surprised when these days happen (because days like this *will* happen). Therefore, if this sounds like a day you can handle, then you're ready. You'll be able to handle being an independent bookkeeper and eventually a virtual bookkeeper, because most of your days will actually consist of warm conversations with some clients, and being told "You're brilliant!" by others (and their accountants). And most days, you'll be so thankful that you don't have to work for a jerk, you won't even mind days like the one I just described.

Who Your Clients Will Be

Whatever you think you know about your future clients – *forget it*. The people you work with are not going to be what you expect at all. I know; I've been there. When I became an independent bookkeeper, I expected that most of my clients would be savvy business professionals who knew about money and accounting. They would understand me when I used terminology like "Fiscal Year" or "Balance Sheet." They would nod and accept my verdict when I said things like, "*You can't afford that – you have no money in your account.*" But that was not the case.

The truth is, most Independent Bookkeepers will go into this business believing their clients are going to be highly-educated and professional...after all, that's what our culture teaches. We expect that everyone will be as honorable as we are, and we are flummoxed when they are not.

Here's what you'll really find when you become an Independent Bookkeeper. Depending on where you're located, most of the business owners you work with will probably NOT have a College Degree. In fact, the majority of people you work with will probably have started their business because of necessity or circumstance – just like you. Either the job they had before "taking the leap into the entrepreneurial pool" wasn't working out, they got laid off, they got fed up with the status quo, or they just *knew* they could do a better job than whoever else was in the market. They opened their doors and immediately started seeing some money coming in – which gave them hope. Then they got into a rhythm doing their day-to-day. They spent more and more time away from their office, and their paperwork piled higher and higher. They didn't start their business thinking about bookkeeping (unless they were in the bookkeeping industry, of course); they got into their business to fulfill a need. Their natural talent does not lie in the number-crunching field – and that's why they will turn to you. Because that is your talent (even if it's not your passion).

How Small Business Owners Will Treat You

If you are going out on your own, one thing you can expect is to be treated differently then when you were an employee. For one thing, the business owners will believe that you can get clients anywhere, and that you don't need them...but *they* need *you*. Even if you need them desperately – maybe they're your only client, or you make more money from them than anyone else – don't let them know that. Because the minute they believe you need them more than they need you is the minute they will start abusing that knowledge and then you. They will become demanding and unreasonable; they will make accusations that will dumbfound you. Because the sad truth is, dealing with money is stressful, and you are the messenger who is going to tell them that they either have it or they don't.

So, as long as they believe they need you more than you need them, they will be friendly and open. They will want to talk to you just to talk – sometimes about business and sometimes not. They will probably be *so* talkative and friendly, you won't be able to get much work done in their office. Since they may not have degrees (and if you don't as well), they will feel like the two of you are on equal ground. They may still talk down to you a bit, and occasionally throw out an order here or there, but their attitude will still be completely opposite from what you're used to.

CONVINCING YOUR FRIENDS AND FAMILY THAT THIS REALLY IS THE BEST DECISION FOR YOU

Most likely, when you first start your business, your friends and family won't understand. Maybe they'll be supportive, maybe they won't. Either way, you are about to get an opinion-storm directed right at your head. You are going to get advice you never asked for, and hear comments that border on innocently-insulting. But no matter what they say, keep the faith. You can do this. In fact, here is what you can expect from each:

Your Family:

When a person becomes a Mary Kay Consultant for the first time, the very first part of their training involves dealing with family members. The new consultant is immediately told, "*Your family probably won't understand, and they probably won't be supportive.*" As harsh as this may sound, I always found the advice to be fairly accurate. You see, your family has a preconceived notion about who you are. They've seen you fail as often as they've seen you succeed. The result is that they often believe they know what's best for you based on their history with you. The analysis of that history can be skewed since it's based on an accumulation of decades of events, and not necessarily how you've "improved with age." So when you tell your family, "I'm going into business for myself," the first thing they'll do is remember the time you went to Vegas and blew all your money on one hand of poker. Or maybe they'll think about the time you were going to sell candles from your home but instead ended up with a 10-year supply of oddly shaped wax sculptures and a home that still smells like vanilla and jasmine wax.

They'll consider your track record, and then they'll decide you'd be safer working for someone else. After all, it's harder to fail at a "job" then it is a business. A "job" is safe; a business is risky.

There are other reasons that a family might not be supportive, but I think it's best to believe that your family wants what they think is best for you instead of getting angry about any history that may exist between you. That is why in Mary Kay, the new consultant is first taught that their family won't be supportive, and then taught to ignore their families. A Mary Kay recruiter will say to a new recruit:

"Imagine yourself inside of a bubble of positive thoughts with your family on the outside. Whatever they say to you, remain oblivious. Don't let their negative comments pierce the bubble."

This may sound ridiculous, but there is a lesson here. The simple lesson is that we can choose to let people's comments get inside our minds and plant weed-seeds, or we can block them and choose to press on nonetheless.

Another expression I've heard to describe it is, "Don't give someone free rent inside your head." The more you worry about what they're going to say or think of you, the more free rent they're getting. In other words, you're spending all of your energy being stressed about what someone else's judgments are instead of spending your energy enjoying life. Forget what they think and get on with making a lifestyle for yourself. Once you're a success, they'll tell you how much they've always believed in you, and that they knew you could do it. (Okay – not everyone will say this, but many will.)

What I'm really trying to say here is – there's no real way to convince your family that this is the best option for you. They'll either be supportive or they won't, and you're just going to have to prove you can do this.

Your Kids:

These are my lil' hatchlings...see the family resemblance? No? Ok, I'll admit it – they look more like my Mom. (*This was taken on a Tuesday, by the way – at the zoo. That was a good "Hooky From Work" day*.)

If you don't have kids, obviously, you can skip to the next subheading. But if you do have kids, and you worry about how your new business will affect them, then you need to "*think about your kids*." Think about all the events in their lives that you miss right now because you have to work the 9-to-5 (like PTA meetings, class field trips, etc.). Think about how tired you are after your current day job, how stressed, and then having to find the energy to smile and pay your kids even a little bit of attention. Think about what you miss when they get home after school, who they're hanging out with, what they're eating before dinner, and what's going on in their lives. Think about the "stranger" that is raising them, whether the nanny, the teacher, the day care worker, or even the television. Now think about this - do you really know what's going on in their lives right now, or are you often too tired and too drained to put your best foot forward when you need to relate to them? Does the majority of your interaction with them involve a dinner table? (Have I gone too far yet? Because I am trying to drive home a point...)

The best thing about being your own business owner is that you get to schedule your time. You get to *tell* your clients when you're coming and when you're not, and they'll be happy to get you whenever they can.

Again...*you* get to decide the timeframe for your work and your play. You can be there when your kids get home and make sure they eat what they should be eating. You can help them with their homework, and go to all their soccer games and school plays. You can be a chaperone for their field trips or dances. And then you can do your work after they've gone to bed or while they're at school. You can even schedule in a massage so that when it's time to deal with your kids, you're relaxed, happy and ready to listen to them chatter for hours without feeling exhausted. Heck, you can even hire them as your subcontractors and pay them for doing photocopying or filing so they can make money too. Being your own boss means you can be a better parent...and your kids will love you for it (unless their teenagers, of course...there's NO pleasing *them* ☺).

And when it comes to convincing your kids, you don't really need to. They will believe in you no matter what. Just keep them in the loop on what's happening in your life, and you will be amazed to see your kids become your biggest support system.

Your Spouse:

Sometimes, the Spouse can be the hardest sell-job of all. They may view your decision to go freelance as "gambling your nest egg." Small businesses can be risky, and they can take a while to build. To them, your new business means that they are going to have to work harder until you succeed or fail. It could mean no health insurance (if you are the one to carry it with your "job"); it could mean less money for the two of you to spend – especially when you have to invest money to stock your business. It could mean less time together because you're going to have to bust your butt to get clients, and maybe that will negatively affect your marriage. Or, once you do get started, they may see you "sitting at home doing nothing" because your day is going to be different than theirs, and they won't understand your daily to-do list at all, which could result in more arguing. And time for romance...when is that going to happen?

These are just a few of the concerns your spouse is going to have, and they are generally the largest objections. Any objections stronger or more vehement than these (like "I forbid it" or "I'm putting my foot down") may indicate a problem in your relationship that needs a bit more work, but that is something you are going to have to deal with when the time comes. You are going to have to weigh it against your overall desire for a happier career versus a desire for a happier marriage. But – I'm not a marriage counselor, so let's get back to the sell-job.

When it comes to balancing your spouse and your job, it's much like balancing your kids and your job. You are the master of your own schedule and you get to decide when you'll spend time together. You'll be working fewer hours but making more money, so you'll be able to have more adventures and material objects then if you work for someone else. You'll be able to pick and choose who your clients are – and are *not* – so you won't have the stress that comes with working for a jerk. There will be a whole lot less office politics, so your whole day in general will just be more relaxed. And once *you're* happy, it's easier to make *them* happy.

As far as health insurance goes...using your insurance for job-stress-related illnesses (like ulcers, migraines, eye strain, backaches, carpal tunnel, depression, etc.) is a whole lot more expensive than just paying for insurance yourself. In fact, if you were to talk to the insurance company that covers your car, you will most likely find they have many affordable health insurance plans. And just like when adding another car or a house to your plan saves money on both policies, adding health insurance can actually discount your car insurance at many insurance agencies. In many cases, you can find cheaper insurance on your own then you can get from an employer – so don't let insurance (or lack thereof) keep you from going after what you want.

Also, you can always try insurance alternatives, like going to clinics instead of doctor's offices, or asking for discounts on your bill when you pay your doctor with cash. Instead of going to Emergency Rooms, you can save money by finding "Urgent Care" centers in your area. Finally, you can get discounts at pharmacies by signing up for their loyalty cards, buying generic prescriptions instead of name brands, and getting discount cards (like the Pharma Card) which will get you even bigger discounts on your drugs.

Back to the Spouse...when convincing your spouse that this is the best thing for you, it's not going to be as hard as you think. All you need is a few tricks up your sleeves and a willingness to allay any fears they have – because they probably will have a few, like I pointed out above. But, here are the tricks you need to convince them that your way is the best way.

Trick # 1: The Subliminal Attack

To get your spouse on board with your change in career, you are going to have to get inside their heads and convince

I say "Trick" in the most loving sense of the word, of course...oh, and "Attack" too. ☺

them that *your* way is the *best* way. To do this, all you have to do when talking to your spouse is *smile and nod a lot.*

I know – "*Smile and nod a lot? Are you crazy?*"

No, I'm not crazy.

If you "smile and nod a lot," you send a subliminal message to your spouse that this conversation is a good and open conversation. The smiling tells them that you are in a friendly state of mind and you are willing to listen. But nodding – that's the sneaky part. It is a positive reinforcement that rewards them for doing what you want – much like giving a child a lollipop after they visit the dentist. It makes the whole interaction feel positive. Nodding is a positive reinforcement because it delivers a feeling of approval, and everyone wants approval whether consciously or subconsciously. Nodding says, "*I like where you're going with this...keep going.*"

On the flip side, frowning and shaking your head is a negative reinforcement that tells the person, "*No – you're going the wrong way. Rethink what you're saying or doing and do it my way so I can approve of you.*" It's called Behavior Modification, and it is an actual science that you can use to change someone without them ever knowing what you're doing.

Like I said – it's sneaky. In fact, when I was in college, I used this tactic to change my awful boss's behavior – the Israeli tyrant. My boss was a sexist dictator from a culture where men liked to raise their voice in order to make a point and stand way too close in order to intimidate. My boss was constantly stomping up and down our hallways, yelling and distracting people from their work, getting in their personal space, and just scaring the crap out of everyone. After two months of behavior modification along with a few negative and positive reinforcements, I turned him into a much better boss. He stayed in his office and stopped raising his voice. He began using his intercom to talk to the other employees, and everyone became much more productive...all because I used the "Smile and Nod" / "Frown and Shake Your Head" tricks, along with a few other reinforcers. So when I say this will work, I'm saying this from experience. *Why not give it a shot?*

Once you begin using these tools, you will know they're working when your spouse starts nodding right along with you. That says they are beginning to come around.

Trick # 2: Get Them to Say the Word "Yes"

One of the secrets Mary Kay uses to sell people on becoming a beauty consultant is to get them to say or think the word "Yes." They do this by asking a series of questions where the only logical answer is "Yes." For example, "Do you want to make more money? Do you want to have fun? Do you want to be able to work less hours?"

Can you see how these questions would apply to your own life? Did you just say "Yes" again? ☺ Can you see where I'm going with this? ☺

The more a person says "Yes", the more they're going to believe that the final answer should be "Yes." Because logically, a "Yes" is a Pro while a "No" is a Con. People want to believe that there are more Pros than Cons when making *any* decision.

Therefore, when you're talking to your spouse, you want them to say "Yes" to you as many times as possible. It is a definite answer that can be tallied and thus sway them to your side. To do this, stick to the positive questions. For example, when you talk about money – which is usually the biggest objection – you want to ask questions that will bring out a positive answer like, "Don't you want me to earn more money?" You do NOT want to ask, "Do you want us to stay broke?" The first question has a fast, *no-need-to-think-about-it* answer – *"Yes, I want you to earn more money."* The second question will make the person give a "No-But" answer – "No, but I don't want us to lose money either" – and you don't want that. A "No-But" answer means that they have just added a point to the Con-side of the argument, and now they're going to come back with a rebuttal to nail that Con home. Don't give them that chance. Keep the conversation firmly on the Pro-side and get the hard, fast agreements that only a "Yes" will bring.

Here are some more examples: (Positive) "Do you want me to be *happy*?" *Yes.* (Negative) "Do you want me to be *unhappy*?" *No.*

(Positive) "Do you want to spend *more* time with me?" *Yes.* (Negative) "Do you want to spend *less* time with me?" *No.*

The only time you really want your spouse to say "No" is in regards to keeping things the same. For example, "I'm unhappy at my job. Do you want me to stay unhappy?" That creates negative responses against the object you want destroyed – your old job.

So again – the more you get your spouse to say "No", the more their final answer will be "No." So stick to "Yes" as much as possible, and try to keep the conversation positive.

Trick # 3: Validate Their Fears and You Validate Them

One of the biggest fears people have – one they rarely speak of – is the fear of being unimportant. Everyone wants to feel important whether they admit it or not. They want to feel intelligent, respected, and needed. They want people to talk to them and actually listen to what they have to say...even people who are uber-shy. Maybe the person gets this need across by raising their voice and yelling. Maybe they write carefully worded notes. Maybe they give the cold shoulder or raise a single eyebrow, which clearly expresses their disapproval. Maybe they keep a diary where they admit their dark and dirty feelings. Maybe they blog, go to Facebook, or spend hours chatting with their friends over coffee. Maybe they go down to the bar and drink with a questionable-looking bartender. Or maybe they even "Smile and Nod a lot." No matter what channel of expression is used, people want to matter to other people.

This is something you need to keep in mind when you speak with your spouse, because it's a trick you can use to sway them in your favor. You see, when you sit down with your spouse and talk about your new venture, they are going to see that venture as a risk, and it is going to raise some valid fears inside *them*. It is your job to validate their fears, which will convince them that they matter to you, but then show why their fear is groundless in regards to your new venture. One of the best ways to validate and allay those fears is to repeat the fear back to them, and then give your rebuttal – gently – <u>as a benefit</u>. Talk to them about how much better their life is going to be when you do this.

Here are some scripts you can use for many of the bigger issues that will come up. (Items underlined once are the negatives that need to be addressed, while items underlined twice are the positives that counter balance those):

1. **Money**: Your spouse says, "If you do this, we are going to have <u>less money</u> (negative)." What they're really saying is, *I'm afraid we're going to have <u>less money</u>* or *I'm going to have to <u>work harder</u> so that we can <u>make ends meet</u>.*"

   - You can answer, "I get that. You believe that if I strike out on my own, it will affect our bank balance. But the truth is, I'm going to be charging my new clients two to three times <u>more money</u> (positive) on an hourly basis then I make right now. So in actuality, I'll be bringing home <u>a larger paycheck</u> running my own business then working for someone else. **<u>Don't you want me to bring home more money?</u>**" (See how I slipped that in there to get the "Yes"?)

2. **Time**: Your spouse says, "Running a business is going to <u>take up all your time</u>." What they're really saying is, *when are you going to have <u>time for me</u>? Is this going to <u>ruin our relationship</u>?*

   - Your answer could be, "I agree. Small businesses can take up a lot of time. However, since I will be charging <u>more per hour</u>, I can <u>work half the hours I'm working now</u> (positive) and still bring home <u>the same amount of money or more</u>. On top of that, I will be in control of my own schedule, so you and I can spend <u>more time together</u> whenever we want. I can <u>work any time of the day or night</u>, and I will finally have time to do the things my job does not allow me to do – like exercising (sexier you means bonus for them – oh, and health-wise too). **<u>Don't you want me to have more time for myself and us?</u>**"

3. **Startup Costs / Day-to-Day Expenses**: Your spouse says, "We <u>can't afford</u> for you to start your own business right now. We have <u>no money to spare</u>, and we already <u>owe a lot of money on</u>...(whatever). Running a business costs money that we don't have." What they're really saying is, *I don't want to <u>gamble</u> what <u>little money</u> we do have on a <u>risky venture</u>. Starting up a business, as well as running one, is <u>expensive</u>, and I can think of at least 100 other things I want to do with our nest egg...like buy new golf clubs.*

   - Your answer could be: "I agree – starting up a business can be expensive. But my type of business is a service business and has <u>very few startup costs and no inventory</u>. That means <u>all I need is a computer and a printer</u> (which maybe you already have or you really need anyway), and I can download the programs I will need from my clients <u>for free</u>. My biggest expense is going to be gas, but <u>car mileage is one of the</u>

best tax deductions allowed, and will actually <u>save us money on our taxes</u> every year, or <u>even qualify us for a refund</u> (which will get him his new golf clubs ☺). Although I would like to get a new laptop now, <u>I can wait</u> until I make some money with my business, or <u>I can finance one</u> at Best Buy and it will <u>only cost $20 a month</u>. So in actuality, going to the movies will cost more than starting this business, and <u>I will make more than enough money to recoup those expenses very quickly</u>. I don't even need to touch our savings to get this business off the ground...**<u>Isn't that great?</u>**"

- (Notice how I keep saying <u>more money – more money – more money</u>. Since this is always going to be the biggest argument, you want to keep pounding the more money benefit home.)

4. **Security**: Your spouse says, "I just don't think this is the right time to start a business. We are in a <u>recession</u> and <u>the unemployment rate is through the roof</u>. <u>Maybe you should wait</u> until the economy starts to turn around." What they're really saying is, *A Job is safe; A Business is not. I'm afraid that <u>if you quit, you won't be able to get your job back</u>, and with unemployment so high, <u>you might have a hard time finding a new job</u>. Then, <u>we'll spend all of our savings and eventually lose our house</u>.*

- I've already addressed the unemployment rates and new businesses earlier in this chapter. You can either repeat that to your spouse, or you can say, "I agree. The economy has definitely tanked, <u>which is why this is the best time to start a bookkeeping business</u>. <u>Other business owners want to save money, and my services will cost them less than hiring a full-time bookkeeper</u>. And if I ever need to find a regular 9-to-5 job again, every business needs bookkeeping, so <u>I will always be able to find a new position</u>.

These are just a few of the scripts you can utilize to convince your spouse that this is the best business for you.

FROM EMPLOYEE TO BUSINESS OWNER

Once you start your own bookkeeping business, thereby becoming your own business owner, you need to stop thinking small. You are no longer merely defined as "bookkeeper," nor do you have to offer only bookkeeping services. In fact, the more services you can add to your business, the more your clients will want to utilize you, and the more money you'll make. So as you read through the rest of this book, make sure you keep one question in mind...

"What Kind of Bookkeeper Do You Want to Be?"

What are you good at – besides bookkeeping? Do you make a "killer" cup of coffee or give a "deadly" foot rub? Can you do a "one-eighty" in the company car while driving 60 mph? Do you know how to make your spouse break out in a cold sweat just by the raise of a single solitary eyebrow? Because if you do, maybe espionage is an additional service you can offer.

Okay – obviously I'm kidding. (Just wanted to make sure you're still with me.) But I am serious about additional services you can offer to your clients. Because if you're good at things like blogging, Photoshop, website design, using Excel/PowerPoint/Word, or know how to defrag a computer, you have complementary skills that could be easily incorporated into your new business.

So keep these things in mind? What Services will you offer your clients? How will you advertise yourself and your company? Will you do Accounts Payable and Accounts Receivable? Will you do Credit Card and Bank Reconciliations? Are you going to do their Payroll, and will you be able to do the Tax Reports that go along with that? Will you be coming into their office once a week, twice a week, once a month, or never? Will everything be done "Virtually" from your home office, some work in your office and some in theirs, or strictly in their office at all times? Why should a business owner hire YOU instead of some minimum wage droid off the street?

These are all things you need to think about before you approach your first client. They are also things you should think about before you quit your "Day Job" because quite honestly, if you're smart (and a bit conniving), you can actually manage to get more money at your current job, keeping them on as your first client, but work fewer hours. You can even hire out an assistant and make extra money for work your assistant does. Whatever you rock at – or even just have a basic understanding of – you can add these services to your business.

If you're having problems figuring out which salable skills you might be able to offer your clients, check out Chapter 11 at the end of this book. That chapter has tons 31 additional ways to supplement your bookkeeping income.

SHOULD YOU GET A DEGREE OR CERTIFICATE?

In the more than 15 years that I've been a bookkeeper, *not once* have I ever – *ever* – been asked to supply a diploma of any kind. No one has asked me if I had a bachelor's, an associate's, or even a mere certificate of completion. I believe the reason behind that strange phenomenon is that most Small Business Owners think they can hire any idiot off the street and pay them minimum wage in order to do the bookkeeping, thus hiring an over-educated bookkeeper would just be a waste of money. (Or in other words, they have no real idea what goes into doing the Company Books correctly. They think they know, because they did it themselves in the beginning...but they really are clueless.)

Instead, when you take on a new client, that Small Business Owner will want to know one thing from you:

Can you do their Books in a way that will involve them as little as possible?

Or in other words – *Can you do their books without stressing them out?*

They don't want to be bothered by Vendors demanding payments, or chasing down Customers for monies owed. They don't want to talk to the IRS or file the related paperwork. They got into business because they love their daily grind and day-to-day bookkeeping is just a pain-in-the-keester.

So, keeping that in mind, the only real reason to get a degree or certificate for accounting is if you actually want to be an accountant, or if you feel you need to brush up on your bookkeeping skills. But this reason is largely a benefit for your peace of mind more than for attracting customers.

SETTING GOALS

Starting a business is like starting a journey. You may like the idea of "going with the flow" and "seeing where the wind may take you," but it's really reckless to take off without some kind of map or plan in hand. If you don't start this journey with a plan in hand and a mission statement in place, you will soon lose your way and end up back where you started – working at a J.O.B.

Therefore, to make sure you know exactly what you're getting into, it's an excellent idea to start with a few business goals. Here's a worksheet you can use to help you set your own goals:

(You can also find this questionnaire in the Appendix entitled "Money Plan Worksheet.")

1. **How Much Money Do You Really Want to Make?**

   a. Right now, I am making $_____ per hour,

      $_____ per week,

      $_____ per month,

      and $_____ per year.

   b. *(For this next part, calculate a <u>minimum</u> of 30% higher than your current wage.)* In order for me to feel comfortable making a living as an independent bookkeeper, I would want to make $_____ per hour,

      $_____ per week,

      $_____ per month,

      and $_____ per year.

   c. **<u>Ideally</u>**, I would like to make $_____ per hour,

      $_____ per week,

      $_____ per month,

      and $_____ per year.

   d. This would be my **<u>DREAM Job</u>** *if* I could make $_____ per *<u>Year</u>*, which is $_____ per month,

      $_____ per week,

$ _____ per day,

and $ _____ per hour.

(Notice how this last one is reversed.)

2. How Much Time Do You Want to Spend Working?

a. Right now, I work _____ hours per day,

_____ hours per week,

_____ hours per month,

and _____ hours per year.

b. To make the <u>same amount of money</u> I make currently, but charge my "new comfortable wage" (*i.e. my currently hourly wage* + *a minimum of* **<u>30% or more</u>**), I would have to work _____ hours per day,

_____ hours per week,

_____ hours per month,

and _____ hours per year.

c. To make a <u>Comfortable living</u> (*i.e. the wage I would <u>like to make</u> to feel good about this career change*), I would have to work _____ hours per day,

_____ hours per week,

_____ hours per month,

and _____ hours per year.

d. To make my *Ideal* <u>living</u>, I would have to work a minimum of

_____ hours per day,

_____ hours per week,

_____ hours per month,

and _____ hours per year.

e. If this were my DREAM Job (...now, be outrageous! ☺), I would only have to work _____ hours per week,

but I would still make $ _____ per week.

Now that you have a general idea of how much you'd like to make, write it down on a separate piece of paper like this:

(THIS IS JUST A SAMPLE!!!)

MY MONEY PLAN

"I am going to start this new business by working a minimum of (your goal hours) *20 hours a week and charging a minimum of $13 an hour (previous $10/hr. wage + 30%) in order to make $260 a week (20/hr x $13 hrs), which was approximately the same as my take home pay after taxes working at my "J.O.B."*

To make a more comfortable living, I will work 25 hours a week (just an example) and charge $20 an hour for a total of $500 a week.

Ideally, I will work 30 hours a week and charge $30 an hour for a take-home amount of $900.

Eventually, I would like to build this business up enough to work 20 hours a week, but still earn $2,000 per week."

Now you may be thinking that there's no way you could ever charge $100 per hour for bookkeeping, or make $2,000 a week doing this job...but I want you to write it down anyway. I want you to write down the "impossible" because as you get farther into this book, you will begin to see how the "impossible" is *completely possible*. Because you see, I did *not* actually say that you would be charging $100 a week. You can make $2,000 per week without actually charging your customers $100 per hour...largely by adding other services to your business, outsourcing those services, and then taking a cut. By keeping the "impossible" at the back of your mind, you will soon find that you are making it happen. (I will go more into detail about other services in Chapter 11.)

Once you have your Money Plan written out, write it down again and again, and post it where you can see it often. You're going to need to read it every time you begin to question

"Why am I doing this? Why don't I just go back to working for someone else?" Because there will be days where you think that, and you're going to need a reminder.

Are you wondering how much you *should be charging*? To figure out what your bookkeeping rate should be, check out www.Accountemps.com. This site has job postings for tons of local areas. All you have to do is type in "bookkeeping job" and your zip code, then voila – tons of recent job postings. Then, decide to charge a minimum of whatever the highest hourly wage is. Even better, tack on an extra 30% - after all, you will be saving your future clients at least 30% in taxes, worker's compensation, overhead, etc. At best, charge double or triple the highest rate...because you're going to need it...and you're going to be faster than everyone else.

Another way to find out how much you should be charging is to "ask an accountant" what other independent bookkeepers in your area charge. You'll be surprised at how many accountants know the answer to this.

Chapter 2

Step 2: Switching Offices

SPOTLIGHT ON A BOOKKEEPING BUSINESS – Virtual Office Goddess

How I became an 'accidental entrepreneur'

I started my office career as a secretary and ended up working as a bookkeeper for various companies – a water engineering firm, an immigration law office, a criminal law office, and a criminal justice consulting firm, all small companies - when the bookkeeper at the water engineering firm left to start her own business and they trained me to replace her. My father owned his own business when I was growing up and I swore up and down that I would NEVER become an entrepreneur! Famous last words!

I had been working for the criminal justice consulting firm for about two years when one of our subcontractors approached me for a referral. "I'm the trustee for a local horse rescue operation and the board just authorized me to find a part-time bookkeeper. It's only a couple of hours a month. Can you suggest someone for me to contact?" Of course, my first response was "me!" After all, only a few hours a month wouldn't be that hard and who couldn't use the extra money, right?

She suggested I start up a business and file for a LLC with the Secretary of State so I could write off my expenses. A few weeks later, she called and said she had a friend who was looking for a part-time bookkeeper and, now that I had my own business, would I be interested in talking to her. The rest, as they say, is history!

Lily E. Chambers, CPS, CQU is the owner and operator of The Virtual Office Goddess, LLC. (VirtualOfficeGoddess.com) specializing in bookkeeping and office support services with over three decades of experience in an office environment. She is also a co-owner and teaches a basic 'how to do your own bookkeeping' class through the Academy of Virtual Education (AOVE.org/bookkeeping.html), and publishes The Virtual Evolution online e-zine (TVEmagazine.com) for entrepreneurs.

One of the scariest things you will do as an Independent Bookkeeper is quitting the job you've been at for so long. You're used to your job; it's safe. You know the rhythms and routines as well as you know your own heartbeat; it's second nature. Striking out on your own, however, is new and therefore scary. But if you'll notice, the name of this chapter is **not** "Quitting Your Day Job." It's "Switching Offices." There's no step in this book that says you have to quit what makes you feel safe and secure. In fact, I am a firm believer that – if and only if you like your current boss – you should turn your boss into your first client. The easiest way to do this is to begin practicing your virtual bookkeeping skills right from your office.

My Lifestyle Guru is Timothy Ferris, and his book, "The 4-Hour Workweek" is my "Manual on Running Any Business." I highly recommend it to everyone – including you. If you want to know how to phase yourself out of your boss's office and into your new bookkeeping business office, then you need to get his book and read the section entitled "Elimination." You'll be amazed at how effective his advice is. And if you don't want to spend $20 to buy it, then at least swing by the bookstore or library and thumb through it, because his advice is too good to miss. But, bring along $20..."just in case."

Having said that, I will add one more little note. If you've already converted your last boss to your first client, and if you've already stocked your office with everything you need (aka laptop, computer programs, multi-function printers, etc.), then go ahead and skip this chapter too. If you haven't, or if you're looking for ideas on products that will work best for your new business read on. Otherwise...see you in Chapter 3.

PICK UP THE SPEED

The first thing you will want to do to prove to your boss that you will be a "fast alternative" to a traditional in-office bookkeeper is prove that you actually *are going to be* faster.

That means you will want to start being more efficient and productive. When you're out of someone else's office and in your own, you will find that a lot of this will already happen naturally because your office phone will no longer be ringing off the hook and people won't be coming in and out of your office at random times. You will have a firmer control on your time than ever before.

The next thing you will want to do to prove you're faster is to become more efficient. If there is something you are going to do over and over for your client, then you will want to create a system that will allow that to happen with minimal work from you. For example, I once had a client in the carpeting industry who used a custom Purchase Order for the contractors that purchased carpet from the store. He would use a 3-Part form for every contractor-order, then keep a copy for his personal file, send a copy to the client, and shoot me a copy that I had to add as backup to the related invoice. Not only were the forms expensive to buy and time consuming to fill out, but then I had to remember to collect that paperwork, find them wherever the manager left them (which was always somewhere strange), enter them manually into the computer, attach them to the matching invoices if and when that invoice finally came across my desk, and then file them away. What a pain! To make the whole process more efficient, I recreated the document in Excel and then locked the worksheet so that only the squares that needed data entry were accessible. The manager could then "Tab" to the appropriate box and enter the information. The Excel sheet would even calculate totals for him automatically. From there, all he had to do was print out copies for his contractor-customers, and a copy for his own records. When the original invoice came across my desk, I could then find the matching file on his computer and print out the copy for my backup. It saved the manager hand-writing time, and it saved me "searching for the copy" time because it was so easy to reprint it should he lose it. It also saved me "waiting" time because I no longer had to put an invoice aside until the backup came onto my desk. Plus, the mess on my desk was smaller.

The point...if there are any forms that can be recreated to save you or your client time, *make them*. Even if you don't bill them for making them, it will make you look like a genius for saving them time, and it will help you do your job faster.

Another way you can speed up your job is to speed up the bookkeeping process. Do your books faster. Cut timely endeavors wherever you can. If you have no idea what I'm talking about, then you can find some time-saving techniques in our book, "How to Do a Year's Worth of Bookkeeping in One Day." It will help you get through some of the basics very quickly. Later in 2010, we will also have released a video called "The One Hour Bookkeeping Method," which can show you how to do books for most small businesses in one hour or less per day, per week, or even per month. The key is all about automation, and we walk you step-by-step through the process in the video. In fact, by the time the one-hour video is done, you should have completed the majority of your bookkeeping.

So – think about ways you can pick up the speed so that you don't have to spend nearly as much time in the office. I will give more examples later in this chapter.

ASK FOR MORE MONEY

For a lot of people, this step is going to be the hardest, especially if you've worked for the same person for a long time. You'll have convinced yourself that you are only worth what you are currently earning, and that your future clients will want to pay those same rates. **You have to get out of that mindset.** The new facts will be these:

1) You are going to save your new clients – *and your boss* – money because they won't need to pay overhead. You won't even need to use their computer because you will have your own.

2) You will save your clients and your boss money because they won't have to pay the Employer taxes that normally match the Employee taxes.

3) They will have less IRS-stress, fees, interest, and penalties that can be associated with paying Employer Taxes (and what business owner doesn't want to deal with the IRS less?).

4) They also won't have to pay Worker's Compensation for you.

5) You will be faster than anyone else who can do your job, so you will be saving them money in that aspect as well.

6) And finally, you're going to be working fewer hours. As a result, you are going to need to make "enough" money – aka *more money* – to survive. If it takes you 10 hours a month to do a business's books, are you really going to wanna make only $100 for that time, or $300? "A monthly fee of $300 for bookkeeping services" will be more

reasonable to a small business owner than having to pay $1,600 a month for a full-time $10-an-hour bookkeeper. Keep that in mind when you pitch your services...***you will cost them less, <u>but you still need to make a living</u>***.

Thus, for your current "boss-turned-client," you are going to point out that they will need to pay you more, but that the ending amount will actually be less then what they are paying you currently because you will not need to waste time on other issues any longer (like taking the large multitude of phone calls you normally take, dealing with office drama and employees, or the constant distractions that come with working in an office). Here's an example you can use:

Let's say you are currently making $10 an hour and you pay approximately 30% in taxes (which is low for a bookkeeper, but it's an easy number to calculate). This means you are having $3 an hour taken from your pay, and you would be taking home an average of $7 after taxes. Your employer would have to match that tax. So, while they are paying you $10 an hour, they are paying $3 an hour to the government, as are you. (Of course, these are not exact numbers. They are estimated for simplicity's sake.) What this means is that your boss can pay you $13 an hour without feeling a difference. On top of that, they are saving another $100 (give or take) per month on Worker's Compensation that they no longer have to pay. You get to keep that full $13 per hour, and you only pay taxes on it once a year when you file your income taxes. At that point, you will have small business deductions which will allow you to "lower your income" – in the government's eyes at least – and you will be able to keep more of that money.

Therefore, your pitch to your boss for more money is that you need to make more money per hour because you are going to work fewer hours and save them more money in other areas.

If you're not comfortable doing this yet, the other thing you can do is wait until you have a few clients under your belt, then go to your boss and say...

"My new bookkeeping business is really taking off, and I am making a much higher hourly rate with my new clients. I want to keep working with you, but I am not making enough per hour to make it worth my while. That means, I either need to charge you more per hour, or I have to quit. Right now, I'm working <u>X hours per month</u> *for you, and I'm charging you* <u>$Y per hour</u> *for a total of* <u>$Z per month</u>. <u>My new hourly rate is $A per hour</u>, *which means* <u>I will need to charge you $B per month</u> *in order to make this worth my while. What do you think? Would you prefer to pay my new rate, or should I begin training my replacement?"*

Remember, it's always the "call to action" that makes people act a bit more impulsively then they should – so spell out the new terms, and then *give a definitive alternative.*

LEAVE EARLIER & EARLIER

I'm going to assume you are working a full 40-hour workweek with your current boss. If that's the case, the first thing you're going to need to do (besides renegotiating your pay) is to figure out where and how you can cut your full-time hours and the time you spend in the office. If you can compartmentalize your time each day, then you can cut out all of the time-wasters that fall into your lap. For example...talking to the boss. Every bookkeeper experiences this whether they realize it or not. Their boss comes into their office at all times of the day with "a question" about money, bills, customers, vendors, etc. The question takes more than "a quick minute" to answer, and soon the boss has plopped down in your extra office seat "to chat." Even though you've answered their question, you still end up talking about *their* love lives, travels, a lunch they had with a client – *whatever*. The next thing you know, you look at the clock and a very unproductive hour (or two) has gone by. Your boss leaves feeling confident about you, their business, and their money, while you now have to bust your behind to get the rest of your work done before you go home. It's situations like this – dealing with the people in your office – where compartmentalizing will come in handy.

How to Compartmentalize Your Work Day and Save Time

To compartmentalize your work day, you will first need to think about all the tasks involved with your "day-job" as a bookkeeper. It's a good idea to make a list of those tasks so that you can figure out how much time you actually spend doing various things and where you can save time. Here's a sample spreadsheet to help you get this started (a blank copy for you to copy and use is in the Appendix):

Various Bookkeeping Tasks	Amount of Time It Takes to Complete This Task Each Day:
Answering Phone Calls and Emails	1 hour
Answering the Boss's Questions	1 hour
Answering Other Employees' Questions	1 hour
Data Entry	5 hours
Printing Invoices and Checks	10 minutes
Stuffing Envelopes with those Invoices and Checks	1 hour
Bank Reconciliations	30 minutes
Filing	No Idea – I avoid it as much as humanly possible
Handling Cash, Checks and Deposits	30 minutes
Running Errands for the Company – like going to the bank, post office, or office supply store.	2 hours

Once you have a visual picture of what you're day looks like, the next thing you want to remember is CCD – Combine, Cut or Delegate. Figure out which tasks you can combine together to save time, which projects you can cut altogether, and then which tasks you can delegate to someone else. Here are some further examples in relation to the spreadsheet above:

- **Combine:** In the spreadsheet above, you can see that it takes roughly three hours to deal with the boss, other employees, and answering phones and emails. That is a lot of time for verbal and/or written communications, and it is not usually spent all at once; it's usually spread throughout the day. Since these are all communication tasks, they can be *combined* into one or two "Communication Time Slots." Instead of doing all of these things as they arise, you can create an "Open Office Door Time Slot" where you will deal with everyone else's problems for a preset period of time.

For example, the first 30 minutes you arrive in the office can be the time you've set aside to focus on your voicemail, email, and talking to the boss or employees. Then, if *you chose to*, you could create a second 30-minute Communication Slot later in the day where you can deal with any issues that came up as the day progressed. Thus, when someone comes into your office with a "quick question" that really isn't a quick question, you can look at them and say, "I'm in the middle of something right now, but I can have that answer for you by (insert Communication Time Slot # 2 here)." As long as you can give a specific time that you can get back to them, most people will be happy to leave your office without their answer as long as they know you will come to them later on.

Thus, by combining these three tasks into one or two 30-minute time slots, you can save yourself TWO HOURS a day of useless chitchat.

Another thing you can do to save communication time is to actually _tell people_ about these Communication Time Slots. Change your voicemail to say that you will return the phone call during the second Communication Time Slot or the next morning during the first Communication Time Slot. Then stop answering your phone, let callers leave a message, get all your messages at once, and make your calls in quick succession. Let employees and your boss know that from the end of Communication Time Slot # 1 to the beginning of Communication Time Slot # 2, you prefer not to be disturbed because that is when you need to focus on your data entry. After a while, they will just know to come back later, or leave you a message, and you will become a lot more productive.

- **Cut**: The next time-saving, be-more-productive step you can take is to figure out what you can cut. In the spreadsheet above, you can see that it can take approximately one hour to stuff envelopes with invoices and checks. That's a lot of time doing a boring and menial task. To cut that time, you can utilize that business's Online Banking features. For example, banks often offer Bill-Pay features, which will allow you to mail checks to all kinds of vendors by simply filling in the amounts online and hitting send. You can send 100 checks in less than 5 minutes this way. The bank's Direct Deposit feature will also allow you to pay many of the business's employees instantly, saving you time printing and handing out checks while saving the employees running-to-the-bank time. For invoices, many bookkeeping programs offer the opportunity to email invoices directly to your customers. This is instant and means you no longer have to count on the post office to deliver your invoice in a timely fashion – which is especially handy if you are only going to be mailing invoices once a week. All it *usually* takes to make this happen is to click on the "Send by Email" button during the data entry process, and then clicking the "Send" button when you're done with all of your data entry. If you could do this for all of your invoices and checks, you could potentially save a full 55 minutes of Envelope Stuffing Time, not to mention money on stamps, envelopes, checks, paper, ink/toner, and wear and tear on a printer.

- **Delegate**: This is my favorite step...what can I make someone else do? From the spreadsheet above, there are two tasks that can obviously be given to someone else – filing and running errands. Why should you be the one to do this (especially if you hate it, like I do)? If that's not enough of a reason to *not do* something, then think about this: which is more profitable for your boss-turned-client? Paying *you* a higher wage to do filing and running errands, or paying minimum wage to an office assistant or receptionist? The truth is, they'd rather save the money. So, why not pass on those tasks to the office gopher and cut out of the office early?

Here's another thought...

You're going to become an Independent Virtual Bookkeeper, *right*? That means, you want to spend as little time as possible in your clients' offices...

Why not hire a local college student with a car as your company's personal assistant, pay them just above minimum wage to do the jobs you hate for your boss and your future clients – *things like filing and running errands* – and then charge extra for that student's services. Sure, you are going to pay taxes on them as an employee, but you will also make a few extra dollars for every hour they work without you having to do any work at all. It's a win-win-win because your clients *don't* have to pay taxes on that person and they save money on your hours; you get to avoid tasks you hate while still offering extra services you can make money on; and some eager college student will be able to have a flexible job that works around their unusual college schedule. Plus, you'll have a driver to pick up and deliver paperwork to businesses you don't want to go into, allowing you to stay completely *Virtual*.

Now that you have an idea of how to Combine, Cut and Delegate time – go hog wild. Start slashing your time left and right until you only need to be in that office part time. Once you do, you will be free to start finding other clients. (You can find a CCD Worksheet in the Appendix to help you do all this.)

DEMAND RESPECT – ANNOUNCE YOUR INTENTIONS AND YOUR NEW BUSINESS

My favorite thing about being an Independent Bookkeeper, besides the money, is the shift in a "boss's" respect level. If a boss is treating you badly and they think you don't need them, or that you have one foot out the door. Thus, they will begin to treat you differently...especially if you're saving them money. They'll look at the work you're doing and they'll analyze the cost of replacing you. They'll calculate the higher wage you're making with your new office hours, and then they'll compare it to the cost of a full-time bookkeeper that makes less and knows less, but who they can bully and harass. They'll see that you're the better deal, and that you make their office run smoothly even with one foot out the door, and they will begin to act accordingly. It's incredibly sad that it takes this kind of drastic action to get someone's respect, but it does work.

Therefore, once you've managed to cut even a few hours out of your week, and if you haven't "had the talk" with your boss yet – *the talk that you are starting your own business* – then suck it up and go corner them somewhere. It *is* scary, no matter how nice your boss is, but I will bet you that the fears running through your head are a lot scarier than actually doing it. Just keep telling yourself, "they will respect me more once I do this." Keep the conversation short and to the point, and watch a whole new relationship blossom once you walk out of the boss's office.

YOU ARE NO LONGER AN EMPLOYEE

Once you are no longer an "Employee" but an "Independent Contractor," it's time to get your business started. You will need to stock your office, start thinking about advertising, stationery, and letterhead. You will need to analyze what you need to make your future company successful, and you will need to get started right away. Because once you've had the conversation with your boss and turned that person into a client, it's time to take yourself seriously. Just remember one thing...if your bad boss doesn't turn into a good client, *dump them*. You will soon have more than enough clients, so don't waste your life on someone who can't see you for the gem you are. *Never, ever, ever put up with being treated like a moron.*

STOCK YOUR OFFICE

Now comes the fun part...shopping. Whether you like shopping or not, shopping for office supplies is like going to Disneyland for me. I have literally spent hours in Office Depot just looking at knick knacks and clearance items. Whenever an employee asks me, "Can I help you with something," my answer is always, "Are you kidding? I probably know this store better than you do." So coming from the standpoint of a *total* Office Geek, here are the items I recommend for any bookkeeping business.

Forget Most of What You Know

If you've done any kind of bookkeeping at all, then you already have an idea of what *will* and *will not* work for you in a small office situation. You know what brand of pens you like, what type of post-its appeal to you most, and the exact size of binder clips you need in order to clip together a package of IRS paperwork. Heck – you probably even know exactly which aisles of your favorite office supply store have those products and how much they each cost per package. But if you've never worked as a Virtual Bookkeeper before, then you need to forget what's worked for you in the past. That stuff is **_not_** going to work for you in a Virtual Bookkeeping situation.

Think about it: When you were an employee, the equipment your last job used was probably selected for that business as a result of a *sudden need*. A computer crashed; a new Dell Desktop was ordered. A printer went on the fritz; someone ran out and bought an inexpensive Lexmark. Suddenly, a customer wanted a fax from the company, so someone ran out and bought a basic fax machine. Most of these items were probably bought without any real forethought as to space, replacement costs, usefulness, etc., and they won't be replaced until they too sputter into a much-needed recycle bin...or until you take a sledgehammer to it. ☺

That's why you need to forget what worked for you in the past and plan ahead. You (as a Virtual Bookkeeper) are not going to have a huge amount of space or a bunch of offices – you will probably work on your dining room table at home even if you have a room "just for your office." You will want to be where the TV is (or the stereo, or your kids) so that you won't feel so bored or lonely during your day. When you are at home, you will not be doing data entry during the usual 9-to-5 shift like you've done in the past – you will be squeezing in your data entry around Family Time, Dinner Time, Phone Call Time, Me-Time, and Visiting Your "Needy Client" Time. In fact, you will not be spending a lot of time in your home office at all. You'll be on the road, up late at nights, or even listening to your favorite shows in the background as you try to work. Your office will constantly be moving from desktop to tabletop and back again. So having said that, here are some things you will need to stock your office with whether before you begin, or as soon as you can. (A Shopping/To-Do list for these items can be found in the Appendix)

1. **The DBA (Doing Business As) Name:** While you may prefer to work under your own name, thus avoiding the need for a Small Business License, consider this: *How long do you plan to work this bookkeeping business?* Because the fact is, there will come a day when you consider "closing your doors." The question at that point will become: *Should I sell my business, drop all my Clients, or pass them off to other people?* Since you have customers, you have a tangible asset. If you're operating under your name, then you would be selling your business under your name, thus allowing someone else to ruin your good name (a bit like identity theft). <u>If you have a DBA, you have a tangible asset that you can sell which is not associated with your personal name or integrity.</u> If you sell the business, you sell all assets and liabilities, so you can actually walk away clean with a hefty payoff. So depending on how you would like to close your doors at some point down the road, getting a DBA not associated with your name is a really good idea, and it's very inexpensive. It's a one-time fee you make at your local government office, and then a small fee to advertise your new business name in any local newspaper. Together, the price is usually less than $100.

One Quick Note: Make sure to keep your business name simple. If your first or last name is hard to spell or hard to remember, don't use them. Consider using something like the name of your city, and the words "Virtual Bookkeeping." That way, when someone Googles those keywords, your company name will pop up first, and it's easy for future clients to remember.

2. **The Business License:** Whether you get a DBA or not, you'll probably want to get a business license (even if it isn't necessary because you are operating the business under your name). A Business License is a very inexpensive piece of paper – only $50 or so depending on how much you make annually – and it will give many of your Small Business Owners "peace of mind." Will they ask you for a Business License? Probably not. But still, it's a good thing to have that will show anyone who asks for it that you are

serious about being a business. You renew it once a year, and <u>it will help you get business financing under your business's name later on</u>, should you so desire to expand. This will be another tangible asset you can sell with the business if and when you decide to sell...i.e., an on-paper history that will allow the next owner to get financing.

3. **Employer Identification Number (EIN):** Whether or not you get a business name and/or a business license, it is always a good idea to get an Employer Identification Number as well. At the end of each year, instead of getting a W-2, you will get a 1099. That means, you will have to give your tax ID number to any and all small businesses you work with. If you don't get an EIN, then you have to give out your Social Security # - and who knows if that new client is really trustworthy or not? So, if you want to prevent Identity Theft with less than questionable embezzlers (like my "alter ego" – Betty Bookkeeper), then you will want to get n EIN and use that on all documents relating to your business's taxes.

   a. You can apply online at: <u>IRS.gov/Businesses/Small/Article/0,,id=98350,00.html</u> or by fax at: <u>IRS.gov/Pub/IRS-PDF/fss4.pdf</u>.

4. **Get a Laptop – Period.** Don't even *bother* telling yourself you won't need one or that a Desktop Computer will do fine...it *won't*. If you decide to become an Independent Bookkeeper, you can expect to travel. A Lot! A whole heck of a lot. On top of that, <u>the smaller the business you work with, the more likely that the business owner you work with *won't* have a computer</u>. In fact, they may not even have a separate office space. I remember a Restaurant Owner I worked with who set up a *hallway* as her office – *literally*. That meant I had people stepping over me to get from the front of the restaurant to the kitchens. Another client actually had *no office whatsoever*, and instead built a lean-to shack in his backyard where he tossed a few used filing cabinets for his paperwork. In both instances, it was important for me to be able to do work at my office instead of theirs, and only pick up and drop off information I needed, including uploading the Backup QuickBooks file I had made. There are even times that I met a client in a coffee shop near their jobsite or home. So, if you don't have a laptop now, and you are serious about getting an Independent Virtual Bookkeeping Business going, then start saving up for this asset. You'll need it.

And if I haven't convinced you yet, imagine yourself on a beach in the Caribbean, your laptop in your lap and a Mai Tai on a nearby table...a working vacation. That *could* be your Virtual Bookkeeping life if you planned it correctly right from the beginning.

a. Must-Have Features For Your Bookkeeping Laptop:

i. A DVD Burner: Don't be cheap and skip the DVD burner in lieu of a CD Burner; they are *not* the same thing. CD's can only burn a fraction of the information a DVD can burn, and you will want to give your clients DVDs when you back up their work.

ii. An SD Card Slot: This will come in handy whenever you need to transfer digital files from a camera to your computer. Although it may not make much sense now, you'll be glad you have it later.

iii. Bluetooth Access: It just comes in handy.

iv. Wireless Access: You will want to be able to get on the Internet anywhere, especially coffee shops. In fact, you may even consider signing up for a monthly service from AT&T or Sprint so that you can get Internet access from the middle of a field, if you so chose.

b. Optional Features For Your Laptop To Consider:

i. A 10-Key Keyboard: The reason I have NOT made this a "Must-Have"

feature is because this is actually a "Preference" choice more than anything. Yes, it can be incredibly handy to have your 10-Key right on your keyboard when you open your laptop, but the problem is, a Laptop with a 10-Key Keyboard is <u>a *very heavy* laptop</u>. It can add an extra 5 to 10 pounds of weight, and it can add a couple hundred dollars to the price tag. If you buy this kind of laptop, you will also probably end up investing in a bag with wheels just to tote the thing around. So now, you have a heavy laptop with a heavy AND bulky bag that you have to schlep from house to car to office and back. On the other hand, you can buy a 10-Key Keypad that plugs directly into your laptop for a cost of $10 to $20, or a Bluetooth 10-Key Keypad for $30 to $40. These are compact, lightweight, and can  fit right in the pocket of any computer bag. On top of that, you can buy a computer that weighs as little as five pounds, and now taking your computer with you is no longer a hassle. So, make the decision for yourself on how important that 10-Key is before you buy a laptop. (*Notice, the Kensington keypad-with-calculator to the left has a calculator screen on it as well, which allows you to quickly tally numbers without having to access your computer.*)

ii. LightScribe Burner: If you've never seen a Burnt LightScribe CD or DVD, you are missing out. This feature allows you to burn any picture or text on the top of a certain type of CD and DVD, and can really give you (and your business) a very professional image. Imagine giving your clients a Backup Disc with *their* Company Name, Logo and date on it. You will convince your Clients you spend a lot of time and money to produce high-quality products, even when you don't. This feature does not come standard on all laptops, but is usually only $25 more if you're buying a "custom computer." So, if you want to give an appearance of being Professional and "Tech-Savvy," add this feature...you won't regret it. (Because quite frankly, if you're not doing it now, your competitors will be doing it soon.)

c. **My Laptop Recommendations:**

i. Anything HP: Personally, I am a HUGE fan of anything Hewlett Packard. The price is mid-range and the quality is excellent. I own three HP Laptops, including a 10-Key and a Tablet. I LOVE LOVE LOVE my Tablet because I can write on the screen with the little touch pen and sign documents without printing them out. But that's a personal preference. (Average Sale Price: $400 to $1,000)

If you do get the HP with a 10-Key keyboard, be sure to watch out for the hinges...the computer is so heavy, the hinges can crack in the first couple years. Thus, you will want to invest in the Warranty if you get the 10-Key.

Also, I like to order my HP's from HP.com because they often have the same sale prices as retail locations, but with tons of customized extras that you can add for free, or very cheap. Plus, S&H is free, and they do have financing options.

ii. Anything Sony: Sony is on the higher-priced end of laptops, but the quality is excellent. The only downside I've seen to owning a Sony is that *usually* Sony only works with Sony. That means you may have to get creative when downloading pictures to it from anything other than a Sony camera or phone. (Average Sale Price: $650 to $1,100)

iii. <u>Toshiba</u> is a Great Low Cost Choice: I've had Toshibas in the past and the best thing about them is the low prices. On top of that, they have hard casings so they are more rugged for someone who might drop their computer a lot. They are definitely a worthwhile purchase for anyone looking to save money, although they don't always have all the features offered by HPs or Sony. (Average Sale Price: $400 to $800)

iv. **AVOID AT ALL COSTS**: One of the benefits about being an Independent Bookkeeper is that you see a LOT of computers. As such, I would NEVER recommend a Compaq (even though it's made by HP) or a Gateway. I've seen major issues with Compaqs, and I've heard Gateway has the worst customer service when a problem arises (this from a very computer savvy person). Acers are super-cheap options, but there's a reason for that...they won't work well with a whole lot of business programs. The IBMs I've seen have been heavy, awkward and incredibly expensive, but aren't really any fancier than a Toshiba. Dells are great because they're inexpensive, you can customize them, and they have decent customer service, but I've seen more Dells freeze up than not and then you have to do a "hard reboot." But again, your laptop choice is always a preference thing.

v. **ALSO AVOID:** Mini Netbooks. While Netbooks are a fabulous deal price-wise, they are *not good* choices for a business. For one thing, the keyboards are small, which makes it hard to type (and EXTREMELY curse-worthy if you type a lot). For another, there are usually NO DVD/CD Burners, only USB ports. And for a third, without a DVD drive, it is nearly impossible to get many computer programs on the laptop –

including QuickBooks. I have tried to download QuickBooks onto computers from the internet before, but even with the QuickBooks key code, you really need the disks to install the program. So skip the Netbooks for your business and go with something larger.

d. **To find the best price on a laptop:** If I don't buy my laptop from the manufacturer's website, then I like to go Best Buy or Office Depot. They often have *incredible* sales and decent financing. On top of that, you can usually take your computer to Best Buy if you need to get something fixed, and Office Depot now offers free computer check-ups whether you buy from them or not. Check their catalogs regularly and you will be amazed at the deals.

5. **Get a Multi-Function Printer**. You want to look for a Multi-Function Printer versus a regular printer because like I said before, you will have limited space. You want it to have a "Flatbed" because you will be scanning paperwork. You also want it to be able to "Feed" a lot of papers through the scanner at once because *you will be faxing a lot of paperwork*. In fact, the feed is one of the most important features to look at...DON'T SKIMP HERE. A wimpy feed will mean lots of paper jams, lots of frustration, a few choice curse words, a whole lot of equipment violence, and eventually, a whole lot of time wasted manually feeding your pages one at a time. (Which sucks, believe me!) Save yourself the headache and pony up the extra $10-$50 for a better feeding option.

a. Features to Look for in a Multifunction Printer:

i. Laser Printers versus Inkjet Printers:

- Laser printers mean toner cartridges. That is a lot more expensive then Inkjet cartridges, and usually larger in size, but they print faster, and they print more copies before they have to be replaced. In addition, the printer costs more money, especially if you go for the Color Laser printer, but the print quality is excellent, and if you don't mind pony-ing up $100 every time you have to buy replacement cartridges, then a laser printer is a great option.

- Inkjet Printers: Both the printer and the cartridges cost less....period. The quality can be really good, but you will buy cartridges more often (although the prices can be as low as $5 each). You will probably also have to do a "head cleaning" more often on an Inkjet Printer, but this is the more affordable choice when starting any new business.

ONE MORE THING TO CONSIDER: While you will be offering bookkeeping services, there is nothing wrong with offering extra services like black and white copies, color copies, high quality labels / business cards / brochures, as well as faxing, scanning, and even converting files to a digital format...all services you can offer that don't take a whole lot of work. In order to do this, you will need a good-quality multi-function printer / scanner / fax machine.

If you are going to offer these services, then go with a laser printer. You will save so much time, and the quality is impeccable.

ii. Replacement Cartridges: Before you buy any printer, always pop over to the cartridge aisle and see how much the replacement cartridges are. You may also want to check a website like www.123Inkjets.com where you can save as much as 80% on the generic versions. Just the cost of the cartridges alone could be a reason NOT to buy whatever printer you're looking at, no matter how cheap the printer is. For example, Lexmarks are generally the cheapest printers you can find, but they're cartridges cost just a little less than the printer itself. On top of that, the cartridges don't print a whole lot of documents before the cartridge has to be replaced – so these are only good deals for people who don't print a lot. *You*...as a VIRTUAL bookkeeper...ARE going to print – *a lot*. So take the price of the cartridges seriously.

iii. A Good Feeder: This is a must-have for a bookkeeper. You are going to be faxing, scanning and copying a lot of documents at once. If you have a wimpy feeder, then you can expect paper jams or an early death to your MFC printer. Therefore, make sure you look at how many papers you can feed at once. This information will be listed in the printer's details or on the box itself.

iv. A Flatbed Scanner: A lot of Business Owners think that having a machine with only a feeder (like a fax machine) is a great low-cost option, but the truth is, it's a bad option for bookkeeping. Bookkeepers need to make copies of checks, bills, tax forms, books, and all sorts of odd-shaped papers. It's a whole heck of a lot easier to have a flatbed that can handle odd shapes and sizes so you can scan portions, if necessary, and put the scans back together on a computer. Therefore, get both the feeder and the scanner model.

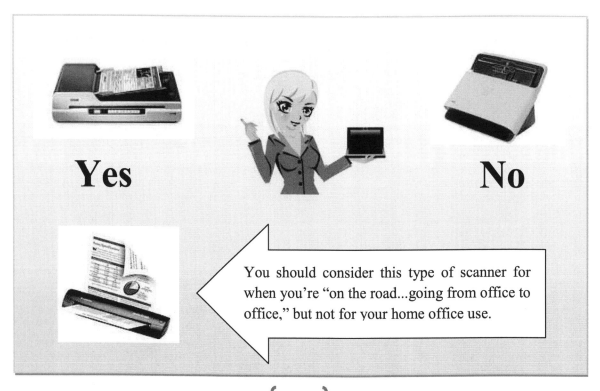

You should consider this type of scanner for when you're "on the road...going from office to office," but not for your home office use.

v. A Fax Machine: You'd be amazed how many multi-function printers are still made without a fax machine. But the truth is, a fax machine is a Virtual Bookkeeper's best friend. You will be sending a lot of paperwork to your clients via email or fax, and having a fax machine lets you do both. Be smart and check for this feature right from the beginning.

vi. All in all, we prefer the Brother printers. The cartridges are cheap (at least in comparison to other toner and inkjet cartridges), it feeds paper fairly quickly, and it prints an excellent quality at a good speed. However, keep in mind that not all Brother Printers are created equally. The cheap ones don't feed a lot of paper at once. So, look for something that looks like these (notice the feeds are angled upward to hold more pages):

But avoid ones that look these because these feeds aren't that great (notice the feeds are flat, and thus usually fit and/or feed fewer pages).

A Good Rule-of-Thumb is: The more pages they feed at once, the better.

vii.   Another thing to look for in your printer is an SD Card Slot like the one to the left (*if you don't have an SD card slot on your computer*). If you're going to be the best technologically-up-to-date virtual bookkeeper ever, you may be taking or receiving pictures with your phone, and the SD Card or Mini-SD Card feature on your MFC Printer will save time if you prefer to do your data entry from physical paperwork.

6. **Subscribe to an eFax.** This may seem like a total waste of money since you will already have a fax machine, but trust me – *it's not*. In fact, having an eFax is *super* important to the Virtual Bookkeeper. For roughly $15 - $20 a month, you will save hundreds of sheets of paper, fax machine wear and tear, ink cartridge replacements, and thousands of hours scanning and/or shredding documents. You will have all of the information that clients send you instantly downloaded to your computer, and you will be able to check those documents from anywhere in the world. Imagine this – you're on a cruise ship in Hawaii (with your laptop, of course), when you get an "Urgent Email" from a client. They can't find the original bill they faxed to you last Thursday, and they need the account number and phone number right away. While sipping your Mai Tai (because obviously I'm a fan of Mai Tais), you simply pull up your email, go to that day, find the file sent to you, open it, and voila – you can email it right back to them. That's what an eFax can do for you...it can make you a *Super* Bookkeeper.

    a. **My Recommendations:** RingCentral.com, or eFax.com...although I really prefer RingCentral because you get a specialized voicemail included with your eFax order. That means that you can have people call or fax your new eFax number, and the voicemail messages get transcribed and sent to your email immediately. Thus, you can listen to your voicemail or read it – very handy when you are at a client's office and can't answer your phone. EFax does not offer this service, and you have to go to eVoice.com and pay a separate monthly fee to get the same voicemail features. (You can also get your new eFax number as a toll-free number at both lines, which is very handy if you stick with the virtual bookkeeping side of things – thus having clients from all over the world.)

7. **Get a Cell Phone – and By That, I Mean Add A Second Phone AND Phone Line to Your Cell Phone Bill. Don't forget TEXT MESSAGING!** The first part of that sentence should have been a "*Duh*" moment for you. Of course you'd have a Cell Phone for your business. What self respecting citizen of the 21st Century doesn't have a Cell Phone, let alone a Business Owner? But you'd be surprised how many Business Owners only use a Cell Phone to talk to their Family, Employees and Subcontractors while ignoring their Vendors and Customers. For a Virtual Bookkeeper, a Cell Phone will be your Office Phone, and it will be one of your most important pieces of technology. Most of your clients probably won't be satisfied unless they can call *You* "direct" at the drop of a hat. This can be rather irritating. In fact, it can be *so irritating*, that you'll quickly realize why I said to get TWO lines. One, you will continue to use for your Friends and Family. The other will be for your Clients, Employees, Subcontractors, and Vendors/Customers of Clients. You will carry both with you when you go about your day. While this may seem cumbersome (and irritating...another favorite word), *you will be far less stressed* if you can shut the business phone off at 5PM during the week and also on the weekends. You may think this is irresponsible as a Business Owner, but trust me on this – *you will want the peace.* So, get a second line added to your bill (it's only $5 to $10 a month more) and share the minutes to save your sanity. While you're at it, consider upping the amount of minutes you've signed up for because you will be using more minutes than ever before.

   a. **Must-Have Features For Your Virtual Bookkeeping Phone:**

      i. A High Resolution Camera: You *can* use your camera to take pictures of your Client's Receipts and save time on scanning. The higher the quality of the resolution, the better for your data entry. *(Check out the Section entitled "Bookkeeping Technology Advancements" later in this chapter for more information on the how's and why's of doing this.)*

ii. A Slot for an SD / Mini-SD Card, or a Mini-USB Port: If you're taking pictures of receipts, you'll want to be able to transfer those pictures quickly and easily. While Bluetooth is one such way to do that, it can take quite a bit of time to do. Make your life easy by choosing a phone with this feature ahead of time.

iii. Bluetooth Access: Even though you'll probably have an SD Card, a Mini-SD Card, or a Mini-USB Port on your phone, Bluetooth Access is still a good idea so that you can utilize a Wireless Headset for telephone calls while driving...because face it, you will be making phone calls while driving. Worst comes to worse, you can transfer your pictures via Bluetooth as well, although the process is a whole lot slower than using an SD card or USB cable.

iv. Text Messaging: If you really don't want to deal with a client on the phone, then you DO want Text Messaging. It makes answering their "quick questions" so much easier when it's texted to you, and you don't even have to be good at customer service.

b. Optional Features:

i. Internet: Internet is completely up to you. I don't use it on my phone, but I do take my Laptop with me everywhere. I also have an iPod Touch when I want to get on the Internet quickly, so I'm doubly covered wherever I go. All I have to do is find the nearest coffee shop or Barnes & Noble, and I'm online for free.

ii. MP3 Player: Again, an MP3 player may not be something you would normally care about, but when you're at a Client's site and you're stressed, being able to access your favorite songs on your phone can be a godsend. Soon, you'll be singing your favorite Shakira song (badly and out-of-tune), but you'll be having the time of your life. (Okay, maybe that's just me.)

c. A Few Cell Phone Recommendations:

i. iPhone if you want the best: Although the iPhone does NOT have an SD Card slot, or any kind of card slot, it does allow for uploading photos to your computer *very easily*. In fact, if you don't mind the extra $30 a month fee for internet access that is required with every iPhone, then in my opinion, this is the best phone you could ever own hands down. It can do absolutely anything you want it to do, and then even more than that. The newest iPhone 4 will have TWO 5.0 Megapixel digital cameras on the front and back of the phone (with a flash), and an HD video camera that will allow for video conferencing. But if you don't want to spend the extra money, consider getting an iPod Touch instead. The iPhone and iPod are the absolute best pieces of technology in our market today, and if you don't have one, you're behind the times. (In fact, even QuickBooks now "has an app for that..." – "that" being online access to a QuickBooks account. How cool is that?) Oh – and unless you buy an unlocked version, this phone can only be used with AT&T. The iPhone 4 will cost $199 with a new two-year contract, or you can get the previous version for $99 with a 2-year contract.

ii. Android Phones: Android phones are basically phones that run Google's mobile operating systems. I've been told my a tech-savvy computer geek who attended Google's convention in 2009 (and who loves his iPhone), that the internet on the Android phones are actually faster than the iPhone, but don't yet offer as many apps. To date, there are a little over 38,000 apps for all types of usage, while the iPhone has over 100,000 apps. Therefore, if you find you don't want an iPhone or iPod, an Android phone would be an excellent substitution. Here are some of the Android Phones:

- Droid Incredible by HTC: This phone is only compatible with Verizon, unless you buy it unlocked. It comes with an 8.0 megapixel digital camera, 8GB of memory, Wi-Fi technology, a mini-SD card, and a touch-screen display. It allows for FM Technology as well. To get this phone brand new will cost you approximately $199, and you will have to sign up for a 2-year contract.

- Nexus One: If you Google "Google Phone," this is the phone that will come up. Like the iPhone 4, it too will have a flash with its 5.0 digital camera – although only one camera. It also has many of the same features as the Droid, but so far, it can only be used with T-Mobile (unless you buy it unlocked and without service for $529). This phone costs $179 with a 2-year contract and the monthly fee is approximately $80 a month at the time of the writing of this book.

- HTC EVO 4G: At the writing of this book, the HTC EVO has not yet been released, but it too is an Android phone that will be released specifically for Sprint's Wireless service. It will come with TWO 8.0 megapixel cameras (one on each side of the phone), an HD video camera, a kickstand, an FM tuner, and even a compass. As far as I could find, this phone is set to be released by the end of July 2010, and will cost $199 with a 2-year contract and $100 mail-in rebate.

iii. A Blackberry: When the Blackberry first came out, it was THE Standard Business Phone to have. Personally, I think they've lost their status to the iPhone, but it's still a good phone to have, and there are still many apps that will work on your Blackberry that also work on the iPhone. So, if you don't want to spend so much on the iPhone, or you would like to go with another service, take a good look at one of the Blackberry Smartphones.

8. **Invest in a Shredder (if you don't have a fireplace):** While I always prefer to watch my backup paperwork go up in a flame of glory, shredding can be just as fun. But with or without your lighter and fire extinguisher, you will need to destroy hard copies at some point. I like to do this when I'm done with a client. I get rid of any backup by both sending hardcopies back to them, or shredding anything they don't want or need. The information I generally keep involves QuickBooks backup, emails or other

correspondence, and that's it. So, consider a shredder a must-have, because you don't want to be accused of fraud or embezzlement later on, which can happen if you still have their account information lying around (or if you have an assistant who turns out to be unreliable).

a. **A Good Feature to Have:** While it isn't always necessary, a really good feature to have on a shredder is the CD/DVD and Credit Card Shredder. That way, you can offer to shred any backup discs or old cards for your clients – for an additional charge, of course – or for free if you just want to make your clients think you're beyond awesome. Also, look for something that can shred paperclips and staples...that way, you don't break it if you decide to add shredding to your list of "Additional Services."

9. **You NEED the Internet:** How you get it is another story. Having it at your home office is a must...just get it.

10. **Get a PayPal Account:** I've been in Mary Kay for about ten years now, and the one thing that every Mary Kay person knows is this: <u>A customer will spend MORE money if you accept credit cards, often as much as 25% more.</u> It's one of those things they teach us in training, and the truth is, it's absolutely correct. For some reason, using a credit card doesn't feel like spending real money to a lot of people. Thus, they will be able to get the extra few things they're holding back on if they can pay with a credit card. The way this works in bookkeeping is that they may ask you to do other services as well. Those services can include anything from making copies to running to the post office for stamps. PayPal allows you to send them an invoice that they can pay with their credit card or checking account, and while it is true that PayPal will charge you 2% – 3% of the amount your customer pays, there are too many benefits of being able to accept credit cards that 2% – 3% is nothing in comparison. For example, not only will you probably be earning as much as 25% more for the extra work your clients will throw your way, but you will probably get paid on time and more often than if you only accept checks. And since PayPal only charges you when you accept money, you only pay when you get paid. Plus, it's a tax deduction you can list under bank fees. (Are you sold yet?)

11. **QuickBooks – A Must-Have, But You Can Probably Get It For FREE:** While it is always a good idea to invest in QuickBooks (since it's basically the most popular

bookkeeping program on the market today), it is not always necessary to have the most current program. Many times, you will find that your client has an old version of QuickBooks, and you can download their version onto your laptop to do their books. While it would be more convenient for you to update them to the newest version, the QuickBooks license you purchased may not allow it. It will be far more likely that the Small Business Owner you are working with will *not* want to be updated, nor will they want to pay for the newest version. Yet, since they will probably own an older version that has probably only been downloaded onto one or two computers at the company, you will be able to use their copy without actually violating their license. For Clients with older versions, you can upload their information into newer versions, but you can NOT put it back into an older version, so you will need to use whatever version your Client is using. Thus, purchasing your own version of QuickBooks may not be necessary. However, having said that, I do recommend you always own the newest version so that you can stay on top of what is happening with QuickBooks and be aware of what new features they add. That way, you can present the newest features to a Small Business Owner with an inefficient version and convince them to upgrade to the new product.

12. **A Car – and Not Necessarily a New One:** You're going to need a car to get back and forth to your clients. BUT, if you don't have a car, or can't get access to one, then hire a college student with a car to help you out. Let them pick up and drop off your work for you, and have them be your chauffer if and when you need to meet with a client. If you do buy a car, don't bother with the big fancy expensive models since this can be off-putting to your new small business clients. Small business clients may look at a big expensive car and think "This bookkeeper is going to cost a lot of money." On the flip side, if you drive a heap, they're going to think you do a lousy job. So, when you do get a car for work, get a nice, decent, mid-priced car and drive it proudly. Call it "the Mothership" and decorate it with fuzzy seats and fuzzier dice...and suction-cup a little flower vase to the dashboard. Maybe add an air freshener that smells like suntan lotion. (Is that "just me" again? ☺)

13. **A Plastic Box or Two for Hanging File Folders to Put in Your Car Trunk:** This is an optional feature, but I highly recommend it. You will be picking up files and taking them to and from your clients' offices. You will not want those things sliding all over your

backseat and getting mixed up. Therefore, look for a decent plastic box (which is less likely to get or cause damage in a hot car), and some green hanging file folders. Put your clients' work into separate file folders and keep this in the trunk of your car. It will make transporting the files from their office to yours so much easier and cleaner.

14. **Finally, Microsoft Office – or at least Word and Excel.** Unfortunately, this is not always standard on a new computer these days. You often have to pay extra for it. BUT, it is the standard for most business offices. QuickBooks can export many different reports to Excel, thus allowing you to manipulate numbers even further. So, get Word and Excel and learn how to use them (if you don't know how already).

That's it. That's everything I can think of that you will need. With all of this, you should now be ready to get to work.

One final quick recommendation…"*Never drink and type…never. Especially when writing correspondence to the IRS."* ☺

Chapter 3

Step 3: Put Out Your Sign Post

SPOTLIGHT ON A BOOKKEEPING BUSINESS – Ross P. Allan Chapman

Fire, flood, tornado, earthquake, & audit, five words that can instill fear in any business owner's heart. Fires permanently close 44% of the business they affect. Over 60% of businesses confronted with a major disaster will close within 2 years.

What can us as bookkeepers and accountants do to assist our clients in this issue, and why did I include audit? Simple, what you advise your client to do to be able to protect themselves if the unthinkable happens can also protect them during an audit from a governmental body. There are some very simple things that can be done here to protect the ability to continue to operate.

Scan every major document associated with the business – by scanning invoices, receipts, insurance policies, leases and other important documents you are creating a permanent digital record of them. Once they are scanned have the client store them off site as well as within their own computer systems. This can be a service you as their bookkeeper/accountant can offer to them as an added service or benefit. Think about those wonderful receipts we get from the gas station, Best Buy, Staples/Business Depot. How long do they actually last. I have had clients pass me a receipt that was 4 months old and I couldn't read it. If they had been scanned I could have entered an item into the capital assets of the corporation, as it was, I had to advise the client to go back to the store and see if they could get a replacement receipt. This further protects the client if they don't have immediate access to their documents, or if they are destroyed. You can now prove everything to your insurance agent in case of claim.

Keep a supply of letterhead, envelopes, cheques and other similar important supplies off site. If there is a fire (even if it is just smoke damage) you will not have access to any of that in the period between when you can get it replaced and the actual event. You can now still continue to pay what bills are necessary during that transition, deal with correspondence and other business activities and not have to pay to have it replaced.

Store a copy of the ledgers and other books of accounts for your client.

Store a copy of all important log-ins, passwords, account numbers, phone numbers in a document that is in a secure location. Bank safety deposit boxes are good, but what happens if you can't get into the bank. Store them in a safe place somewhere off site. Again, another service you can offer your clients.

These are some pretty simple tricks to help your client and help yourself. Lastly I would recommend that you all talk to a Business Continuity expert in your region. They have lost of helpful advice that goes well beyond what I have mentioned here.

Ross P. Allan Chapman is the owner of a bookkeeping practice under his name own and located in Toronto, Ontario, Canada. With over 13 years of experience in the for-profit and not-for-profit fields of accounting and bookkeeping he has held positions including Controller of an International Business Services company, Treasurer of an International US based 501 (c) 3 corporation and Manager of Finance for a Canadian based non-profit. He specializes in bookkeeping/accounting for independent artists, as well as small business enterprises, sole proprietorships and corporations. His website is located at RossChapman.Name and you may follow him on twitter @RossAChapman.

Once you decide to go into business for yourself, then it's time to put out your sign post. What this means for you is that you need to announce that you are in business and start doing what you can to get clients. You need to develop a marketing strategy that will catch the attention of your future clients and make you stick out in their brain. You need to develop a brand that "brands" you and your company into the subconscious of the people you want to work with. As scary as this may sound, it's really not that difficult, and that's what this chapter is all about: marketing.

This is one of the most important chapters you can read in this book. I know you are going to be tempted to jump right over and get to Chapter 4, where you learn where to find your clients. But if you don't have your marketing strategy in place before you start making contact, you might not even get a chance to speak to the client. So read this chapter thoroughly, and start brainstorming as you do, about how you are going to market yourself.

CREATING YOUR BRAND

Have you ever heard the expression "branding?" You may have heard of it with cattle – branding the hides to mark which cattle belong to which ranch – but have you heard of the expression in the business world?

Assuming you haven't heard about branding, or that you aren't exactly certain what it is or how it can help you, I'm going to give a quick rundown. Basically, branding in business is the same as branding cattle. With cattle branding, a rancher is selecting a specific logo that ties to their ranch, and they are marking it on every single asset they own – namely, their cattle, fence posts, car signs, business cards, websites, saddles, etc...basically, whatever they can mark as their possession.

In business, branding is also putting your mark on everything you own. Some brands are logos or pictures that are easily recognizable – like the Nike's checkmark logo. You see that logo and you immediately think, "running shoes." McDonald's Golden Arches is another brand that is recognizable. When you see that logo anywhere in the world, you immediately begin salivating for French fries and a Big Mac. Some other obvious brands are the AT&T bars, the Wendy's Fast Food red-haired girl, and the castle in the Disneyland logo. People just have to see these logos and they know what they are, even if there are no words with that logo. On the flip side, if you even say the words Disney, AT&T, Nike or McDonalds, those logos immediately pop into your head – largely because the name and logo are branded together.

Another type of brand that is common are catch phrases such as "Just Do It," "More Bars in More Places," "Can you hear me now?", and even "Like a Good Neighbor..."

Some brands are songs, like "I wish I was an Oscar Meyer Weiner," or "J-E-L-L-O."

Other brands consist of a very particular style or reputation. For example, Jim Carrey has a very distinct brand of comedy, one I like to call "extreme slapstick." Janeane Garafalo goes for the "bitter plain Jane" style of comedy. Quinton Tarantino makes dark, twisted and often bloody movies that make you first cringe and then ponder. James Cameron likes to create brand new worlds in his movies, like in the movie "Avatar." For actors, branding is often called type-casting and many actors fight it. For directors, it can make people run to the theater without even knowing what the story is about. Either way, when people in Hollywood don't deliver their brand, they disappoint their customers – namely, their audience.

Some companies use their names as their brands, like "As Seen on TV" or "QuickBooks." Both of those names give you an idea of what the product is. The first is some product that was sold in an infomercial; the second is a fast bookkeeping program.

In the retail world, branding can be a look or an environment. Think about Wal-Mart. The image that probably comes to mind is very cheap products stacked in a building with a white interior and blue accents. Now consider Target: mid-priced products displayed in stores of white with red accents. Now consider Red Lobster, Olive Garden, In' N' Out, Chuck E Cheese, and even Starbucks. All of these restaurants have very specific looks from branch to branch – a look that people can identify with and therefore feel comfortable about.

If you've ever travelled outside of the country for any length of time and felt homesick, but then saw a McDonald's sign...you understand the feeling of comfort a brand can bring. Just walking into a McDonald's after weeks of eating strange food can actually bring tears to your eyes.

Not that I've ever cried over a Big Mac.

(Ok, Maybe I have....but it was a *GOOD* Big Mac.)

So in case I'm not being clear enough, branding can be described as a logo, a catch phrase, a song, an environment, a reputation, or even a style, all melded into one solid, memorable element intended to "brand" a company into a customer's mind. Its purpose is to generate a feeling or a belief in a customer simply when they come into contact with the business or business product. When used correctly, it catapults a company into the top echelons of their market. And when you use it correctly, it can make you the Go-To Bookkeeper in your area, and possibly even on the Internet.

One more important thing to remember about branding...Branding will give an impression about you. The impression you should focus on is being the answer to every problem your client has – not just bookkeeping. YOU are the Super Bookkeeper. You can handle anything they throw at you, and you can solve any problem they have. (Even if you can't, that's the message you are going to want to send with every piece of branding you display.)

Creating Your Brand

Having done my spiel (i.e. monologue) about what branding is, let's look at what you can do to brand your business, and therefore your product, so that you and your company will be memorable. You want your brand to cross all channels of branding so that your business really sinks in with your clients.

Now, if you already have a business name, some of the following information can still be of help to you. However, if you don't have a business name yet, consider ALL of the following things **as a package** before you choose a name. If you think of the following items as interlinked elements, you will be much more successful at creating a brand then if you "winged it" right from the beginning (i.e. just dove into the deep end while holding your breath). Here are the things you need to consider as a whole when creating your brand:

1. **Naming Your Business:** What name have you chosen for your business? Does it relate to your name, your location, or your industry? Is it an easy name to remember or a difficult one? Is it easy to spell? Where will it be located in a phone book or directory?

2. **Choosing a Logo:** What image can you select that would represent your chosen business name, your industry, your office location, etc? What pictures relate to the business name

you have chosen? Is it an attractive logo? Is it easily recognizable, or does it look like another companies logo? Is it a standard logo or a custom logo?

3. **Creating a Catch Phrase:** Have you ever heard of an Elevator Pitch? It's a common phrase in the Mary Kay world, as well as the publishing world, because it's based on the premise that you have to make an impression on your customer in less than 30 seconds. You have to spout off something witty, funny, or philosophical in the time it takes to ride an elevator. Therefore, thing about what phrase, expression, song or rhyme you can come up with and deliver in one sentence (for your business cards and website), or in one elevator ride.

4. **Selecting a Website or Blog Domain:** Is the business name you want available as a website domain name? Is the domain name easy to spell? Can you get the ".com" version of the title, or do you have to go with some less popular domain like ".org" or ".net?" Is there any related names you can choose instead?

5. **Your Email Address and Signature:** Once you choose your website, you want your email address to reference that website so that people can easily remember your address if they need to contact you. For example, ETBarton@OneHourBookkeeper.com is easier for people to remember when finding me then etnsuz@yahoo.com, which is my personal email. I usually answer people from the etnsuz address because it is my main address, but it is very difficult for people to remember that address, while the first one is much easier. I'll admit, it is a difficult name to remember, but when I created etnsuz, I was travelling with my friend Suzanne. We created ETnSuz together so that anyone we met would remember us as a unit and write to us at one site – a yahoo site. However, Suzanne never checked the email, and when our travels were over, it became my personal email. I use etnsuz as my brand across all sorts of social networking sites, even though ETBarton is easier for people to remember.

6. **Your Name or Pen Name:** For anyone who's ever read the "About" section on our website, they know that I like to keep my thumb on the pulse of the publishing industry. In fact, I am an active member of a national romance writers Group, as well as a board member of my local chapter. One of the funniest things about being in a romance writers group – besides getting to read a lot of kinky love scenes – is the names. Everyone in the group has a pen name, including me, and some even have multiple pen names.

Obviously for me, my mother did not name me E.T., but Erica. Yet, in my romance writers group, people know me as Talia Clare. Both E.T. Barton and Talia Clare are brands I am creating for my ideal customers – which are my readers. I write business articles, credit articles, and bookkeeping articles as E.T. Barton and I publish them in various places on the internet. I write Historical Romance, Mainstream Romance, and Writing Advice articles as Talia Clare. I also write my father's memoirs under Erica Hamilton, my maiden name. Therefore, when someone sees how I published any blog I write, they will know exactly what type of article that article is going to be. In this way, you too can brand your personal name into a pen name or nickname of sorts that is easy for your customers to remember.

7. **Your Mission Statement:** You may think you don't need a mission statement – and maybe you don't – but you should at least have a goal in mind for your business. What exactly is it that you are hoping to do? Are you simply hoping to make money and be independent? Or do you have a particular client-type in mind? Are you looking to make yourself a niche-bookkeeper, someone who works in one particular industry...like construction, retail, restaurants, or maybe for used car lots. If you can come up with at least one solid sentence that states what you hope to do with your company, you can use that as a part of your brand.

Putting It All Together

Okay – so now you've thought about your company name, your logo, your catch phrase, your business name, your website and even your email, it's time to put it all together. I'm going to give you a few personal examples of branding in hopes of inspiring you.

1. **My Uncle David** (that's right, I said my Uncle): My Uncle David is a manager at a large retail location in Florida, so he has no need for branding of any sort. As far as he's concerned, he's working his dream job and living a successful and fulfilling life. And yet, my uncle branded himself years ago so that people would remember him. His last name is "Hamilton." Guess who's on a $10 bill? Alexander Hamilton. My uncle likes to call it a "Hamil-Ten" so that people remember who is on the $10 bill. Every time an

occasion calls for gift-giving, he gives – you guessed it – a "Hamil-Ten" (and he makes sure you know it's a Hamil-Ten). He does it at weddings, for Christmas, for birthdays, etc. And every time we get a card from Uncle David on one of those gift-giving occasions, the first thing we say before we even open the card is, "Ope, here's our Hamil-Ten." He's branded the $10 bill as his personal brand, and people think of him whenever anyone says, "Who's the President on a $10 bill?" He's monopolized on his name, a logo and a catch phrase, and people remember him for that.

2. **Mary Kay Beauty Consultants**: Branding is huge in the Mary Kay world. The company itself has millions of consultants world-wide, and each of the more serious consultants – the ones who move on to become Directors and eventually National Directors – all create a brand early on. Whenever a consultant recruits, they begin to create a sales unit. In order to establish themselves from the thousands of other sales units, they name their groups...usually something related to their names and their business. When I joined Mary Kay, my director's last name was Avila, and she called her group Avila's Angels. Her group was a smaller group within her Director's group, Carmen's Classics, named after the Recruiter Carmen, and the "Classic" Mary Kay skin care regime. When I created my group, we called ourselves Hamilton's Hustlers – because we hustled. (I even came up with a fun little rhyme, but I won't bore you with those details.) We took a name and some part of the Mary Kay brand, then rebranded ourselves so that other Mary Kay Consultants would remember us. We would then create signs, ribbons, magnets, business cards, and brochures – anything we could with that unit's name so that other groups would remember us when we went to conference. It was a great technique, and a whole lot of fun...because branding can be fun.

3. **Me – An American in Dublin**: When I was 21, I studied abroad in Ireland for a year. It was one of the most fun years of my life because I was a unique element in that country. I was an American surrounded by International students, and no matter how obnoxious I was, people dismissed it as, "She's American; she doesn't understand our ways." During that year, I perpetuated that dismissive philosophy by quickly branding myself as different. When I would introduce myself, I would stick out my hand and say, "Hi. I'm Erica from America." The rhyme was my catch phrase; being American was my brand; my mission was to make people dismiss any offensive behavior as simply part of being

American; and my name just happened to be Erica (very convenient, if I do say so myself).   People instantly remembered me after I introduced myself because I was different, and I had a brand.   I was American in everything I did and said, and all they had to remember was the rhyme "Erica from America" to recall my name.   Once they had that brand settled in their mind, I suddenly had a license to be as outrageous and hyper as I wanted to be, and people would just think, *"She's American; she doesn't understand our ways."*   In this instance, my name, accent, and catch phrase allowed me to cement my reputation all into one little package – my American Brand.

The point of all this is that branding doesn't have to be scary; it can be fun.   In fact, the more fun you can make your brand, the more memorable you will be.   So play with the seven branding elements I named above, and keep in mind how they can all work together to make you memorable.

Now, let's start developing some of those brands for you...

Naming Your Bookkeeping Business

In Chapter 2, I touched on the fact that one day – who knows if it's in a couple years or at the end of your working life – you will want to quit being an Independent Bookkeeper.   You will be ready to try something new and move on.   (I know...it's *shocking* that I'm talking about *ending a bookkeeping business* in a book about *starting a bookkeeping business*, but in case you haven't figured it out yet – I like to be shocking. ☺)

Here's the facts.   You will want to quit one day, or at least retire.   However many years you've spent doing this business, you will have to make a decision about what you're going to do with your clients.   You can either tell all your clients you're quitting and let them scramble to find someone else, train your bookkeeping replacement, give your customers to another bookkeeper, or sell your company to the highest bidder.   Your company has clients that other bookkeeping businesses will want, and they'll probably be willing to pay you for them.

Here's something to consider: If you name your business after yourself, then sell your company, you are selling **your personal-name-rights** along with that company. You are selling any and all rights to get business financing in your company's name, the credit history of that business, and the reputation that goes with that business (the business that was named after you). Do you really want to sell your personal name to another bookkeeping business and never be able to start another bookkeeping business in your name again? Because, if you decide to start another bookkeeping business, your personal name will be a stronger sellable asset later in your life then the name of your first bookkeeping business. You will have created a personal reputation that you can market later, as long as you haven't sold your naming rights to another business.

Here are some other elements to consider when choosing a name:

1. **Your Services:** It's an excellent idea to put what you do into the name of your company, that way, people know what services you offer just from the name (...like QuickBooks – you know right away what it is). So adding the words bookkeeping, books, accounting, accountant, bookkeeper, or virtual bookkeeping/bookkeeper to your company name is always a good idea. However, if you also offer office administration services – like copying, scanning, digital backups, website design, etc. – then you may want to go with terms like office administration, virtual assistant, virtual entrepreneur, office goddess...you get the idea.

2. **Your Niche:** Do you know who your ideal client is? What type of bookkeeping have you done in the past that you are comfortable with? For example, have you worked at construction companies in the past? Are you comfortable with all the paperwork that goes along with the construction industry? Or maybe you've worked at a lot of bars and have many, many contacts in the alcohol industry. Maybe you've worked at restaurants and know all about dealing with farmers directly to get organic products. Whatever industries you're most comfortable with, you can specialize in and capitalize on as your

brand. You can be The Construction Bookkeeper, The Bookkeeper for Bartenders, or The Restaurant and Retail Bookkeeper. Your niche would be a great way to brand and market your business.

3. **Your Location:** Putting your location in your business name can also be an excellent idea, especially when it comes to setting up a website or becoming searchable on the Internet. Often times, when people Google for bookkeeping services, they will narrow down their search by adding their location. If you include the name of your location in your business name, then it's very likely that your business name will be one of the first ones to pop up. Since you want to be virtual, you want your website to pop up first. Thus, location is a great idea, and a wider range is even better. For example, maybe name your service after the county instead of just the city – like Los Angeles County's Best Bookkeeping Services. That will help you attract a wider range of customers who are looking for you when they Google for bookkeeping services in their area.

4. **Your Catch Phrase:** When I first created a brand for my company straight out of college, I called it BusAssist (pronounced BizAssist). My catch phrase was "Business Assistance for all your office admin needs" and my product was office administration services. Unfortunately, people thought the name was "Bus" Assist – as in something you drive, and I quickly realized that I needed to rebrand my company. Thus, a couple years later, when I decided to really make a go at the whole self-employed business world, I took my original name and rebranded it as "Pro BizAssist" with a new catch phrase of "Professional <u>Business</u> <u>Assistance</u> for all your office admin needs." The new spelling on Business helps people pronounce it correctly, while also branding the catch phrase and business name together. Now, when people ask me what my business name is or why I named it that way, I can spout off both the name and catch phrase in one breath, and people will remember it.

5. **Alliteration Techniques to Make Your Name Memorable:** Remember how earlier I said that I used the catch phrase, "Erica from America" as a way to get people to remember my name? Not only is "Erica from America" a great brand personally when I'm in another country (but not so great when I'm IN America), it's effective because it's an alliteration technique. According to Wikipedia, the definition of Alliteration is...(this is direct from their website):

> **Alliteration** is a literary or rhetorical stylistic device that consists in repeating the same consonant sound at the beginning of two or more words in close succession. An example is the Mother Goose tongue-twister, "Peter Piper picked a peck of pickled peppers ...".
>
> In poetry, alliteration may also refer to repetition of a consonant in any syllables that, according to the poem's meter, are stressed as if they occurred at the beginning of a word, as in James Thomson's verse "Come...dragging the lazy languid Line along" [1].
>
> Alliteration is usually distinguished from the mere repetition of the same sound in positions other than the beginning of each word — whether a consonant, as in "some mammals are clammy" (consonance) or a vowel, as in "yellow wedding bells" (assonance); but the term is sometimes used in these broader senses.

In other words, Alliteration is a play on words that makes a phrase or name memorable. It can be a rhyme, a repetition of consonants, or a phrase's meter or rhythm.   "Erica from America" is memorable because it's a rhyme.   The Better Business Bureau is memorable because each word starts with "B." "Hamil-ten" is a play on words, and thus is also memorable. So when choosing a name, if you use Alliteration, you will make it that much easier for your customers to remember you, and thus find you later on. That is the goal.

6. **And Finally, Your Reputation:** It never hurts to throw your reputation into the title of your business...like "Los Angeles County's BEST Bookkeeping Service." You could also go with "L.A.'s FASTEST Bookkeeping Service" or "L.A.'s MOST ACCURATE Bookkeeping Service." Reputation declarations – like these – listed in your name give you something to live up to, but they also intrigue your clients. Your clients will want to know if it's true or not, and they may hire you just to find out. So it never hurts to list your *desired* reputation in your business name, as long as you plan on living up to it.

There you go...six great elements and methods to help you figure out a name for your business. Even better, each of those methods is going to help you to brand your business name as a whole. So play around with those concepts and mix and match until you find something you believe will make you memorable to your future virtual bookkeeping clients.

Logo

Once you have your business name, you have to start thinking about your logo. Remember, your logo is the visual image of your company's name and it's the second most important bit of branding you will do. It stimulates the visual senses of your future customers, and thus helps cement you in their subconscious. So pick one of the six elements you used to choose your name – Service, Niche, Location, Catch Phrase, Alliteration, or Reputation – and begin looking at pictures that most closely resemble those elements. For example, if you Google Los Angeles, you might see pictures of beaches, palm trees, or even Hollywood Stars from the Walk of Fame. (Yes I know – Hollywood Stars are not in L.A., but people associate those stars with L.A. all the time...which means, it would be a great way to promote a business located in Los Angeles – and even better if you're actually located in Hollywood.) Remember, logos can also be several letters together – like AAA, or BBB.

- Once you have an idea of what you would like as your logo, the next thing you want to do is hire a graphic artist to create a custom logo for you. I went to Elance.com to get the logos for the OneHourBookkeeper.com, and they cost me approximately $30 a pop. That is 1/10th of the price a local graphic artist would charge (which is a really great deal if you ask me). When you buy a custom logo, you own the rights. No one else can use it without asking your permission. That's a valuable asset you can sell, and it is key in helping you brand yourself.

I'm a logo...I'm the logo for the E.T. Barton pen name, and I am now used on every piece of paper, business card, envelope and social networking site where information from E.T. Barton is posted. When you see me, you know the brand that is attached to the information being shared. I was designed by Rin Kurohana, a freelance graphic artist at Elance.com, and Rin was chosen from dozens of competing artists because she had the style best suited to the One Hour Bookkeeper site. (And she was the cheapest.)

When you finally decide on a logo yourself, start marketing it. Put on everything that has to do with your business – from the signs on your car to the business cards in your wallet. Because even if people forget your business name, they will remember the logo.

Catch Phrase – Your Tagline and Elevator Pitch

Quick Note:

A **Catch Phrase** is exactly what it sounds like...a Phrase that "Catches" someone's attention. It's usually catchy and sticks in your head like the song, "It's a Small World." It's hard to get – or silence, even when you *really want to* – and you fit it on a business card.

A **Tagline** is a sentence on a website that tells visitors what that website is all about. It also tells search engines, like Google, what that site is about so they can recommend your site to people looking for you and your services (i.e. free marketing).

An Elevator Pitch is a sales pitch you would deliver to your ideal client when the two of you get on an elevator together. It takes less than 30 seconds to say, and it has to be catchy so that your ideal client remembers you when they escape that elevator. Having said that...

Even though the definitions for Catch Phrase, Tagline and Elevator Pitch are different, *these three things don't have to be different*. In fact, I recommend that you make these three things the SAME thing in order to Brand you and your business into the minds of every Virtual Bookkeeping client you ever get. Figure out a catch phrase that's small enough to fit on a business card, but filled with tagline keywords that tell your client what your business does, and put it all together into one sentence that can be said in less than 30 seconds. Once you do, you will create one of the most powerful marketing tools available to help you sell your business.

Here's what I mean:

We'll start with the tagline. When you come up with a tagline for your **_virtual_** bookkeeping business, you are going to put that tagline on your business right at the top of your website. That tagline needs to tell your visitors what your website, and essentially your business, is all about. To do this effectively, you need to focus on Keywords. A Keyword is a word or phrase that people use to search for *anything* from services to products and even product reviews. People use keywords when they want answers to problems...like "how do I find a bookkeeper in Los Angeles that is cheap?" They would probably Google "Cheap Bookkeeping in Los Angeles." That is a keyword phrase, and it could also be your tagline.

When you add keywords to your tagline, and then post it on your website just below the name of the website, you make your website more attractive to your current and future customers, as well as all the little Google Spiders. (Yes, there is such a thing as Google spiders...they are like tiny little robots searching your website for keywords so that they can promote your website to the right people.) Because Google and other search engines biggest service is to help people find solutions to their problems, they want your site to have keywords that can help their spiders match your site to their information seekers. You can capitalize on this free marketing service by adding keywords and keyword phrases to your tagline that Google can understand...like "accounting & bookkeeping." If you've ever been to our website – OneHourBookkeeper.com – then you've probably already noticed our Keyword Tagline, which is "How to Save Thousands on Accounting & Bookkeeping." "Accounting & Bookkeeping" is a keyword phrase that is commonly Googled by various people. "How to" is another popular Google phrase. When put together, we tell our readers that we are teaching people "How to save thousands on Accounting & Bookkeeping," but we are also telling Google that we are a "How to" website. By doing so, Google ranks us in a list of websites that also talk about those issues, and it moves us up the list as we gain more and more visitors, or as people narrow down their searches.

To find Keywords that you can add to your website's tagline – and your website in general – check out Google Adwords or Wordtracker.com. Both offer search results for various keywords, as well as competition for those keywords, and related search terms.

Once you've done a Keyword Search and have some keyword ideas in mind for your tagline, the next step is to put them together into a One-Sentence Catch Phrase that will become your final tagline. This tagline will be printed on your business cards, letterhead, envelopes, email signature line, etc. It should tell someone exactly what your business does, and possibly your business's mission. It should be catchy, have some type of rhythm, and – if possible – use some alliteration techniques.

After you've created your Tagline/Catch Phrase, you can add another sentence or two on it to further explain what your business does. By doing so, you would create an Elevator Pitch. The key is, make it memorable and make it short.

A really good tagline/catch phrase to go with is "As Low As $100 a Month." It speaks directly to your clients' goals, which will be inexpensive bookkeeping. That is one more thing to keep in mind when choosing a tagline...what are your clients' goals and how can you answer those goals with your tagline?

YOUR WEBSITE

Once you have a name, logo and Catch Phrase in mind, it's time to start packaging those things together into a brand that will settle firmly in people's minds. The next thing we will deal with is your website. Every business today has a website, and if you're going to be a virtual bookkeeper, you are going to need one also – especially because you want to be *virtual*. To be virtual, you will be collecting bookkeeping clients from all over the country (and possibly the world), but never see them. That means your website is going to be your virtual business card.

While it never hurts to have a website that is professionally designed by a website designer (who is going to charge thousands of dollars), spending a lot of money is no longer necessary thanks to the Internet and website/blog templates. There are so many great website development companies out there with pre-designed layouts, that it seems foolish to actually pay anyone else to do the work. However, there are a lot of things to consider before you actually launch your website, like...should you have a blog or a basic website? Are you going to accept credit cards, or count on the mail? Do you want the option to make extra money with your website by displaying ads or creating an online store? And – do you really want to be a virtual bookkeeper or a face-to-face bookkeeper?

A Blog versus a Basic Website

The number one thing to think about when developing your website is "Should I blog or should I just stick with a website?" The biggest difference between a blog and a website is that blogs change all the time, while websites rarely change. It's harder to change the look of a blog once you've selected a background, while a website is 100% changeable and everything can be placed exactly where you want it. Since blogs change more often than websites, blogs often get more visitors than websites. Since websites are 100% changeable, it's easier to create online stores with a website then it is with a blog. Finally, blogs are often free to set up while websites usually cost a monthly fee.

When it comes to blogs and websites, blogs have a way of giving you "credentials" that websites don't. (I put "credentials" in quotes because the more you share somewhat logical information, the more people will think you're an expert *because of your blog*.) Blogging is a way to share the jargon inside your head for free, which can then impress upon potential customers that your services are worth buying. It is a one-sided conversation that will prove to people that you are honest and worth hiring, which is why everyone has a blog these days. When you have a website, the only way to convince people that you are an expert is to actually list your credentials and post your resume right where anyone and everyone can see it.

I could go on all day, but here's what website selection really comes down to...

1. **Do You Blog – and should you?** Blogging is the newest trendy approach to business websites and they're changing the way business is done. The biggest reason is that blogs are personal and new information is added regularly, so customers keep coming back, and they often feel like they get to know you on a personal level. With a blog, you can also submit your articles to social networking sites more often, which may draw a larger audience (and eventually customers) to your site from other sites.

2. **Setup Costs**. While you can have *both* a website and a blog for your business, trying to connect them together may be difficult if you're not website-savvy. The biggest problem you will usually have is setting your site up for the first time. Yet generally, once that's done, you will find things are very easy to change or add in both blogs and websites. In most cases, **you can have a site up in under an hour**. Blogs are very easy to update quickly, and usually consist of pasting information into a square and hitting "Publish." Websites take a bit more work to update, and can be more difficult depending on who hosts you, but they are easier to customize.

3. **How often you will be making changes to your site**. Will you be adding new information regularly, or products? Because if you plan on updating your website regularly, you don't want to invest in a program that requires a lot of time and know-how for simple changes (like Dreamweaver or FrontPage). On the other hand, blogs are easy to update because they only update one area of your site – the main blogging area. If you need to move stuff around on the site a lot – like items for sale – then go with a website. If you just want to update information, then go with a blog.

4. **Design and Layout**. Both websites and blogs have thousands of different templates, themes and backgrounds you can choose from. You just have to search through the online catalogs and pick the style that you feel best suits you and your business – or the style that most closely matches your letterhead (if you have some already). Then just click and launch. It's usually that simple for both types of sites.

5. **Monthly Costs:** Cost-wise, you can usually start a blog for free, while websites cost a monthly (or annual) fee to maintain. The biggest downside to a free blog is that you will have the name of the blogging company right in your url (for example, www.your-company.wordpress.com) which can deter people from coming to your site regularly since that's a whole lot to type. Also, you can't usually make money with a free blog, although I recently heard that you can with Blogger.com. Apparently, Blogger is owned by Google, so they allow you to put Adsense ads on your site cheaply, easily and for free. But if you don't go with Blogger for blogging (especially because most blogging experts agree that Wordpress is the best), then pay a Hosting Site like JustHost.com to host your site, and you can use the Wordpress Plug-ins to supplement your bookkeeping income. (I go more into detail about all this later in this chapter.) I like JustHost because you can

buy your domain name for $15, host your first site for $4 a month, and host any additional domain names for free. Once you set it up in JustHost, you just click on the Wordpress link and put in your desired Wordpress login info. From there, all of your blog / website updates are done on Wordpress. And if your site ever gets hacked, you have a backup at Justhost that you can simply reinstate and get your site back immediately.

    a. If you decide you really don't want to pay for a website or blog – or at least you don't want to right now while you're starting out – you can actually get a free blogging account and then get around the blogging company name being placed in your URL by paying for the domain name you truly want, and then creating a "Masked Forward" to your free blog. What that means is that you pay for your chosen domain name (about $5-$15 a year) and then you point it to your free blog site. When you choose the "Masked Forward" option, people coming to your site never see the free blogging name in the domain address. It's a great, inexpensive way to get your domain for cheap without investing a lot of money in hosting or website development.

What NOT to Do in Picking a Website Domain Name:

Now that I've given you some thought on what you *should* be doing for your business's website, I'm going to give you some thoughts on what you *shouldn't* be doing on that same website. Here we go...

1. **Don't Use Complicated Words or Names:** Do yourself a favor...when you pick the name of a website...go with something simple. If your first or last name is hard to remember or confusing (and you know if it is), then don't use it in the website link. You want people to be able to find you and to remember your company website's name without going "How was that spelled again?" So something like..."*Supercalifragilisticexpialidocious*_Bookkeeping.com" would be bad, even if you spelled it "*Super-Cali-Fragilistic-Expi-Ali-Docious*_Bookkeeping.com." Instead, maybe

shorten it and try "SuperBookkeeping.com" instead, or go with the name of your city or county – as long as it's simple, easy to remember and easy to spell.

2. **Don't Make The Website Name Too Long** – as also shown in the example above, keep it short. A long name doesn't fit nicely in any kind of communication, whether Word documents, letterhead, or even on business cards. Short is quick and easy to type...that's the goal.

3. **Don't Make it "Forgettable**." We've all done it. We've all forgotten someone's exact website address and ended up at the wrong site. We assume a website name should be obvious, but it instead ends up being complicated. For example, "American Airlines;" they are NOT at AmericanAirlines.com. Instead, they are at <u>AA.COM</u>. And AA (i.e. Alcoholics Anonymous) is at <u>AA.ORG</u>. And then of course, there's the Auto Club, which is not at AutoClub.com, but is at <u>AAA.com</u> instead. That's not confusing, right? Personally, I forget American Airlines' website every time I want to go to them. I have to Google the site each time to make sure I end up at the right website. The end result? I fly United instead. Their website's easier to find...<u>United.com</u>. Therefore, name your website something associated to your business, and name it something your clients can remember.

4. **Don't Use "Characters."** Putting "&," "-"or "_" signs in your website name is a HUGE pain-in-the-keester for your clients to type. It slows your client down, and you don't want to slow them down when they come to your site. It's also easy to forget the characters, so they may not end up at your site at all. On the other hand, typing "and" or leaving out the dashes is much easier and faster for someone to type. So, be super easy, and super convenient in everything you do – including naming your website.

5. **Don't Use Numbers** – unless of course the numbers are part of your business name. For example, <u>123Inkjets.com</u> is a great Business Name (and thus website name by association) because 1) the 123 is easy to remember, and 2) the numbers at the beginning of the word pretty much guarantee the website first billing in any Phone Book Directory they list themselves in. Any number sequence that's really easy to remember can help move your local yellow pages listings to the top of the list. BUT, on the flip side, picking a website like SuperBookkeeper**99**.com is not a good idea. Even though the 99 may be memorable, people are still going to ask you, "*Why 99?*" If your answer is, "*Because*

SuperBookkeeper.com was already taken and the name generator suggested the 99"...well guess what...you've lost your client's attention at the words, "already taken." And when they go to search your website, they're going to forget the "99" part in your website name. Instead, they'll end up at the original SuperBookkeeper.com website – your competition – and they'll forget all about you.

a. **Other Examples of good numbers:** 123, 321, 1800 (*as in 1-800*), 50, 100, 101, 1001. Basically, anything ending in 1,5, or 0 is usually easier to remember.

b. **Examples of bad numbers:** There was a great website I went to once. It was called 46things.com – or was it 47? Or 48? Or maybe it was 30 something. Whatever it was, I LOVED the website, and I found it because it was suggested by a book I read. But guess what – I never found the website again. I couldn't remember the name, and even when I tried Googling it, nothing came up. The idea and concept behind the website was fantastic, but because the number was not easy to remember, they lost me as a reader and potential client. And if they lost me – they've probably lost many other people as well. After all, I'm just an Average American Girl. (Other numbers to forget about – 1866, 1877, 1888, and anything ***not*** ending in 1,5, or 0. They're harder to remember.)

Making Money with Your Website

Whether you go with a blog or a website, the one thing you are absolutely going to want to do is make money with that website. Of course, you can make the usual income through customers coming to your website and looking for your services. However, you can also make money from your website by placing ads, selling products, using affiliate links, and even asking for donations. When it comes to a website – and especially using that website to support your business – you are going to want to take advantage of as many income streams as you possibly can.

Consider this: Being a bookkeeper means that you are dealing with people's money. If you make yourself the type of bookkeeper where people say, "I have to ask my bookkeeper where to buy a computer for the cheapest price," you have the opportunity to earn some of that money as a referral commission. You see, there are thousands of companies that will pay you for bringing your clients to them, and it's often a percentage of whatever the sale is. This is called Affiliate Income. You get a commission for referring your client's to that business, and the retail company writes your commission off as "Marketing Dollars." (This is similar to when Real Estate Agents introduce their Buyers to Sellers and make a commission off the sale – a commission that comes out of the Sellers' money.)

"But is that Ethical?" you may be wondering. *"Is it fair for me to make money off of my customers – especially without them knowing?"*

Being the money-grubbing little booger that I am, I say absolutely. In fact, I say, "You are doing your clients a HUGE favor." You see, when you become an affiliate to a company, you get access to all of their best sales, rebates and coupons – discounts your clients would never find on their own. You can save your clients as much as 50% on a product, and then still make 2% to 50% of that sale. In other words, your clients saves money, and you earn money because you are taking the time to find them the best deal you can possibly find.

But, there are plenty of other ways that you can make money with your blog, which I will get into as I go along. For now, since Affiliate Income is the easiest and fastest way to increase your bookkeeping income, I'm going to go into a bit more detail about that.

How Do I Become an Affiliate?

First off, to become an affiliate, you have to have a website. (Surprise, surprise...we're only in the website section, right?)

Secondly, you have to have a *legitimate* website name – with an account that you pay to host – and not a free Wordpress or Blogger account. Most free blogs will prevent you from being able to put Affiliate Ads, or any kind of ads, on your blog. Therefore, you have to upgrade to an account that will host your blog and get the name "Wordpress" or "Blogger" out of the domain name.

Third, you need to sign up for an Affiliate account. For office supplies, computers, equipment, travel, electronics...basically anything you would need for a business...I go to Commission Junction at CJ.com for my affiliate products. This company has thousands (and probably hundreds of thousands) of companies that want you to sell their products for them. For informational products, like eBooks on everything from grooming your cat to creating a million dollar product, I go to <u>ClickBank.com</u>. Both accounts are free, and both are easy to use. You simply find the products or coupons you want to display, select them, and then click the "Get HTML" button. The Affiliate Websites then create a custom HTML for you (which is basically a secret code that tracks every purchase coming from your website) and you copy and paste that HTML into your blog or website. Once you hit publish, the HTML turns into a coupon on your website that you can access to order products, and every order will gain you a commission.

Fourth – once you have the Affiliate account on your website and an idea of what products you would like to sell, it's time to take orders. Wait until you hear your clients say, "I need ink cartridge replacements, but I don't want to spend a lot of money." When you hear that, that is your opportunity to say, "Let me do some research for you. I bet I can find you a great deal – cheaper than you would get at the local office supply store." Of course, they will like the idea that you are doing the work, and they will be happy to let you try.

Five – now that you have the order in hand, go back to Commission Junction and do a "Search" for the product that your client wants. (Yes, you can actually search for one product.) You will immediately get a list of products as well as how much the commission is and a general price range for the products. Apply to the programs that have the best prices until one of them gives you instant approval, and then get the HTML. You don't even have to put the HTML on your website. As soon as you see the "http://" sign with the fancy code, that is your special link to the site, and you just have to put that in your browser to make a commission. "Wham, Bam, Thank You Ma'am – instant money in your account."

By doing this, I regularly make an extra $1,000 a year for less than one hour of my time here and there. So if you want to be the go-to bookkeeper that everyone thinks is a genius, and you want to get paid for it – you have to start using your website for affiliate income.

And don't forget – you make a commission every time YOU buy something too!

Making Money with Google Adsense:

Now that you have dollar signs rolling through your head for making Affiliate Income, let's get into other types of income.

If you've ever Googled anything in your entire life, then you probably have a vague recollection of Google Adsense. It's those tiny little ads that you see at the top and to the right of the screen when you get your Google Search results. *Those little ads are specifically ordered by various companies, and they pay to be shown whenever certain key phrases are typed into the Google Search Engine.*

"What does that have to do with me?" you may be thinking. Simple. *"Those little ads are specifically ordered by various companies, and they pay to be shown whenever certain key phrases are typed into the Google Search Engine."* You see, Google will automatically assign specific search terms – known as keywords – to your website based on the words that you use in your website. If you decide to place a Google Adsense ad on your website, then Google will customize that ad to fit your website's keywords, and pay you a commission every time someone clicks on the link. In the beginning, you could make only a few pennies or dollars per month, but as you get more traffic to your site, and as you place those Adsense ads in key locations, your income will begin to snowball into bigger and bigger amounts. In fact, there are plenty of bloggers out there making tens of thousands of dollars per month from Google Adsense ads placed on their blogs.

Just keep in mind, the key to making a lot of money on Google Adsense is not just placement, it's usually based on visitors (aka, "traffic"). The more visitors you get, the more money you can make in the long run. The best way to get traffic is to blog. Therefore, don't expect to make a whole lot of money in the beginning unless you plan on making blogging a regular part of your business. However, you can make an extra $10 to $20 a month in the first year for simply putting ads on your website or blog and doing nothing else.

How to Start a Lucrative Virtual Bookkeeping Business
By E.T. Barton and Robin E. Davis
www.OneHourBookkeeper.com

YOUR EMAIL

Believe it or not, your email is another way to cement your brand with your future clients – but a lot of people don't take advantage of it. Instead, they stick with their free personal email address that maybe they've had for years, and they put that on their business cards and website. But here's the thing; when you order a website, you get a minimum of one free website with an @yourwebsite.com ending. Even though that sounds like it would be easier to use the email you've had forever instead of creating a new website-related email address, anyone who does that is actually missing an opportunity to advertise their business, and they're making it *more difficult* for clients to find them.

Think about it: my personal email is etnsuz@yahoo.com. My business email is ETBarton@OneHourBookkeeper.com. Which one will be easier for YOU to remember? The obscure one I started more than a decade ago? Or the one that has both my pen name and my website name in it? And if you saw etnsuz, would you know that it goes with the Pen Name E.T. Barton or the One Hour Bookkeeper site? Of course not. That's why I took advantage of my free website address and personalized it – so people would remember the email, the website, and my name. It's one of my many branding tools.

Now before you dismiss this advice with the usual, *"I don't want a new email address. It would be too hard to remember to check both emails. I just want everything to come to one email."*...**STOP**. You CAN still have all of your business email come to your personal email without a lot of work. All you have to do is set up an "Automatic Forward" from your email address to your personal address, and then you never need to remember to check your business email again. That way, you can still advertise your business email on your card without asking people to remember your personal, non-business related email.

One more thing to remember about email...keep your email address as simple as possible. If your first or last name is hard to spell, use your nickname.

Good point. Another Email-No-No is...DON'T put a number in your email address just because the email you want is not available. I once emailed all of my personal financial information to a mortgage broker who had a number in his email, but I didn't remember that. So I ended up sending all of my personal info to some stranger. I was really NOT happy about that, but the mortgage broker didn't think it was a big deal. IT WAS! Therefore, don't do that to your clients. They're going to send you confidential information. Make it easy for them to send it to you. FORGET THE NUMBERS!

BUSINESS CARDS

Business cards are one of the lowest and most effective marketing tools you can create for any business – whether independent bookkeeping or something else. There are a million and one places to go and get them nowadays, and they generally cost as little as $15 for 500 cards. Now while a lot of people may tell you to just print up some quick cards, it's obvious to professional business people when cards are printed at home versus by a reputable company – and they will come to their own conclusions if your cards look homemade. While you may find it charming to have "homemade" business cards, you aren't actually impressing anyone with them...and having a business means *you are selling yourself at all times in all ways*. Your business card is your first line of sales – so keep that in mind when you order. How do you want to be thought of? As a "homemade" bookkeeper who can't afford $15 for professional cards? Or as an astute business owner who is willing to invest in their business?

I say – go professional all the way.

Where to Buy

If you want your business cards designed specifically by a reputable, trustworthy, eager-to-please company, then head over to Office Depot and swing by their copy center. There, you can find a catalog of thousands of promotional items for any business, and all you have to do is pick and choose. They've got everything from very simple to very fancy.

Having said that, Office Depot is not necessarily the cheapest option out there. Personally, when I need any kind of promotional items, I go to iPrint.com, which is Yahoo!'s site for promotional items. You can design anything you want personally, upload your company logo, move things exactly where you want them to be, and often order a very small amount for a very low price...and you can do this all from the comfort of your own dining table. I recommend checking them out before you go anywhere. (Click on the link above and you can actually save 20% on everything you buy at iPrint.com.)

What to Put On Your Business Card

In my virtual business, I see a LOT of business cards...*a lot!* I see every kind of paper, shape, cut, texture and wording. I see too much information and too little information. I see fancy logos and *what-the-heck-is-that* logos. So to say I have an opinion on business cards is to put it mildly. Having said that, here are my lists of what you *should do* with your business card:

Do:

1. **Put your website on your card**. Again, your website is the place where they can go to learn more about you and your business. And if you want to be virtual, this is one of the most important branding tools you can use.

2. **Put your catch phrase on it.** You want to imprint your brand on everything, and a catch phrase will help you be memorable.

3. **Put Your Logo on it**...for branding purposes.

4. **Put your voicemail number on the card** – *preferably a virtual voicemail number*. You don't have to put every phone number on your card, or even your cell number, but it is a good idea to put some phone number on your card where people can leave messages. For

me, a voicemail phone number especially comes in handy when I'm travelling and I want to run my business while on vacation. So get a voicemail number and put it on your card.

    a. (I like <u>RingCentral.com</u> because your voicemail number is also your eFax number, and they offer extensions to that phone number for free...you can even get an 800 number for little or no additional cost.)

5. **Put your Text Message number on your card.** More people today are texting than ever before. In fact, as I write this in the coffee shop, three is a girl at the table next to mine texting someone. Texting is way-more convenient then picking up the phone and making a phone call. It guarantees that you won't be stuck on the phone talking to someone when you're in the middle of some other important project. So, include your text message number so that business owners can text you when they "just have a quick question."

6. **Put your email on your card**. Everybody's on email today – *everybody*. Why? Because it's easier to shoot out a quick email then it is to text message (as long as you're computer is already booted up). Not only that, it's usually free while text messaging can cost as much as $0.40 per message. Since you want to be virtual, people need to get hold of you in Cyberspace. Therefore an email is a must.

7. **Put your eFax number on your card**. Mom and I were recently arguing over having a land-line fax machine versus having an <u>eFax</u> and which was a better option. (Of course, I won). The facts are, you may think you're saving money by not getting an eFax and using a land line instead, but the truth is the eFax is way more convenient then having a land line. Imagine yourself doing books at a client's office when another client suddenly calls in a panic. The second client tells you that they got a notice from the IRS and they are freaking out. You tell that client to fax it to you right away so you can see it. Either they can fax it to you at your house (and then you have to run home to see it, leaving your first client hanging), they can fax it to your second client (which is not really a good idea, professionally speaking), or they can fax it to your eFax and you can open it on any computer in that office without wasting your client's paper, or without your first client even knowing. Plus, you have it saved digitally in your email, and you can access it again and again from anywhere else in the world (including the Caribbean, should you happen to be there). Furthermore, by saving your eFaxes in your email, you could turn

your personal or business email into a digital filing cabinet, where files are stored for as long as you wish to keep them.

8. **Take Advantage of the Back of the Card**. A lot of people forget about the back of the card and leave it blank. Or even worse, they let someone else advertise on the back of their card (like cards from VistaPrint.com – it saves money on the business card purchase because VistaPrint is advertising on your card instead). The back of your card is what I like to call "Prime Real Estate." You want to put as much information as you can on your card, and if it all fits on one side – great. But on the back of the card, you can provide a mini-service for your clients. You can add lines for them to take notes, or a calendar for them to circle an appointment date, or an actual appointment memo on the back. You can even put your catch phrase on the back. The reason I say this is that many business owners will use the back of a business card to take notes about the person that handed them the card (namely you). Make an impression by giving them something extra on the back. Maybe it's silly and maybe it won't make much of an impact, but it will begin to cement your reputation – as the bookkeeper that provides full-service treatment, right from the moment you hand that card over.

MAGNETIC CAR SIGNS

(Again, I like iPrint.com for this. They are a Yahoo! company, and if you use the link here, you can save 20% on your sign.)

While some people may think having a magnetic car sign to advertise your business is tacky or unprofessional, it is actually a very effective way to get clients, especially small business clients. Having a magnetic car sign says, "*I'm approachable. I'm not a big fancy corporation, but I am serious about what I do. My focus is not on huge advertising campaigns – it's on people. If you hire me, you and I will build a professional relationship.*" That's the general message your future clients will get when they look at your car sign...and that's the message they want.

On the flip side, a lot of businesses like to get the clear plastic stickers for their windows also advertising their business. The only problem with those signs is that heated glass will eventually melt those signs permanently into the window and you will have to use a razor and cleaner to get the sign off. Not only that, you can't take the sign down easily if and when you get too many clients. Trust me – it's a bummer having to tell a potential client that you can't take them on, and then possibly losing them forever.

Having said that, make sure you use your brand on your website – meaning your catch phrase, name, website information, and your logo. When you have all these branding elements in place, then you are ready to start making your car signs. But before you order your website, here are some other things to consider:

1. **Placement**. A lot of people place their car signs on their car doors. The only time that placing a magnetic car sign on a car door is effective is when you're parked in a parking lot or at a curb. Think about it. While driving on the freeway or down the street, people don't like to turn their head and try to read a sign on someone's car door. It's too dangerous. And yet, getting stuck behind someone in traffic often results in people killing their wait time by reading bumper stickers and license plate holders. Following you on the street can also result in people reading your car sign. (I've actually had someone call me and say they were driving behind me and saw my sign and wanted to know more about my services; that's how effective a magnetic car sign can be when placed on the trunk.)

2. **Measurement**: Since the car sign is best positioned on the back of your car, you want to measure the flattest space on the back of your car and design your sign accordingly. Most likely, this means that your car sign will be 6" tall, and 12" to 24" long. This also means that you will probably be covering your car logo or trunk keyhole. Since the sign is magnetic, it won't be a problem because you'll be able to easily lift it whenever you need access.

3. **A Very Basic Design**: Since your advertising space is going to be fairly small, you need to be precise about what you advertise. Most likely, you will want to use your basic catch phrase, your website, your logo, and a phone number. That is pretty much all you will have space for. So put your best design work into your sign, because it can get you clients from where you least expect it, and make it as large as you can make it so that your sign can be read from a distance.

ANNOUNCE YOUR NEW BUSINESS

Once you've got your branding and business cards in place, it's time to start advertising that business like there's no tomorrow. Hand out your business card to anyone and everyone you come in contact with. Put your magnetic car sign on the back of your car, and start driving in the areas where your ideal clients are (...namely rich areas in your local community). Feel free to invest in other promotional products if you wish (like pens or mugs), but business cards and the magnetic signs are usually all you need.

Don't forget to announce your new business at other locations as well – like your social networking sites (i.e. Facebook, Twitter, and LinkedIn) and update your profiles at those sites with your new website and job-skill information. I especially like LinkedIn for business contacts because its target demographic was business people right from the first day of inception, and it allows people to advertise their businesses, resumes, job skills, and even post job listings. Facebook is just personal, so it's always a great place to post information about you, and Twitter is just ridiculously good for advertising in general. I don't know why Twitter works, or how it does, but I do know that I get a LOT of traffic from Twitter just because I share articles I like there. Therefore, it can't hurt you to sign up for a free account.

Of course, you can sign up for other social networking sites as well, but honestly, I find these three – Twitter, Facebook and LinkedIn – to be the most beneficial for making relationships with people.

Finally, don't forget to tell the people you know in your life personally that you've started your own business – like friends and family, previous employers who might like to hire you every now and then, or accountants you've worked with in the past. Especially contact the accountants. They can get you a lot of business right away, and will probably send you the most referrals.

That's it. You are branded, and should now be ready to actively market yourself and your business to the world. Read on for the most effective ways I've found for doing that.

Chapter 4

Step 4: Finding Your Clients

SPOTLIGHT ON NETWORKING – Rosen Professional Services

Networking with BNI – By Jason Rosen

BNI can be a great resource but there are a number of caveats. The first is it really depends on the people in the chapter. If the group has the right connections it can be a gold mine of referrals. On the other hand you can find a chapter that appears to have all the people in all the right positions but they fail to produce usable referrals.

The key here is to get to know some of the members ahead of time and get a feel for their real willingness and capability to provide referrals. It is also helpful to know if you feel you can provide referrals to the other members.

Another thing to keep in mind is that chapters are dynamic. That means BNI chapters can change over time. A chapter that has strong members and a healthy number of referrals can turn into a dud. On the other hand, your chapter can attract the right member and that can make all the difference in the world. This is important to consider as it means you have to perpetually evaluate your chapter's performance and how it helps your business.

Lastly it is important to know that your ability to participate and share referrals. Too often, I would see people come into the chapter and wait until they received a referral before they would offer a referral. The net effect is that everyone would sit on the sidelines waiting for the other to make the first move. This does not work.

Networking is a full contact sport. This is true regardless of the networking forum. BNI is certainly one of the largest networking groups, but there are many other viable networking groups. Networking done properly can be fun. Explore different networking options and see which one is a good fit for your business.

Jason Rosen, Owner of Rosen Professional Services helps clients turn FEAR into Focus, Energy, Action and Results by providing specialized business consulting, CXO services and coaching to small and medium sized businesses and their owners. Jason has more than 15 years of experience in the financial services industry working with premier wealth management firms such as JP Morgan Chase and U.S. Trust Company. Jason has served as an Assistant Director of BNI Connecticut and as Chairman of the Solopreneur Council at the New Haven Chamber of Commerce.

The concept for the "One Hour Bookkeeper" name and brand actually did not come from trying to be funny or memorable. The truth is, if I had gone for funny or memorable, I would have picked "The Lazy Bookkeeper." Not only would I have picked that name because it makes me laugh every time I see it or think of it, but I would have picked it because it applies in my case. I have always called myself "The Lazy Bookkeeper" because 1) bookkeeping for any new company begins to bore me right around the 6-month mark, and 2) if there's an easier way to do bookkeeping – one that will save me time and get me out of an office sooner – I will find it and do it.

Number 2 has turned out to be one of the driving forces of my life. There are so many things I *want* to do versus the things I *have* to do, that I've had to figure out what works best. I've researched and tested many, many concepts regarding nearly every aspect of my business, and cut the chaff – so to speak – on anything that wasn't highly effective. Thus, the marketing concepts and ideas that I mention in this chapter *will* work for you, if you are brave enough to try them. After it works for you once, do it again and again to get as many clients as you feel you need to get for your personal security. However, please keep in mind, my hopes for you are not that you make a million dollars in bookkeeping, but that you create a freeing lifestyle which allows you to really live and enjoy your life. My suggestion is always this: *get just enough clients to allow you to feel secure, and then go out and have <u>fun</u>.*

Oh – and in case you were wondering – the "One Hour Bookkeeper" brand also came from my laziness skills. I was able to create a system that cut so much time from my bookkeeping process that I can now do a large majority of bookkeeping in one hour. While writing this book, I am also working on a one-hour video to teach other bookkeepers how they too can do their bookkeeping in one hour. So stay tuned...

WORD-OF-MOUTH / ASKING FOR REFERRALS

If you ask any independent business owner (not just bookkeepers) their number one method for getting customers, they will tell you "Word-of-Mouth." Word-of-mouth is cheap, and in many cases free. It's a "Sell Job" meaning that someone is *"selling a product"* to someone else by giving their open and honest opinion. The first person is effectively backing the quality of the product.

Here's another way to think of it: have you ever gone to a boss and said, "You have to hire (*insert name of friend here*). They will do a great job for you. They're reliable and hardworking, and they'll fit in perfectly at this company. You really should hire them." If you have, then you've done a "Sell Job" to your boss. You're vouching for someone, listing all the benefits of hiring them, and encouraging your boss to make a choice. Even if the conversation goes more like this – "You have to hire my friend. They're *not* very bright, but they are hardworking and I think you'll like 'em." – you're still doing a "Sell Job." You've listed the benefit that most applies to the boss.

A few more examples of this would be:

- Movie reviews. People go onto various websites, like Flixter.com, and they post their opinions about the movie. The review will either sell a reader on going to the movie or waiting until the movie comes out on video. Every review is a "Sell Job," whether to see the movie or not see the movie.

- Vacations. How many times have you tried to talk friends or family into joining you on a vacation? You list the cost, the location, the weather, the beauty of the hotel, the shortness of the flight, etc. That's a "Sell Job."

- Watching a TV Show. We've all done this one...you call your best friend and you say, "Did you watch my favorite TV show? It is so *good*. It's funny, and sexy, and I really want to get-it-on with the star of the show." (No? Just me? ☹) Well, whatever you said to get your friend to watch that show – that is a "Sell Job."

- Ice Cream. If you have kids or have ever even babysat, then you've been the focus of a "Sell Job" at least once in that child's short life. They probably turned their big, innocent eyes to you at some point and asked for ice cream (or pizza, or a toy). When you say no, they immediately launch into all the reasons why you should change that no to a yes. *"I ate all my dinner. My room is clean. I took my bath. I'll brush my teeth afterwards. If you let me have ice cream this one time, I'll never ask for ice cream ever again."* (Clearly a lie, but still, you get the point.) This isn't just a "Sell Job"; it's a "Snow Job."

You're probably thinking, *"What is the point of all this? I know what Word-of-Mouth means. Get on with it."*

The point is that your Number 1 source of getting clients is going to be through Word-of-Mouth, which may be a hard concept for you to deal with. It may be so hard, in fact, that you dismiss it out of hand and focus on some of the other marketing strategies I list in this chapter. But you're not gonna wanna do that. Instead, you need to wrap your head around the concept of Word-of-Mouth because you're going to have to ask people to refer you to other people they know. You're asking someone to do a "Sell Job," and sometimes, it's hard to ask for that kind of help.

Therefore, when you ask your friends and family for referrals (a.k.a. – a word-of-mouth "Sell Job"), don't think of it as "I'm asking them to do something they're not gonna want to do." Instead think of it as, "I'm asking my friends and family to let people know that I have this business, especially the people who they believe I can help. I'm just asking them to be open and honest and to tell people about my services, if they believe in me as a person." Because the truth is, your friends and family won't be selling your business; they know nothing about your business. Your friends and family will be selling *you* and what they know about you. They will be *vouching* for you.

If you're still on the fence about this – especially if you're trying to prove to everyone that you can be a successful business owner all by yourself – then here's something else to think about: When you ask someone for help – or referrals – you are getting them invested in you and your business. You're getting them to support you whether they realize it or not. On top of that, people usually want to help people. It makes them feel important and needed. So by asking them for help, you're giving them a chance to be a factor in this new life you're creating. You are telling them that you value their opinion and you want them to be part of what's happening in your life. This is one of the best ways to turn doubters into supporters.

How to Ask for Word-of-Mouth

If you are afraid to ask for Word-of-Mouth, then here are some ideas on how to do that without having to feel like you're begging.

1. **Send Out an Email Blast Announcing Your New Business:** An Email Blast is a whole bunch of emails that are customized to each recipient. You can do this by typing one email after the other and changing the names in the greeting line (which can take forever). You can also try to send out one email to a bunch of people at once, but you will most likely end up in their Spam box. Another way to do this a whole lot faster and easier (especially if you have more than 20 people to email), is to use Microsoft Outlook and Word. Begin by making sure all of your contacts are already in Microsoft Outlook. If they aren't, you can easily "Import" them from another email account. Then, create your message in Word and use the "Step-by-Step Mail Merge Wizard" to customize the message. With the Mail Merge Wizard, you can insert a custom greeting line (like "Dear Jane"). As you go through the Wizard, it will prompt you to choose your contact list, and you will choose Outlook as your Contact List Source. Then, you can finish the message and click "Send Emails." Within minutes, you can send hundreds of custom emails to everyone you know announcing your new business. Doing an Email Blast this way will help keep your email message out of their Spam folders. (For more thorough directions on how to do an email blast step-by-step, go to the Appendix.)

2. **Post the "News" About Your New Business on Your Social Networking Sites:** Even if you send an Email Blast to people, it's still a good idea to post it on your Social Networking sites for all of the people who you've never really met in person, but who are still your "friends."

3. **Also, Update Your Social Networking Profiles to Include Your New Business.** Make sure to include information about your services, websites, and backgrounds. On sites like Facebook, this will create a posting to your Wall as well.

4. **Offer Rewards for Referrals:** This is a bit of a desperate move, and it can be costly if done wrong. But, at the same time, people like to get things in exchange for their assistance. You could offer something like a free lunch or a $25 gift certificate to

somewhere. The choice is up to you. The key here, however, is to say that you will give out the gift certificate when the new client actually hires you and you work a certain number of hours with them. Keep the number low so that way your friends and family won't feel it's impossible to get the reward.

5. **Change the Signature Line in Your Email to Announce Your New Business:** If you've never used the Signature feature in your email, you're missing out on getting free advertising. So, go ahead and include the name of your new business, email, phone number, address, website, tagline, etc. into your signature line. This is especially helpful for when you begin communicating with clients because they will never have to work hard to find your contact info. It will be in every email you send.

6. **Post or Send "Special Deals" Every Now and Then:** When you post a special deal to your blog or networking sites, you keep your product fresh in people's minds. On top of that, people don't mind telling other people about great deals they saw at your site. So, always be thinking of deals you can offer to new clients – things like "free 1 hour consultation," "Half Price Auditing for a Company's books (of course, you'll want to have a high price point on this so you can still get your basic hourly rate)," "One hour of free office organization when you pay for one hour." These are just a few ideas to get you started.

NETWORKING

In business, word-of-mouth is basically networking. However, networking has one further feature that word-of-mouth does not have. That feature is "Quid Pro Quo"...or in other words, "I do for you if you do for me." Sometimes you pay for this service; sometimes you can do an even swap. Either way, there are millions of ways to network for any type of business. For example, with our blog – OneHourBookkeeper.com – I network with other bookkeeping professionals. They may do a blog for me that promotes some aspect of bookkeeping I want promoted, and I give them a prominent place on the site for a period of time which allows my readers to learn more about them and their business. It's a win-win situation, and that's what you should always be looking for in any networking situation.

As such, here are some networking companies that you can look into which should help your new bookkeeping business.

BNI (Business Networking International) – BNI.com

(Be sure to read the Spotlight on Jason Rosen at the beginning of this chapter.)

This one company can be the most beneficial company you ever use to grow your business. Its main concept is to have business professionals help other business professionals by passing out each other's business cards to their clients, and then bringing back pre-approved referrals to the other members of their chapter. Imagine it – one giant collective pool of customers that a limited number of professionals can access, and those customers are eager to hear from you.

Here's how it works:

1. You check out a chapter that you like, and then apply to join that chapter. In the application, you specify exactly what your services are, and what you specialize in.

2. The chapter reviews your application to decide if you should become a member. Each chapter only allows one "industry type" of professional into their group, so if there is another bookkeeper, you will be denied entry to *just that chapter*. That means, when you are approved to join any chapter in your area, ***you will be the only bookkeeper in that chapter.*** There may be an accountant in that chapter as well, but their services will be specified as dealing with taxes while yours is doing data entry. (If I were you, I would specifically look for a chapter WITH an accountant, because an accountant will bring you more clients than anyone else.)

If you get denied membership to a chapter you really want to be part of because there is another professional in that chapter who has services similar to yours, ask the president of the chapter to talk to that professional and figure out which services you can offer that complement theirs. This way, you and the other professional will become a stronger team. If they still say no, just look at another chapter in your area, or consider starting a new BNI chapter.

3. You pay an annual fee of about $300. Yes, the fee is fairly high, but it's still cheaper than a Yellow Pages ad, and it is far more effective at gaining clients.

4. You get together once a week for breakfast or lunch, depending on the chapter you chose. The meetings are usually one hour in length, but schedule an hour and a half just for schmoozing. You do have to pay separately for your weekly meal, but it's usually around $10 and usually includes "being served" by a waitress.

5. At that meeting, one of the professionals in the group will give a speech about some piece of knowledge they have which they think might interest you. This will help you get familiar with that person their services, and it will inspire you as to who to approach for that person.

6. At some point during the meeting, everyone will swap referrals. Some weeks you will receive no referrals while other weeks you can receive several at once. The biggest benefit of these referrals is that the person giving you the referral has already told that person about you and your services, so they will be expecting your call, and they will be receptive to your sales pitch. It takes all of the scariness-factors out of the cold call situation.

Keep in mind: BNI is all about helping each other...not just getting referrals and leaving. You have to give referrals to get them. If you don't, you may be asked to leave the group. So, keep your friends, family, clients, and associates in mind at all times. That way, membership will be a win-win for everyone.

Additionally, when you find professionals for your friends, family, clients, etc., those people will soon see you as the most amazing go-to person they know. They'll call you first whenever they need anything. Trust me...you *want* to be that person.

7. Eventually, it will be your turn to speak. By then, however, you will know everyone in that group, so it'll just be like talking to your friends about what you do. This one group alone can help you build your confidence as a business owner like no other group I've ever participated in.

Local Chamber of Commerce

A very popular choice for networking is your local Chamber of Commerce. It's usually a cheaper group then BNI, but there are going to be other bookkeepers there also promoting their business. I will also take you longer to build up your reputation and get people to think of you when someone asks for your type of services.

Other Small Business Groups

Other types of groups you can look to join are groups that are specifically tailored to your industry, sex and race. For example, there are bookkeeping groups, like AIPB (American Institute of Professional Bookkeepers), groups specifically for women in small business, and groups of professionals who are minorities. These groups can help you with everything from finding clients to finding grant money. They offer each other support while also helping each other grow.

ACCOUNTANTS

After word-of-mouth and networking, accountants will be the next best place to get clients. They already have a list of small business owners – your ideal clientele – and they don't generally focus on the day-to-day bookkeeping issues that you'll be dealing with. They prefer to have the books handed over to them already wrapped up nicely so that they can file the necessary paperwork that will satisfy the IRS. Sometimes, they will hire bookkeepers as employees at their own company to help the small businesses that need bookkeeping, but in my experience, they would often rather hire a subcontractor – like you – to handle the day-to-day stuff instead becoming an employer. As I stated in Chapter 2, these fees include overhead, employer taxes, workers' compensation, etc. On top of that, a bad employee could ruin their professional reputation while hiring an outside bookkeeping company creates a veil of protection between themselves and their clients.

How to Approach Accountants

The first accountants you should approach when you come to this process are any and all accountants you've worked with in the past. They will already be familiar with you and your bookkeeping methods. Thus, when you let them know you've gone into business for yourself, they'll already know what to expect from your "company" and they'll be receptive. Also, since they've worked with you in the past, they'll be more willing to open correspondence from you and take your phone calls.

Therefore, for the accountants you already know, pick up the phone and give them a call. Ask for the accountant by name, and in a friendly, casual manner, let them know that you started your own bookkeeping business and the first person you thought of was them (even if they were the last person you thought of). *Ask them* if it would be okay if you sent them a little bit more information about your services. By asking permission, you're letting them know that you are low-key and "not pushy" – which is a benefit they can sell to their customers. Ask them if they would prefer the information via fax or snail mail. Then, thank them for their time and get off the phone. Try not to take up too much of their time unless it's clear that they want to chat with you. The faster and more direct you keep the conversation, the more professional you will appear.

Keep in mind – when talking to an accountant – *never* ask for the address or fax number. Don't waste their time. Either call back and ask the receptionist for the information you need, or look it up on the internet.

Also, when sending information via snail mail, always hand-write the address. Printed labels say "this is impersonal promotional materials – throw me away!" Hand-written addresses say, "this is personal information from someone you know. Open me quick because I might be important." And don't forget the return address. A missing return address says, "I'm a bill."

I said it in the last chapter, but it bears repeating. Get a Magnetic Car Sign. While the vinyl ones may look more professional, they can be impossible to remove. Over time, they will melt into the surfaces they are adhered to, and if they are on the outside of the car, they will begin to peel at the edges and look jagged. Magnetic signs, on the other hand, are easily removable for when the day comes that you need to remove that sign from your car. While you may be thinking to yourself, "*I will never want to remove the sign from my car,*" you will find a day comes when you realize you have enough clients and you don't want anymore. At that point, you can just toss them into your trunk and wait until it's time to advertise again.

Having said that, get creative here. Don't just get magnetic car signs for you. Get them for your spouse, your teen drivers, and any assistants you hire. Think about who you know that you can bribe to put one on their car. After all, this is a numbers game, and the more people who see your sign, the more people will contact you.

For design tips, go back to Chapter 3 – Putting Out Your Sign Post – and read the section on Magnetic Signs.

CRAIGSLIST AND CLASSIFIED ADS

My general opinion on advertising in placing classified ads is – quite simply – don't bother because you'll just be wasting money. In my experience, most small business owners won't look to classified ads when they need to hire office personnel. Instead, they will either call up a temp agency and ask for help, or they will place their own ads saying what they need and how much they are willing to pay per hour. They will list a contact phone number, a fax number, an email, or a post office box where resumes can be sent. This way, they get a plethora of applicants they can choose from instead of choosing just one.

This is something you can take advantage of. Why spend your money to say, "I'm here - pick me" to no one in particular when you can just answer the ads that small business owners are placing. You can fax or email a personal resume to the contact person for free, and be considered right alongside everyone else. The biggest difference, however, is that you are going to include your catch phrase on your resume, and you are going to include a cover letter explaining briefly what you do. By following this process, you will be throwing your hat in the ring. The end result will be based on one of three things: 1) They may not pick you because they want someone in their office "regularly" (like a minimum of 20 hours per week) and you are not a "regular" applicant; or 2) They will pick you because as a fellow business owner, they will know that you have a reputation to protect and some experience in the business world that could be helpful to their business, or 3) They will hire you because you will help them realize that you are the best option for them.

Therefore, if you don't get picked, don't get all butt-hurt over it. (Yes, I said butt-hurt. It's California slang for "Suck it up.") Instead, dust off your resume and send it out to a few other ads. Remember, getting clients is a numbers game – like shotgun spatter. The more you send out in the world, the higher the likelihood that you'll actually hit something.

The Best Ads to answer are the "Part-time" bookkeeper ads. Because, the point is to build your business, not end up as someone else's full-time employee.

Craigslist

Craigslist is just another place where people place their Want Ads, but with one minor difference. Craigslist is free. It's free to browse and it's free to post. As mentioned above, the easiest thing you can do is respond to ads people are already posting. However, if you would also like to advertise on Craigslist – after all, it is free – then realize how it works. Craigslist is basically like a blog. The newest ads are always placed at the top, while older posts drop to the bottom. Only a limited number of ads are shown on the first (and main) page before they get shifted to Page 2 (and most people would rather stay on Page 1). In addition, many people don't open a large number of those ads because clicking on every ad means they will be redirected to a page that may have what they're looking for, but probably won't. If it doesn't, they have to go back to the previous page and look for the next ad that might fill their need.

The point here is – to play the Craigslist game successfully – you have to play by the rules. That means 1) create an attention-grabbing headline, 2) give a brief but thorough description in your ad so that people will want to respond, and 3) post regularly (if you get responses). Here's how you're going to do that:

1. **The Header:** What is the one thing that catches your attention in headlines when you browse Craigslist. For me, it's *always, always, always* **Prices**. The biggest reason people surf Craigslist is because they want to find what they need, but they want to find it for a deal. (After all, posting is free.) People who don't put specific prices in their headlines often get their ads ignored. Therefore, to create a catchy ad, be specific about what you're offering, and put your *minimum monthly* price in the headline. Don't put an hourly wage as a wage that is perceived as "too high" will cause people to skip right over your ad for other ads that are cheaper. Instead, list something like:

   a. ***Full Charge Bookkeeping for as low as $100 per month*** – (Make sure to list the area you are willing to work in within the Location box.) As you can see, this tells someone looking for bookkeeping right up front that you're affordable, and what you do. This will get more people to open your ad and – since there are tons of bookkeeping ads on Craigslist – will set you apart from your competition.

Now, I do realize that you're going to want to ignore me about pricing. I've heard many, many bookkeepers say, *"I don't want to list my prices until a potential client talks to me first. I feel it's important to build a rapport ahead of time, and then we can work out a package deal. Until they get to know me and all the things that are included in my price, listing prices is just going to scare them off."*

My response is: "WHY WASTE YOUR TIME?" If people like your ad, they'll contact you. But then guaranteed, they're going to ask how much you cost. Your hourly wage may scare them off no matter what kind of rapport you build, and you've just wasted your time chatting. By listing your price and FAQs ahead of time, you are weeding out the cheapest of the cheap and attracting the serious-minded. Thus, when someone finally does call you, they'll be more likely to "just get started" with you then string you along. Thus, my policy on pricing is…"Let it all hang out."

2. **The Body of the Ad:** What you say in the ad is just as important as the header. In fact, it's a good idea to browse your competition's ads just to see what they're doing what you like and don't like, and then try that. However, whether you copy someone else or create completely new copy, here are some general guidelines to help make your ad stand out:

3. *Be Brief...Very Brief.* I once read that the average internet user stays on a site for 9 seconds total before they move onto the next article or website. Imagine that. You have 9 seconds to catch your reader's attention.   If you have one huge paragraph of information, the person who came to your ad will quickly hit the "Back" button. If you have a novel of information – even if broken up in paragraphs – you will also lose your reader. Therefore, don't make the mistake of listing all of your personal and educational information. Especially, don't bother telling your ad-viewers how you're going to save them thousands of dollars in bookkeeping costs by preparing their taxes and calculating their depreciation. Instead, stick to the main benefits of using your company, because those are you sale points.

4. **Use Bullets or Numbers.** This is a blogger's trick that really works to capture a reader's attention. By using bullet points, a blogger allows a reader to "Skim" through all the main points of their message, and only read more on the items that catch their attention.

5. **DON'T Use Industry Jargon.** Just because you know what is on a balance sheet, or what amortization is, doesn't mean you should throw those words into your ad. Remember – your clients are going to be small business owners who probably won't give a crap about bookkeeping, even their own bookkeeping. They just want the bookkeeping taken off their hands so they can focus on what they do best. Therefore, use the more common bookkeeping terms that any business owner will recognize – terms like: invoicing, billing, collections, payroll, taxes, dealing with the IRS, etc.

6. **List Your Website.** It's amazing how many ads don't list websites where readers can find more information – especially since a *brief* ad does *not* answer all the questions they're going to have. Your ad is meant to be a teaser that will make them want to contact you. You will list your basic benefits, and then you will direct them to your website where they can find more information. *Just don't forget one thing...*add the http:// before your website. If you forget to add the http://, Craigslist won't recognize it

as a link and won't convert it to a link, thus your clients will have to retype your website's name, and they may be too lazy to do that. When you add the http://, your ad will create the link so that even the laziest client won't mind checking the site out.

    a. It's also a good idea to have that link go directly to a Frequently Asked Questions page so that the business owner can get most of their questions answered before they contact you. Again, the point is not to have people waste your time, but to only have the most serious people contact you.

7. **Finish With Your Contact Info.** The other thing that always amuses me is when people forget to add their contact info. You're a business. Feel free to add your website, name, business name, phone number, fax number and even your email. This way, you make it incredibly easy for someone to find you and your site instead of forcing them to look you up on the internet. Because remember...if it takes them more than 9 seconds to find you, they'll move on.

8. **Finally, Post Regularly.** When you're browsing the other Service ads, make sure to check the last date on the bottom of the first page. The busier a page is (meaning the more ads people place), the fewer dates will be on that page and it could be that only today's postings show up. The slower the page is, the more dates there will be. You will want to keep your business on the first page of postings, and the number of days listed on that page will tell you how often you should re-post your ad. Otherwise, you're completely wasting your time posting an ad in the first place.

The Cover Letter and Resume

There's a general rule of thumb I live by when it comes to getting any job in any industry. (Okay, there's hundreds of rules I live by, but this is a good one...) That rule is K.I.S.S. – "Keep It Simple Stupid." Of course, the "Stupid" does not apply to you or me, so actually the rule should be "Keep It Simple FOR Stupid." The "Stupid" you are keeping it simple for is the person you are passing your information to.

Okay – this is making no sense, right? Here's another way to put it.

When I was in junior high, I had this fabulous English teacher named Mrs. Radshaw. Generally, she ignored me because I loved English and didn't need a lot of attention in regards to learning the lessons. But the one lesson she taught that planted deep in my psyche was "to always write like you were writing for *'Dumb Dora.'*" (It wasn't that she knew any Dora's who were dumb...it was just an alliteration technique.) She went on to say, "Assume that Dumb Dora doesn't understand a lot of English and therefore doesn't understand what you're talking about. You are going to have to explain everything to her in very simple terms. So you (the writer) need to assume that whoever's reading your work doesn't understand the same things you understand, and you need to write accordingly."

So getting back to the Resume and Cover Letter, Keep It Simple (for) Stupid...and Dumb Dora. Stick to the basics, which are:

- Your Resume is meant to list your skills, your education, and your job history.
- Your Cover Letter is meant to introduce you (and your personality) to the person receiving your resume.
- Your Resume is meant to tell someone about what you can do for them.
- Your Cover Letter is meant to tell them why they should hire you instead of someone else.
- Your Resume should be no more than TWO pages long.
- Your Cover Letter should be no more than ONE page long.

When writing the resume you're going to send, create it just like you would for a regular job. Separate your skills, job history, and education into different sections. List the other skills that can put you ahead of the competition, like how fast you can type, which programs, you can use, languages you speak, etc. Detail out your name and contact information at the top of the first page, and don't forget to add your website and tagline (such as "Bookkeeping as low as $100"). This will help grab their attention right from the beginning.

On the cover letter, use block formatting (no indentations and a space between each paragraph), and keep it to two paragraphs. Explain in the first paragraph who you and your company are and why you are responding to their ad. In the second paragraph, explain why they should hire you instead of someone else (i.e. you will save them in wages, taxes and overhead, you can do the work faster than anyone else, and if they hire you, they also get the benefit of whoever you hire to help you with the work – thus they are getting two people for the price of one). Add a "thank you" line, where you thank them for taking the time to considering your resume, and then sign it. Done. Simple.

SOCIAL NETWORKING SITES

I have yet to see how Social Networking Sites actually bring in any clients, but there are other benefits to being part of Social Networking Sites. For one thing, when someone does a search to find out more about YOU as a person, and your business, your website may not be the first website to pop up, especially if your website does not have a long history or hundreds of thousands of hits. On the flip side, social networking websites – like Facebook, LinkedIn, MySpace and Twitter – have *millions* of hits and they will often pop up first. If your name isn't listed with these sites, you are missing out on having clients searching for you to actually find you. Thus, by joining these Social Networking sites and creating thorough business-related profiles, you are increasing your odds of being found quickly and easily by your potential clients.

Did you know that if you Google "Robin Davis," the first person that pops up is a photographer? Next is a Chief Justice, and then a Certified Financial Planner. None of those are me. I have no official website, and I've only been blogging for a few months. Thus, there are hundreds and thousands of websites you would have to sift through to find me at this point in time. But, I can definitely be found at Facebook, MySpace and LinkedIn.

LinkedIn

LinkedIn is the business professional's answer to networking. It allows anyone to post a resume, website links, and even job listings for free. On top of that, there are thousands of industry related groups that you can join where you can ask questions and actually get answers.

Want to know which bookkeeping programs work best for construction companies? How about how to operate the Time Tracker program on QuickBooks? Or maybe you want to know the best way to post a very complicated transaction. You can join any group at LinkedIn and post your question, and within 24 hours, you will often have many excellent answers. Thus, not only is LinkedIn a great way to network, but it's also good for acquiring industry-specific solutions.

Don't forget to check out their Job Boards while you are there, just to see if anything rings your bell.

Some groups at LinkedIn to join for bookkeeping: Accountemps, American Institute of Professional Bookkeepers, Bookkeeping in Bunny Slippers, Successful QuickBooks Consultants, and TopLinked Financing and Accounting Professionals. (You will find me posting regularly at those groups.)

Facebook

Facebook is another great place to post a profile because it's a more personal social networking site with plenty of business opportunities. Not only is it really easy to share personal information that allows potential clients to get to know you and thus feel comfortable with you, but it's also a great place where you can join forums and get questions answered. On top of that, it's super easy to add "friends" that you don't even know because Facebook will actually suggest friends based on how many "friends" the two of you have in common.

Just beware of the games...they're *addicting*.

GOOGLE ADWORDS / ADSENSE

If you want to make your bookkeeping business a virtual bookkeeping business, then you need to place online ads at some point, if for nothing other than to get people to come to your website. One of the best ways to do this is through Google Adwords. With Google Adwords, you can specifically target people who are looking for your services, BUT – and this is a big BUT – you have to be very specific about the services you are offering in order for Google to bring your ideal client.

Utilizing Google Adwords

Advertising with Google Adwords revolves completely around "keywords." Keywords are the words people pick when searching for information. If they're looking for a virtual bookkeeper, they will type "virtual bookkeeper" and get a million results. They will get so many results, in fact, they will narrow their search by adding more words. Those words might consist of their city AND "virtual bookkeeper." This will take them to other websites which have or use *all* of those words in their websites, although not always together. At that point, the searcher will begin clicking on different sites, or they may add more terms to narrow the results even more.

On the flip side – for you as an advertiser – you have to try to guess what terms your ideal clients might search for. Google Adwords charges a different price for each keyword phrase you use. (Notice I said "phrase" and not just "keyword.") You can actually search for Google keywords by using Google's Search-Based Keyword Tool. It will tell you how often an expression is searched per month, along with how much it would cost to have people come to your site, and how much competition you having in using that word.

As an example, let's search the term "Los Angeles Bookkeeping." Google Adwords shows the best keyword phrase and price would be the following:

As you can see, the most popular relevant Keywords are "Bookkeeping Los Angeles" and it has 33 monthly searches. On top of that, you would have to pay $3.82 every time someone clicked on your ad and went to your site.

In other words, your ad could be shown to 30 people a month looking for you and your services, but unless someone clicks on your ad, you pay nothing. When they do click on your ad, whether they buy your services or not, you would pay $3.82.

If you don't see the "keyword phrase" you want to use in your advertising campaign, that could mean that no one is *looking* for your keyword phrase, or it could mean that no one is *advertising* with your keyword phrase. Either way, you could make a bid as low as $0.10 per click and be the only person advertising that expression.

Before you do that, however, there is one other great way to check how often a term is "Googled." Wordtracker.com offers a 7-day free trial of their word tracking services, and can give you a better analysis of the keywords you would like to use. For example, when I put "Los Angeles Bookkeeping" into their search engine, it shows the following results:

Keyword (?) (3)	Searches ▼ (?) (50)	In Anchor And Title (?)	KEI (?)	KEI3 (?)	Google Count (?)	Google Count (quoted) (?)
1 ☑ bookkeeping services los angeles (search)	28	2	131	14.0	648,000	97,900
2 ☑ bookkeeping los angeles (search)	21	12	8.48	1.75	650,000	–
3 ☑ books by michelle bookkeeping firm in los angeles (search)	1	0	–	–	35,600	0

Per page: 100, 1000

As you can see, it also says that the phrase "Bookkeeping Los Angeles" is more popular than "Los Angeles Bookkeeping" and the expression has 650,000 Google Results. In addition, "bookkeeping services Los Angeles" has 648,000 results, but was searched 97,900 times with quotations marks around the words for more specific results. This shows that you could reach as many as 97,900 people with your ad, but only pay for the people who click on your link.

(Another good program is Wordze.com, which offers a 30-day free trial and charges monthly. The nice thing about Wordze is that they offer all of the "misspelled keyword options" as well.)

What does this mean for you?

1. You could create a Google Adwords campaign and bid $0.10 per click for the expression "Bookkeeping Services Los Angeles" and hope to capture some portion of those 98,000 people searching for that phrase. Or...

2. Even if you *don't* pay for the Google Adwords feature, *you need to be using these keywords on your website*. If you change your tagline to something like "The Best Bookkeeping Services Los Angeles has to Offer," you've used the *exact* keyword phrase that Google recognizes, and this could move your site up in the "organic" search results very quickly.

Therefore, if you wish to seriously use your website as your calling card – especially for virtual bookkeeping, then you need to be using this tool. Even if you only use it for the free 7-day trial, make sure you get as much information as you possibly can out of it. These words can be used with every blog you write and speed your website to the top of the search results.

FACEBOOK ADS

In the same way that Google Adwords can put you in front of your ideal clientele, so too can Facebook Ads. The biggest difference, however, is that with Google Adwords, your ad is made up completely of words while Facebook Ads allows you to show images. This comes in handy because you can show your logo, or a product you're selling to your ideal clientele *without* them having to click on the link. Additionally, you only pay when your ideal customer does click on the link and goes to your site. You set the price you would like to pay per click, and your ad could be placed in front of thousands of people without you ever having to pay a dime. (Again, the point here is to not necessarily to make your brand *known* so much as to make your brand *remembered*. If someone recognizes your website's name, they will be more likely to try you out versus someone whose name they've never heard before.)

OTHER SITES THAT ADVERTISE BOOKKEEPING SERVICES

Here are some other sites you can check out that regularly show job listings for bookkeeping. All you have to do is specify the type of job you are looking for and the zip code, and you should see tons of recently posted jobs instantly.

- AIPBJobs.com

- Accountemps.com

- AccountingCoach.com

- SimplyHired.com

- Accounting.Careerbuilder.com/ag.ic/Bookkeeping.htm

- Monster.com

- HotJobs.com

- Vault.com

International Job Postings – For Jobs Anywhere in the World

- Elance.com

- ODesk.com

- Freelancer.com

- BidsCC.com

THINGS THAT PRODUCE <u>MINIMAL</u> RESULTS – (In Other Words, Don't Waste Your Time or Money)

Normally, I would never bother telling you *what not to do* in advertising because I don't want ideas that aren't effective to stick in your head. But, I've seen a lot of bookkeeping business advice, and I know the advice most "marketing professionals" will give you. This advice is *general* advice (for *general* businesses), and if I don't at least address these topics, you may come to the conclusion that I either don't know what I'm talking about, or that maybe I haven't heard or tried these other topics. My answer to that would be: I am aware of these topics, and I don't believe they will be as effective as the tools I've already provided. The information I provided is *specifically tailored* to the independent bookkeeping industry and the ideal bookkeeping clients. Those simple, inexpensive tools will get you 80% of your clientele, while the rest of these will get you less than 20%. Why waste all your time and energy focusing on the 20% when you can attract the 80% quickly and get better, faster results.

Anyway, here are the *General* Marketing Tips that most professionals will advise:

1. **Newspaper Ads:** I once looked into placing an ad in a newspaper for my bookkeeping services, and I got on the line with an ad salesman. After he and I talked for a few minutes, he told me outright, "You know, an ad isn't going to be as successful for your bookkeeping business as you might hope. I just sold ad space to another bookkeeping service last month, and that person placed a coupon for services in our latest circular. I called him just the other day to see how the ad worked for him and to see if he wanted to renew, and he told me that he hadn't gotten any referrals at all." Now, I just have to say, if an ad salesman is going to admit that a bookkeeping ad is not going to be an effective form of getting clients, then you need to think about if a newspaper ad is going to be effective for you. Why waste your marketing dollars? There are cheaper and more effective ways to get clients.

2. **Yellow Pages Ad:** The one thing about the Yellow Pages is that the customers who use them usually get confused fairly quickly. After all, there are no testimonials in the Yellow Pages that say which companies are better than others. For example, Chinese Food. When you look in the Yellow Pages for Chinese Food, you have no idea which one is the best. You may quickly figure out which one is your favorite based on past experience, but if your Chinese Food place doesn't deliver and you can't leave the house, you will flounder on which delivery company to go with. The end result will usually involve picking the restaurant with the biggest ad, the listed menu and prices, and the delivery radius. Knowing whether or not the food is good remains a gamble until the food is delivered. The same goes for bookkeeping services. You can't prove how good you are in an ad without a testimonial, and most people won't believe a testimonial in the Yellow Pages because it's a paid advertisement. Another result is that many people turn to the Internet instead in order to find a reputable service company along with

testimonials. Therefore, instead of getting a Yellow Pages ad, consider listing yourself on as many internet directory sites as you can, and ask previous clients, current clients and employers to submit testimonials. This way, you'll appear to be reputable, even if you're not.

If you insist on getting a Yellow Pages ad, then at least be smart. You're going to want to pay for the biggest ad possible, and put in as much credible-looking information as you can think of. This is very costly and has to be renewed annually, but the ad won't be effective unless your ad is the best in the book. So, if you're going to ignore me and go this route – *GO BIG*.

3. **Coupon Books / Welcome Packages:** While there is always the option of doing coupons that can be added to discounts books or "Welcome to the Neighborhood" packages, this is a lot like shooting an arrow into the dark hoping to hit a target. For one thing, the usual intended recipients of these booklets are not business owners, they are average people and it's hit or miss that the receiver will actually be someone who needs your services. On top of that, you have to pay to have your coupons added to these packages every time these packages are created. In my opinion, it's a far wiser decision to just skip this process and go with something more effective.

4. **Randomly Placed Fliers:** I know many business owners who like to use fliers to advertise. They place those ads on cars, bulletin boards, and even on store counters. Again, this is a hit-or-miss type of marketing and you should consider whether it's worth the huge amount of time it will take to pass these all out. However, it can also be a low cost way to advertise if done properly since a ream of 500 sheets of paper is only $5 to $10, and you can print out the fliers for a very low price, or copy them at Kinkos for around $0.10 a page. Although I don't recommend passing out fliers, I know some people will still feel most comfortable passing them out. So, if you are absolutely going to insist on doing fliers, then put them in places where you know small business owners go. One example would be coffee shops that have conference rooms. Another would be your local copy shops, or even a church. These places often have bulletin boards where you can post those fliers specifically designed for networking, and business owners or managers tend to go there often. Still, in my opinion, it's best to post your business cards instead of fliers. I believe it gives a more professional image.

Chapter 5

Step 5: Nailing the Interview

SPOTLIGHT ON A BOOKKEEEPING BUSINESS - Checks & Balances Bookkeeping Services

When you ventured into your new bookkeeping business did you:

A.   Take each and every client who called?
B.   Re-arrange your personal life to accommodate them?
C.   Say "how high" when they said, "jump"?
D.   All of the above!

You're most likely guilty of at least one of the above statements when you began your business - I know I was. I have since learned to 'set boundaries' with my clients. Here's a few suggestions on how:

1.   Establish a certain day of the week/month for each client. There may be times when you'll have to reschedule things around, but always make sure you go back to their designated time.
2.   Set a 'block of time' for each client. Although it's important to finish all your work in that client's scheduled 'block', it may make you late for your next appointment. Prioritize by doing time sensitive work first.
3.   Train your clients to work around your schedule. Not the other way around.   This tells your clients two things – 1) that you are an established business and 'in demand' and 2) as busy as you are, you value their business and wish to work to accommodate them.
4.   Learn to 'make yourself available' without overwhelming yourself. E-mail is a God-send. It allows you to stay in touch with your clients without the annoyance of your cell phone going off. And having your Outlook, Yahoo, G-Mail, etc. messages forwarded to your phone ensures that you'll always stay connected to your clients.
5.   Don't be intimidated. This is where boundaries come into play the most. Your clients must know that they cannot call you Saturday night to come in and get last minute work done Sunday afternoon – even if they are meeting with their accountant on Monday morning. Your time is your own.

"Part time bookkeeping for full time businesses" – that's Elena Oppedisano's motto. Elena began Checks & Balances Bookkeeping Services in 2005 when she saw a niche for small/independently-owned businesses. These business owners needed to build their business, but also have to wear 'all the hats' - including that of the bookkeeper. Elena's business caters to these types of businesses who only need a bookkeeper when necessary - whether once a week, once a month, once a quarter or "once in a while."   No need to keep someone on staff, purchasing accounting software or even a computer! She works both on and off-site, as well as remotely. Work is transferred either by pick-up/delivery, fax, email or my UPS overnight service. She provides her clients with both convenience and peace of mind. Find out more at ChecksAndBalancesLLC.com.

From the moment you step into your future client's office, the interview process is going to be different then you expect. For one thing, you will be on equal footing with the person you are interviewing with. You are NOT a single individual begging for a job. You are a "company" and a professional that has something worthwhile to offer. They will want you for that.

As such, the best thing you can do when you enter a client's office (or meet with them at a coffee shop), is to assume that you already have the job. Go there with the intent of getting them started right away. By this, I mean, "Be prepared." Have your bookkeeping package with you, put together, and ready to go. Let them do most of the talking, and just "Smile and Nod a Lot." (Yes, that will work here as well...and if you don't know what "Smile and Nod a Lot" means, go back to Chapter 1 and read the "Subliminal Tricks" subsection.) People want to feel like they're witty and intelligent, so letting them talk about themselves will give them a good impression of you.

WHAT TO WEAR

When you go to the interview, you'll want to be dressed professionally, but you don't have to wear a suit. Remember – the business person you are about to meet is probably a small business owner who won't want to be talked down to or intimidated. So wear something like a professional pair of slacks, a decent business top, and a simple pair of business shoes. The goal is to look approachable – not like someone from a huge corporation.

YOUR SALES PITCH

I could go into a huge spiel about all the things you're going to say that will get you hired, but there's no point. The fact is, every small business owner and every interview is going to be different. The best thing you can do is let the business owner do most of the talking. But keep this in mind: the main reason that a business owner approached YOU is that they need and want a bookkeeper. They also need and want to save money. They need and want to be left alone when it comes to that money, so they want someone they can trust handling all of their cash issues.

Having said that, the key to your sales pitch is not going to be how smart you are, or how much training you have. **The key is going to be how you can take all of their bookkeeping stress away, and how affordable you'll be as you're doing it.** As you let them talk, pay attention to what they're saying. They will probably list all of the things they're worried about because they want to know you're going to take care of those things. Once one of their problems catches your attention, you can BRIEFLY tell them how you saved another client from the same problems and how you did it. Just remember to keep it simple – assume they don't understand bookkeeping terminology – and remember to keep smiling. Your goal here is to be likable, to seem approachable, and to appear trustworthy and professional. If you can pull that off, they'll be "chomping at the bit" to hire you.

One last thing: keep the interview confidential. By that I mean, you can mention other clients, but never mention them by name or business name. Once you start blabbing that kind of information to the person who's interviewing you, they are going to assume that you can't keep your mouth shut, and you're going to blab their business to your other clients. So don't make the mistake of naming names. Be as general as possible when talking about other clients, and keep on the topic of problem-solving.

THE TWO-WAY INTERVIEW – Searching for Your Ideal Client

When you go into an interview with a potential client, don't be surprised if you feel "a bit desperate" to get that client. That's common when you're first starting out, especially because you may really need money for your bills or startup costs. The thing is – you don't want to take on "just any old client." You want your ideal client! In fact, you want "the Perfect Client."

I know how crazy this sounds. When I first joined Mary Kay to be a consultant, one of the things my recruiter told me was to "Pre-Qualify" my customers. She told me, "Everyone has skin, so everyone needs Mary Kay products, but not everyone *deserves* them. And you definitely shouldn't be wasting your time with anyone who *doesn't* deserve them." At first, I thought she was being a bigoted idiot, and that she was telling me this so she could push her Hoity-Toity "*I'm-better-than-everyone*" Agenda. I have used Mary Kay products since I was 15 years old, and I really do believe that Mary Kay products are the best and that everyone should be wearing Mary Kay.

So I proceeded to ignore her advice...especially because I felt a bit *desperate* to become a successful Mary Kay beauty consultant.

Within my first few months of selling Mary Kay, I realized she was right. The ideal Mary Kay client is someone who cares about their skin and their appearance. They are women who may or may not be looking to earn extra money, but also who don't mind spending a little more to get the best products they can. They are open and friendly, and love to hang out with their friends. But I had to learn the hard way. By approaching the non-ideal client, I wasted tons of money and energy trying to recruit people who just led me on for the attention and the free products. Some of those clients openly slammed the products I loved so much (which oddly enough, usually led to me getting more sales from other customers), and I got nowhere fast in the Mary Kay world. Soon, I let the Mary Kay dream slip right out of my life.

Starting your own bookkeeping business may feel like a dream right now, but the reality is so easy to achieve. You just have to hold onto the dream with all your might.

Thus, your "interview with a new client" is actually a two-way interview. You are interviewing for their bookkeeping job, but they are also interviewing to be your client (even if they don't realize it). You need to be vigilant when interviewing with a prospective client, and you need to ask yourself, "Do I really want to work with this person? Is this someone who will be a pleasure to work with, or will this person be a Succubus (or Incubus)?" (Definition of a Succubus / Incubus – a soul-sucking demon who haunts your sleep. If you've ever had a boss that stressed you out so much, you couldn't fall asleep at night, then you already know one...)

As you go through the interview, here's what you want to look out for:

1. Who was doing their bookkeeping before you? If it was another bookkeeper, why is that bookkeeper no longer there?
2. Are they going to insist that you be in the office whenever you do your bookkeeping, or will they trust you to do it "out-of-office"?
3. Is this person an Ego-Maniac who is spending all of his time bragging about themself? Or are they talking about their business?
4. Do they seem to care about your expertise? Are they letting you get a word in edgewise?
5. How far behind are they in their bookkeeping?
6. Where do they feel they need your help most of all?

7. Are they behind with Vendors or the IRS? And if they are, how far behind?

8. Do they appear to be someone who spends a lot of money on themselves, while their office is suffering?

9. What is the condition of their office? Is it run down or shabby? Do you feel comfortable or uncomfortable?

10. And finally, what is your overall feeling about this person? Do you get a good vibe or bad vibe from them? Is their "Aura" pink and fluffy or black and creepy?

> Okay, I don't know anything about Auras, but I do know believe in "Vibes." I also believe that a person should always follow their instinct. If you have a bad instinct, blow that client off. This is your life, and it's too short to waste with people who weird you out!

Later in this chapter, I go into more detail about the signs of a bad bookkeeping client, so I won't go into too much detail here. But again, my advice when going into the interview is: Always follow your gut...and if they remind you of an ex-boyfriend / ex-girlfriend, then definitely don't work with them. (You don't want to get caught up in all that old drama again! Trust me.)

YOUR BOOKKEEPING PACKAGE

Since you're going to assume that you're starting a client right off, you're going to need a bookkeeping package to give them. Whenever I go to a new business, I like to have a folder I can give to my clients. In that folder will be everything they need to know about working with me and my company. It may include my resume and job skills. It may include a pretty little brochure of all the services I offer with various pricing (...after all, you always want to try and "up sell" them on other services you offer). But no matter what "informative" items I put into the folder, I always make sure it's actually put together and NOT something I'm scrambling to slap together while in their office. Because putting your package together last minute, or even going empty-handed, will give the client the impression that you "wing it," and that is not something they are looking for. So, before you go into your next client's office, take the time to put together your bookkeeping package and always keep them in your car – "just in case."

Here is a list of items to consider putting in YOUR bookkeeping package:

1. **The Folder:** I like only one type of folder when I begin with a bookkeeping client...and it's not actually a folder at all. I call it a folder because that is the "general packaging" terminology used when most businesses introduce themselves to other businesses. In actuality, I like the Expanding Poly Envelopes for my "folder," preferably with an inside pocket for a DVD or Disc. It looks something like this...

They cost approximately $1 to $2 per folder, and I prefer them because they are going to pull double duty. When you give a client a generic manila file folder, or even a booklet folder with an inner flap, they will usually toss that folder into a filing cabinet and never look at it again. When you give them a Poly Envelope, then they can use that poly envelope many, many times...and you *will* make them use it over and over again. In fact, this is going to be the MAIN way that you correspond with your clients *if you turn them into Virtual Clients*. Think about it. The main point to this book is to turn your regular clients into Virtual Clients. That means, you want to stay out of their office as much as possible. If that client does not have a fax machine, then you will want to pay a college student to swing by their office and pick up whatever paperwork the client has for you. These envelopes are durable and can be temporarily sealed with a string instead of glue. Your client can toss these poly envelopes onto the front seat of their car, and any time they get a receipt, they will put the receipt in that folder. If they want to write you a quick note – it goes into the folder. Since it can be closed and tied with a string, the possibility of them losing their receipts will greatly diminish (and they will still lose them, with or without the poly envelope).

- o Remember, the key is to make this CONVENIENT AND EASY for them. If it's not convenient and easy, they won't do it.

- o Also, by giving your clients a file folder to carry with them at all times, or keep in a dedicated place just for your services, it will be easy for you to swing by and pick up everything that needs to be entered at once. Furthermore, this will help you later on because any assistant you hire will know to "just look for the folder" when they do the picking up and dropping off.

- o Finally, once you or your assistant picks up the poly envelope, that envelope will be exchanged for a NEW empty poly envelope. As such, it is a good idea to get TWO packages of poly envelopes and assign each client with one color, thus giving them the TWO same-colored poly envelopes. Then, every time you pick up a filled poly envelope with your clients receipts, you can leave an empty poly envelope so that your client never has to do without one. It's the best way to make the virtual side of bookkeeping work with your client right from the beginning.

If you really don't want to spend $2 per envelope, you could get the basic manila shipping envelopes for less, but I find that the poly envelope lasts a lot longer, and are just plain prettier. I feel they give a more professional image – but that's merely a preference-thing.

2. **Full-Sheet White Labels:** Once you have your poly envelopes, you will want to create a special full-sized label for the outside of that poly envelope. You could pay a company to create the fancy full-sized labels, but I would just go down to Office Depot and pick up their pack of 100. The non-glossy surface makes it easy to print and easy to write on. Since it's full-sized, you can create all kinds of labels for your poly envelopes and put all

kinds of information on them – like your logo, billing address, phone number, fax number, website, and your email. You can also create a space to write the company's name, the owner's name, pickup/delivery dates, and the day(s) and time slots you will be doing work for them. This way, you will be able to keep all of the necessary individual information packets separate and prevent any mix-ups later on with other clients (and so your assistant won't get them mixed up either). As a bonus, with the owner's name on the package, you'll never forget that person's name.

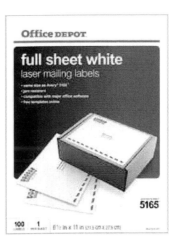

3. **A Pricing Sheet:** It's always a good idea to have a Pricing Sheet of all the services you offer and the various prices you charge. This way, the client will see that you are more than just a bookkeeper – you are someone that can solve multiple problems in their business. This will also keep you at the forefront of their mind whenever they need additional services. Go over the pricing sheet with them, and then pull out your Two New Client Services Checklist. (I go into how-to set your pricing later in this chapter, and in Chapter 11, I list more than 30 ways to supplement your bookkeeping income...so be sure to check those out.)

4. **TWO New Client Services Checklist:** When you start with a client, you will want to give them a "Training List" of sorts. This Training List is simply a checklist listing all of the services you provide. This could be Accounts Payable, Accounts Receivable, Payroll, Tax Reporting, etc. You will then give them the check list and have them check off the things they want you to do and sign on a line at the bottom. This way, they will have a visual image of what you will be doing for them, and you will have a mini contract that they signed acknowledging what your agreed-upon services will be. Once they've done that, copy the information over to the second identical list, and have them sign that one as well. This way, you can take a copy with you, and they will have a copy for themselves. (Feel free to sign both copies as well, this way the client will feel like it is actually a contract between your two companies...but make it clear, it is NOT a contract...it is just a list of agreed-upon services so that there will be no misunderstanding later on.)

5. **A Time-Saving Checklist:** Give them a list of things they can do to help save both of you time, and thus save them money. For example, switching their bank account to a bank that can download QuickBooks files; using their credit card or debit card as much as possible; using a second checking account instead of the main checking account that you will be making payments from, etc.

6. **A Mini-Mini Informative Brochure:** Notice I use Mini Twice...again, that's for a reason. People often get carried away with their brochures, especially informative brochures. They want to come off as incredibly intelligent, or they spend a lot of money to make really beautiful brochures and then they want people to REALLY read them. Small business owners won't necessarily want to do this. In fact, they will probably find bookkeeping boring, so it's a really good idea to keep the bookkeeping jargon to a minimum. Instead, make your brochure have information they actually want to know – like how to protect their bank accounts from embezzlers – and you will end up cementing yourself as an expert in your field.

7. **A Letter of Engagement.** QuickBooks actually has a really good <u>Sample Letter of Engagement</u> that they let people use. You can find it by simply Googling "QuickBooks Letter of Engagement" and then choosing the one that leads to QuickBooks parent site: <u>Intuit.com</u>. These letters are a great tool because they are mini-contracts that give your client detail of what you will and will *not* do with their company. By having them sign it, they are acknowledging what they can't ask you to do, and this will help you out if you ever need to take them to small claims court. Although I do not provide the actual QuickBooks Letter of Engagement, I do list out the exact address in the Appendix...so check out the section under "Bookkeeping Package" to get the exact link to QuickBooks's Sample Letter of Engagement (which comes in a Word Document, so you can use it for your own business).

8. **Extra Business Cards.** It never hurts to throw some extra business cards into the bookkeeping package. When you do, the client can take one and tuck it into their wallet, purse or briefcase. If you include multiple, then when someone else asks for a bookkeeping reference – which happens more than you would think between business owners – they can give the new business owner your business card. Even better, you're your client that if they refer your business to anyone and that person uses your services,

you will give them a reward. It could be a gift certificate to a restaurant, a discount on your services for a month, one hour free of bookkeeping, or just a cash bonus. A lot of times, when there's a reward involved, small business owners will be thrilled to promote your business for you.

> a. **Also, in a Quid Pro Quo manner, you can refer business to them.** If you like the client and think the client's services will be beneficial to other clients, ask for some of their business cards and let them know you would be happy to refer them to your clients as well. This is a win-win for both of you because you come off as being a valuable business tool for that client, a bookkeeper-with-all-the-answers to all your clients, and they will usually promote the heck out of you in gratitude.

YOUR PRICING STRATEGY – HOW TO CONVINCE THEM THAT YOU'RE WORTH THE HIGHER HOURLY WAGE

There's this glitch in the minds of small business owners when it comes to bookkeeping. Usually, that glitch is this belief that saving money is more important than hiring a good bookkeeper. They think anyone can do bookkeeping, especially if they've done it themselves in the past. They often don't realize that they may have been making a lot of common bookkeeping mistakes because as far as they see it, "at least they know their bank balance." As such, their biggest concern won't always be that you're doing it right. They're biggest concern is going to be saving money. Maybe saving money means they'll want you to help them with the IRS "asap", but most likely, it will mean they want you to be *cheap...really cheap.*

On the flip side, you need to make a living – *and you need to remember that*! You and your family come first. Period.

Having said that, you need to have your prices firmly in your head before you walk in to that client's office. However, you also need to know how to market those prices so that your future client will feel desperate to have you! At this point, you have two real choices. 1) You can tell the small business owner what your hourly rate is and watch them become all shaken and pasty, or 2) you can offer a package price.

Consider this: If you were looking to hire me and I told you, "My fee is $100 per hour," you would probably not want to hire me. In fact, you'd probably think, *"What the heck are you – a doctor? Am I getting a physical with that $100?"* Basically, you'd be running for the hills.

But if I told you, "My fee is $100 for one hour, and I can do an entire year's worth of bookkeeping in that one hour," it would make you rethink spending $100 for my services. In fact, it would probably make you eager to pay me that $100.

Thus, the key to an effective sales pitch is NOT to focus on why you're worth $100 an hour. <u>The key is to focus on the Benefits your client will receive when they pay your $100 fee.</u> It is a subtle difference that can mean the difference between getting a new client and losing one.

You see, in a client's head, they can't visualize what you will be doing for your hourly rate. To them, bookkeeping is usually nothing more than keeping a checkbook...and "anyone can do that." When you sell them on your services, you need to paint a picture for them. You need to answer all of their needs when you describe your prices, and you need to make the picture sound so appealing, they want you to start right then.

To recap on how you're going to do your sales pitch: Don't tell them your hourly rate; tell them your package price and what you're going to do for that package price. Let them tell you what they need, and then tell them about the benefits of working with you, including how you're going to answer their problems. Don't forget to finish off with how much your monthly fee will be when they maintain their accounts with you on a regular basis.

How to Set Your Pricing

By now, you should have an idea of what you want to say to your clients, but do you know how much you want to charge? Unfortunately, I can't tell you what you should be charging because every state is different and has various "average rates for bookkeepers." In fact, even cities within a state have different average bookkeeping rates. For example, in Los Angeles, I could easily charge $50-$100 per hour and no one would bat an eye. But in

Bakersfield, roughly two hours north of Los Angeles, a business owner would laugh me out of the office if I said $100 an hour. The average there would be closer to $20-$40 an hour. So in order for you to set your pricing, you need to do a little research. You need to figure out what the range is for your city's bookkeeping services.

In Chapter 1, I suggested how you could deduce what your bookkeeping rate should be. But in case you missed it: simply go to Accountemps.com and look for job postings in your local area. You can do this by typing in "bookkeeping job" and your zip code, then voila – tons of recent job postings. A minimum you should be charging is whatever the highest hourly wage is plus 30% - after all, you will be saving your future clients at least 30% in taxes, worker's compensation, overhead, etc. Even better, charge double or triple the highest rate because you're going to need it, and you're going to be faster than everyone else.

Another way to find out how much you should be charging is to "ask an accountant" what other independent bookkeepers in your area charge. Accountants often know this answer off the top of their heads.

Here's the facts: When you see a company's books, you will know how long it will take for you to do that company's books. Once you have an idea of how long it will take to do their books, quote them two flat rates based on the number of hours. The first rate will be a higher "Catch Up" Rate – where you catch their books up and bring them current – and the second rate will be an hourly rate. Feel free to give a discount for a large number of hours, but don't sell yourself short just because someone tells you they're hard up for money. You need to make a living too.

The other thing to remember: Those two rates you quote will be for In-Office Bookkeeping. If they want you in their office, they have to pay extra for it. When they give you the speech about "being on a tight budget," that is when you want to throw out the Discounted Out-of-Office rate.

Discount for Out-of-Office Services – The Virtual Bookkeeping Sales Pitch

Whether you have clients you are working with already, or you are trying to get new clients, using the "Discount for Out-of-Office Services" sales pitch is a great way to get business owners to agree to let you work from your home office. That is the whole goal of this book: to become a Virtual Bookkeeper.

Here's the basic pitch (...this is me speaking to YOU, and not your client). When your clients agree to have you work on their books remotely from your home office, <u>YOU save time and money</u>, which allows you to pass on that savings. When you work remotely from your home office, you don't have to rush into anyone's office; you can do the books at any time of day or night which frees up your 9-to-5 time slots to go out and find more clients. You don't have to drive in traffic, which saves you stress, your time on the road, and gas money. You also don't have to go out of your way for anyone, which means you don't have to drive from office to office and you can fit in more clients in one day. So in effect, you become more productive. YOU save a lot of time and money, so pass that savings on to your clients to make them jump at the idea of having you work from home.

When I meet a new client, I give them my basic In-Office Package Sales Pitch. I say something like, *"Well, I understand you need (blady, blady, blah) services. I charge $110 a month on average for in-office bookkeeping services. That fee will cover all of the services you're telling me you need, plus processing of the tax paperwork, reconciling all of your accounts, and dealing with phone calls from your Vendors and Customers during normal business hours should they have questions. You can simply pass on my phone number to them, and I will handle whatever bookkeeping issues arise with them. My fee is an average of $55 an hour for my In-Office services. However, if you wish to save money, I have an Out-of-Office Virtual Bookkeeping Fee where I do your bookkeeping remotely from my office, and you save $10 a month, or $5 per hour less. All of the bookkeeping will still be done on the computer in your office, but it will be done remotely. That means that I log into your computer from my home office and open your QuickBooks account, then do the bookkeeping as if I were in the office. When I'm done with the bookkeeping, I hit Print, and all of the reports will be sitting on your printer for your review. I can even print checks in your office remotely, so that all you would* *have to do is sign and mail the checks. That discount includes pickup, delivery and filing of your paperwork.*

"Now if you wish to save another $10 a month, then on the day before I am supposed to do your bookkeeping, simply have someone fax me the paperwork you need me to deal with, and it will be processed. Then, the person that faxed me the paperwork would simply put those receipts into a folder in your filing cabinet marked by month. When I receive the receipts on my end, I automatically convert them to digital files and save them on your hard drive for you. So, by working remotely and having an office assistant fax me the monthly or bi-monthly paperwork, you save $20 a month, plus you get all of your receipts saved digitally as a complimentary service for using our Virtual Bookkeeping Services. What do you think? Would you rather pay the higher $110 a month fee for On-Site Services, or would you rather save $20 a month for the Virtual Bookkeeping package and get complimentary Digital Backups of all your files?"

This is just a Quickie-Sales-Spiel, but as you can tell, there are a lot of benefits for the customer that I list here. First, I start by saying that I will be solving the problems they're having, and then doing even more for them. Then, I give them a really good "Package Deal" rate without stressing my hourly rate. I list more benefits, and then I hit them with my hourly rate so that *only then* – after they're sold on the higher priced package – they will see that an even better deal is available for going virtual. Then, I give them the better deal without them having to ask. I finish by telling them why they should choose the virtual bookkeeping package, and then I ask for a decision. When they make their decision, either decision is a good one for me. Either, I make an extra $20 a month for coming into their office, or I make $10 an hour less but save time driving to their office and dealing with whatever problems arise on-site.

Now it's your turn. Figure out what benefits you can offer and how you should pitch it in a way that is beneficial to your clients.

Don't forget to approach the clients you do have with this sales pitch as well. Tell them that you are restructuring your business so that you can accommodate several new bookkeeping clients, and thus you are offering discounts on your services. Give them the option to pay less for becoming virtual clients, and hopefully soon, you will be 100% virtual.

YOUR BEGINNING COSTS – WHY THEY WILL BE HIGHER

When you begin working with any client, you are going to find that they will need a certain amount of organization and "catching up" with their bookkeeping and office procedures. Generally, this is because they have been without a bookkeeper for a while, or maybe because the previous bookkeeper was not very organized. Either way, that client is going to need you for a fairly large amount of time in the beginning so that you can go through any paperwork that needs to be processed or filed. You will need to explain this to your client up front so that they don't think you're trying to screw them out of any package deals you both agreed on. Be honest and forthright, and try to give them an estimate of how much time it's going to take you to bring them current. By doing so, you can avoid any nasty little comments or distrust right from the get go.

Remember to OVER-estimate these setup hours. That way, if you finish early, you will look like a genius. If you underestimate your time and then go over, they're going to think you're a cheat. (For example, what would you think of a contractor that came to your house to fix your bathroom and told you "two weeks" but then took a month? You would not be too happy at the extra cost and time.)

HOW TO SPOT BAD CLIENTS

I'm going to say something that not a lot of business owners will say to a new business owner. That advice is: ***Do not take on bad clients***. I don't care how desperate you are, or how badly you think you need the money. The fact is, taking on a bad client will always end badly. You'll do a whole lot of work for them; they'll get behind on paying you; and when you go to collect, they'll do whatever they can to take you down...even if that means getting mutual business resources to stop working with you. (By that, I mean, they will try to get your accountant to fire you, or other clients they know you work with to fire you.)

So again I will say - ***Do not take on bad clients***. All you will do is waste your time and energy, then end up feeling disillusioned about the way the relationship ended, as well as the status of your bookkeeping business in general.

Warning Signs that a Client is a Bad Client

When I see any of these signs happening in a company, and the business owner is too stubborn to listen to my advice on how to bring it around, I drop them as a client. Because the simple fact is – if Vendors and Employees aren't getting paid, I won't be either. Thus, if you're a virtual bookkeeper and you don't know whether or not to take on a new client, these signs are definitely ones you should be looking for. If the signs are there, then this business is going under and you're going to get jilted by the Small Business Owner eventually. (Although, they will probably wait until they believe their books are in good order before they jilt you.)

1. **The Vendors aren't getting paid in a timely manner.** This is one of the first signs of trouble for a company. When they can't pay their vendors, they have one of three choices...close the account and pay what they can, find a new vendor who's willing to take a chance on them (bad credit and all), or just ignore them and get sent to collections. You'll recognize this sign when you hear about vendors calling in and demanding to be paid, or when you go to the usual vendor's retail location and are told that they will not sell to you unless you pay with Cash. Once this sign happens, it's very possible that it's "all downhill from there."

2. **The Employees' Paychecks are bouncing regularly.** This is the number one sign that the Company is nearing the end for two reasons. The first is that businesses will always pay their employees first. If they can't pay their employees, they've reached the bottom of their money barrel. The other reason is the government. The government is very hardcore when it comes to employees getting paid on time, as well as getting "their" money in the form of payroll taxes. If a Company cuts a check that they know is going to bounce, and the government finds out, the Company will have to pay huge penalties for writing each and every one of those checks. You see, the one thing that is a huge no-no in the Government's eyes is an Employer screwing over their Employees – which some

business owners do without qualms. So if Employee Checks are bouncing, you can bet it won't be long before some disgruntled employee runs to the IRS to complain. Even if you're not that employee, the end result is that the Company will have to cough up a huge amount of money they probably don't have, and it will force them to close shortly after.

3. **The Company owes the IRS a large sum of money.** Speaking of the IRS, as I said before, they are very hardcore when it comes to getting "their" money. Penalties and interest are often as high as 33% – instantly, not annually – and the Company will have no choice but to pay if they've screwed up somewhere. The screw up could be as simple as not correctly paying or reporting payroll taxes, and Boom! instant Bank-Draining Payment Plan.

4. **The Company has high balances on nearly all of their credit accounts.** This is basically the same thing as number one, only it is more recognizable because suddenly, the Company will no longer be buying their supplies from one retailer or another. It also occurs in the form of credit cards being declined, and more vendors demanding cash at the time of purchase. The reason this is so important is that a Company needs a certain amount of money to keep their doors open – money Companies often don't have because they're waiting for payment from their customers. When the credit is no longer available, that means jobs will be left unfinished and uncollectable. Unfinished and uncollectable means the need for more credit, which is going to be denied. It's a vicious cycle.

5. **Fewer and fewer customers purchasing from their company.** I don't care what anyone says – "Every business is a sales business, and nothing happens until something gets sold." (--Mary Kay Ash) So if sales are lagging and customers are starting to go elsewhere, then this is another big sign that Business is in trouble. Without money coming in regularly, any business will begin hemorrhaging in the bank account department, and without credit, there's nothing to keep them afloat during those difficult times.

6. **The business owner cares more about buying toys then buying business necessities.** This doesn't happen often, but every now and then, you will come across a business owner who really has all of their priorities out of whack. They will spend thousands and even hundreds of thousands of dollars on a car or a plane, but they won't spend even a few hundred dollars on a new business computer. They'll always have the newest truck

or be off to the latest cool vacation, but they're whole office will need a massive overhaul. This may not seem important when choosing to work with a business owner, but the sad fact is, eventually that business owner's money problems will get to ridiculous to solve, and guess who they will blame...not themselves. Oh no! They will blame the person with the checkbook in hand. They will blame YOU! Their check register will get smaller and smaller no matter how hard you work to keep them afloat, and eventually, they will just say, "Sorry, I can't afford to keep you on anymore. I have to terminate your service." At that point, you'll probably be relieved because these types of business owners come with a whole lot of "bookkeeper stress." One day, they won't care about the bank balance at all; the next day, they'll want extreme detail of every dime you've tallied. Some days they'll ignore you; other days, they'll watch you like a hawk. You can take them on if you're really desperate, but always keep an eye on the door (and by that, I mean, always be looking for the client that will replace them).

7. **The business owner is "just plain weird."** When you're working in the bookkeeping business, you will see a lot of strange people – people that just don't understand anything about money or Profit & Loss Statements. I like to call those people "artists." I'm not saying anything bad about artists – in fact, I happen to have a passion for artwork – but artists are a very interesting brand of people. Still, artists are great to have as clients because they have a passion for what they do. What I mean by "Just Plain Weird" are not the artists at all, but the people that make you want to rip your hair out...the ones that don't leave their offices or want you to work in a dark, creepy space. I like to think of them as "a little bit neurotic." You'll know these people because they'll question everything you do and then blame everything on you. It's very stressful, and you don't need them. You don't need the high blood pressure, migraines, sleepless nights, and creepy feelings that come hand-in-hand with working with these types of business owners. The best thing you can do with these types of clients is clean up their books fast and get out, but don't waste your time on month-to-month services.

8. **And finally...They tell you they fired their last bookkeeper for making ONE mistake.** Technically, there's nothing wrong with taking on these kinds of clients, but I do advise you to steer clear of them if you can. Working for a perfectionist can be difficult and stressful, especially since bookkeepers are human and not robots. In my

experience, "mistakes" are usually made within the first few months of working with any client, largely because every business owner has their own systems for doing things, and bookkeepers don't have a lot of time to figure those systems out. It's easy to drop the ball when you first start. If you take on a client who fired a bookkeeper for making one mistake – and the mistake seems like a common bookkeeping mistake – then that client will probably fire you the first time you make a mistake. So if you decide to take on a client that tells you that, realize the relationship will probably be brief, and keep your eye out for a client to replace that one.

Of course, there are lots of other signs, but from a Bookkeeper's point of view, these are the ones I *know* lead to not-getting-paid, ridiculous situations, and very bad business endings. So steer clear and keep an eye out for your ideal clients at all times. If you can get just a few good clients under your belt, you can create a successful virtual bookkeeping business that will thrive for a very long time.

Chapter 6

Step 6: You're Hired...Now What?

Creating the Client's Virtual Office

SPOTLIGHT ON A BOOKKEEPING BUSINESS – Sum Solutions

When I started my freelance accounting practice over ten years ago working virtually was not as widely accepted as it is today. At that time my client base was split evenly down the middle – providing services 50% onsite at the client location and 50% offsite at my office. Over the years I was able to migrate my onsite clients into becoming virtual clients by showing them how working remotely was really no different than working onsite and **eliminating their fears**.

A client will usually object to working remotely because they don't understand or cannot visualize how working remotely works. Their fears take over and believe me they can imagine all kinds of problems that will keep you working onsite at their location!   It is your job to show them just how easy working remotely can be BUT you must remember two things:
- People don't like change, and;
- You must have a process on how you will work remotely with your clients.

So the first step to successfully working remotely with your clients involves you answering these four very important questions:
- How will your client(s) get their accounting information to you?
- How will you return original documents to your client?
- Where will the accounting file (data) reside?
- How will the accounting file be protected?

It is up to you to define the structure of how you and your company will work remotely with clients. Here are some things for you to think about as your answer those questions from above and define your remote working structure.

Structure, Structure, Structure – whether you work remotely or at the client location, creating a consistent structure of when and how work is to be completed are essential. For example:
- You work on the client account the same day of the week, every week
- You provide your client with a list of information that is needed on a regular basis and also a list of items that are missing.
- You take the responsibility to follow up on those missing items.

The less your client has to think about and the more consistency you can provide to them more likely your client will be to cooperate.

Having the Right Tools – if you want to work remotely then you need to use the tools that will make working remotely easy. This includes using a remote hosting service that allows you and your client access to their accounting file from where ever they are. Remote hosting services also offer a daily offsite back-up of all data files. This feature becomes a benefit to your client whose current back-up routine may not be as good as it should be.

Another tool you will want to consider is a scanner. As I moved to being a 100% virtual office, I incorporated the cost of a scanner into my client's set-up fee. This way, my clients can easily scan their documents and email or fax them to my office without incurring the cost of a delivery service.

(Continued on the next page)

Keeping the Lines of Communication Open – when you work remotely it is very important to be in contact with your clients on a regular basis. The worst thing you could do is disappear into your remote office and forget about the personal aspect of your client relationship.

In my office, we have created a process that is followed to ensure that we speak with our clients at least once a week. Our communication process also includes the scheduling of several face-to-face meetings throughout the year.

Another tool you may want to consider is Grasshopper. In my office, we use this service because it provides my company with one phone number for the client to call. They simply enter the extension of the person they are trying to reach and they are then forwarded directly to their cell phone. If the staff person cannot answer, Grasshopper takes a message and emails it to you.

It does take a little trial and error to work out all of the kinks and once your clients have begun to work remotely with you, they will begin to wonder who else they can work with remotely!

Guided by an entrepreneurial spirit, Linda A. Hunt offers over twenty years of progressive experience in management accounting and operational procedures, with the past 11 years focusing on establishing and implementing financial and operational controls for small to medium sized businesses. In 1998, Linda founded SUMSOLUTIONS after recognizing the need for quality, cost-effective, day-to-day accounting services specifically designed for the small business marketplace. Under Linda's leadership, SUMSOLUTIONS quickly became one of Connecticut's fastest-growing providers of accounting and business management consulting services. Her consultative background has enabled Linda to successfully cultivate and maintain productive associations with attorneys, auditors, brokers, lenders, and other prominent business leaders. Then in early 2009, Linda had an employee buyout and moved completely away from providing accounting and small business consulting to exclusively working with other freelance accounting and bookkeeping professionals. She now teaches and shares with them the very same systems and methods that have helped her to create my very profitable freelance firm.

Visit her at www.sumsolutions.com to learn more about her free resources, products and programs.

You've got the client and you're ready to go. Only one problem...your client probably *isn't* ready to go. Or at least, your client's office probably isn't setup for your "virtual bookkeeping services" – at least not yet. With a large majority of your clients (not necessarily all), you are going to need to do a crash training course to get their office to work with yours. Of course, you don't want to tell them that you're doing a crash training course – they might find that offensive. But you will want to have a packet of information ready to go (other than your initial bookkeeping package), and you may want to spend a bit of time in their office getting them organized.

"But wait," you're probably thinking. *"I thought this was supposed to be about* virtual *bookkeeping. Why would I have to go into their office?"*

Logically, you wouldn't. But, more than likely, your client's office has been flooded with paperwork. They are going to have receipts in strange, unusual, and questionable places.

By the time they come to you, they're probably already going to feel overwhelmed. If you actually choose to take the time and get them organized, they are going to think you are a godsend. They will be grateful right from the get-go, and they will be more willing to do anything you want them to do. The less work they have to do in working with you, the longer they will be your client. Therefore, when you first start working with a client, you will want to go into their office and get them caught up with everything, enter their financial paperwork into QuickBooks, and then file everything away. That way, when you stop going into their office, they won't mind so much. They will have confidence that you can do a great job from anywhere, and they have a clean office to prove it.

(Of course, if you have a local college student assistant, you can send your assistant in your place to get them ready, and you can keep doing your day-to-day from home instead.)

Step 1 – SETUP REMOTE ACCESS TO THEIR COMPUTER

If you're going to be virtual, you're going to need Remote Access. Remote Access allows you to work on your clients' computers without actually being in their offices. While it's true that you can work from your computer and simply email backup files to your clients, it will be far, far easier to simply work from their computer. It will be easier for you because you won't have to explain how to upload the files from their email into QuickBooks, and you won't have to spend any time answering the million and one questions they will have about what changes you have made. It will be easier for them because uploading your files will be more complicated then they want, and in their minds...a complicated file = a complicated bookkeeper. Remember, your clients will want everything simple, and they will probably want to be out of the picture as much as possible, so keep things simple as often as you can.

While there are many, many products and websites you can use to make remote access a reality, not all of them are financially beneficial. For example, the online edition of QuickBooks would be a last choice for me for three reasons. They are:

1) QuickBooks *does* offer online accounts for clients, but switching from a desktop edition to an online edition is like switching a QuickBooks file from a Mac to a PC. It's creating a whole new file that needs to be uploaded, and then the previous edition needs to be

deactivated and ignored until you switch the program back for good. Trying to upload it every time you make a change to the file would quickly turn into a nightmare, especially when the programming is "similar-but-different." Something can always get lost.

2) The online QuickBooks edition is "a website" where you switch to various "web pages" to update your information. As a result, usage means you will soon find yourself losing a lot of time waiting for your browser to upload each and every page. And if you have dial-up...forget about it.

3) The online QuickBooks edition does charge a monthly fee of $35 that your client would have to pay. You could volunteer to pay it yourself, but then you have to add that price to your package fee, and you may no longer be considered a "deal" in your client's eyes.

On top of that, some clients are a bit neurotic; they won't want to deal with the mess that keeping their books outside of their office might bring.

Thus, in my opinion, a fast, inexpensive, easy-to-use option that allows your clients to keep their books in their office would be GoToMyPC.com. This site allows you to download and install a single simple file to your client's computer, and then you can access that computer from any other computer in the world through the internet. The cost is $12 a month, and you don't have any of the page loading issues you get with QuickBooks Online. Plus, the file does not have to be uploaded, and your client can access their file in their office at any time. It'll give your more "neurotic" clients the peace of mind they need, your "cheapie" clients the deal they crave, and your "can't be bothered" clients the simplicity they long for. The only question you have to consider with GoToMyPC.com is – who's going to pay for it.

Who Should Pay for Remote Access

I know what you're thinking..."*I don't want to pay for remote access. The client should. After all, it's their business and their books.*" (And if you're not thinking that – you should be. ☺)

Either way you go – whether you pay for it or your client does – adding a computer to any GoToMyPC account is going to cost $12 a month (at the time of this publication). But what you really need to consider before you say "my client will pay for it" is *reliability, accessibility, and culpability*. Consider the following:

1. **Reliability**: GoToMyPC debits from a credit card or debit card every month. Your clients may not be reliable when it comes to their credit cards and debit cards. Heck – you may have trouble getting them to pay you. Thus, if their GoToMyPC account is linked to a debit card and that balance goes negative right before the payment is deducted – or if they hit their limit on a credit card and the payment gets denied – you will be denied access to that computer. You will then have to harass your client for $12, or you will have to spend time getting GoToMyPC to take a different payment source. You, on the other hand, are completely reliable. You know you can make the payment, and you won't have to be the "debt collector" when it comes to keeping your remote access open. So, if you think your client won't make timely payments, or you don't want to rely on them to make timely payments, you may want to pay for it yourself.

2. **Accessibility**: Let's assume your client is not a deadbeat and will be reliable when it comes to payments. If that is the case, having your client pay for their GoToMyPC.com account means that they also can access that computer from any other computer in the world. They may *love* this idea for the simple fact that it will mean going on a vacation or jobsite and not having to take a laptop with them. Furthermore, if they're at home and need to check the QuickBooks bank balance before placing an order through their checking account, they won't have to run to the office and boot that computer up. For them, there is the underlying benefit of convenience. On the flip side, if every client you have has their own accounts, then you are going to have to remember a *lot* of login IDs and passwords. You will have to close out of one customer's account before logging into another. For you, it can be very *inconvenient*. However, if you add their computer to your account, you will have one accessible list of all your clients' computers in one place. You will be able to see which computers are "turned on" at any given time, and which are "turned off." For you, that means you could have one master password to access both your account and each computer without having to log in and out every time you need to switch.

3. **Culpability**: Finally, you need to consider your rights versus their rights. If the file is your file, then at no point would you want them to have access to your master file. Doing so could compromise your other clients. Thus, you need to make it clear from the beginning that "your company" will be the only company that accesses your computers. If and when you terminate your contract with that client, remote access will need to be shut off. If it's in your account, it's very easy to remove their computer from your file, and they can then create their own account if they wish to continue the service. If access is in their account, they would simply change the passwords for their computers to keep you and your "employees" out, and they could keep paying for the access themselves.

Can you tell which type of access I prefer? If you haven't guess, I prefer paying for it myself simply because I'm a lazy control freak. I like only having to remember one Master Password and then being able to access all my clients from one page instead of constantly switching back and forth. I'd rather be hanging with my kids than doing data entry all night. But that's just me...

For Clients Without Computers

Believe it or not, you will probably end up with clients who don't have computers. If that is the case with your new client, that means you will be handling all of their bookkeeping on your computer, and then sending them reports. The easiest way to do this might be to email them the reports, or even snail mail the reports. They also may want the reports delivered the day after you do your data entry for them. You need to figure out ahead of time where the books will be kept and how you will communicate their bookkeeping information to them (and eventually their accountant).

Step 2 – THE BANK ACCOUNT

Once remote access is settled, the next thing to tackle is your client's bank choice. If they are at a bank that can download QuickBooks files then *great*, they don't have to do anything and neither do you. But if they are at a bank that doesn't download QuickBooks files, you will want to encourage them to switch banks. This is going to be difficult, and may seem cold-blooded (especially because this often means switching from a local community bank to a national "big bank"), but you need to remember the financial benefits for your client. If that client remains at a small bank that does not have QuickBooks access, you are going to spend 10x *more time* doing data entry for their books then if they were to switch to another bank. You are going to be entering directly from their bank's online screen or physical statements, going back and forth on the screen or the page for each transaction that needs to be entered, double checking that you haven't made a data entry mistake, and then correcting the mistakes you do make. These are all time-consuming steps. You also have to be careful not to miss any transactions, which you may not know until you do the bank reconciliation. This could take 1-2 minutes per transaction, which multiplied by hundreds of transactions a month can add up to a significant increase in your hours and your fee.

On the flip side, downloading transactions from QuickBooks and having QuickBooks post those transactions to the various cost accounts can often be completed in a matter of minutes. For you, this would mean less money if you have an hourly agreement with that client, but if you have a "Monthly Package Deal" with that client instead, then you will be making more per hour while working less. You would spend a whole lot less time on their books but still get your monthly fee. So, it's a win-win for both of you (unless you have to do all the data entry and don't get to charge an hourly rate).

Thus, when you pitch this to your client, point out that you will have to spend 10 times as many hours doing data entry if they stay with their bank. Then, ask them point blank, "Is staying with your bank worth the extra $300 a month that it's going to cost you in bookkeeping fees (*or whatever your hourly rate is times 10*). Because even if you don't hire me, someone will have to spend time entering all that data."

Another thing you could say if they are still on the fence is, "Don't worry. I don't need you to switch all of your accounts. Just switch the <u>main business *checking*</u> account. All of your personal accounts, savings accounts and credit card accounts can stay with the bank you're at, and I will still be able to save you hundreds of dollars a month on your bookkeeping." For a lot of business owners, this will probably be the clincher.

Once you've sold them on needing a bank account with the "QuickBooks downloadable files" option, the next thing you want to do is suggest a few banks in your area that you know have good deals on business checking accounts, excellent customer service, and the accessibility you need. So, have a list ready when you walk in.

You may even want to approach the banks first and see if they offer any "Referral Bonuses" for bringing new clients. You could get your clients an extra $25 to $50 for switching, then make an extra $25 or $50 for yourself as well. It's a cha-ching situation all around.

Here are some other things you will also need to discuss with your clients in regards to their bank accounts:

Separate Checking Accounts

This is another issue you're going to have to push if you want to keep a good relationship with your client. You see, once they have a new checking account and a new bookkeeper, the first thing many business owners will think is, *"Now I can go spend money."* And you know what they're going to use to spend money with – the new debit card from the new checking account. After all, that's where there money is now.

You are going to have to nix that idea in the bud right from the beginning. If you don't, you're going to go insane trying to control their spending, and you're going to look like you don't know what you're doing. Why am I saying this? Simple. The new debit card is going to mess with the bank balance you're trying to keep for them. You want to look like a fantastic bookkeeper, and one of the ways you're going to do this is to always have the bank balance readily available. But, if your client is drawing money from that account faster than you can reconcile it, you're going to look like a fool.

The solution: have them open TWO checking accounts – one for the checks and payments that need to be made, and one for them to debit from. If they don't want to do this, then encourage them to pick a credit card for their business use so that they don't mess with "*your* bank balance" (and by "your," I don't mean the client).

Online Banking

Once the issue of Bank choice and dual checking accounts have been settled, the next issue you will want to tackle is "Online Banking." If your client does not have online banking access, then you will want to sign them up. When they have online banking, you will be able to utilize their Bill Pay feature, which will save time in regards to writing and signing checks, and then stuffing and mailing the checks in envelopes (not to mention the price of stamps). Even if you aren't the one to access their online banking account when bills need to be paid, it will make the virtual bookkeeping experience a whole lot easier for both you and your client whenever it comes time to cut checks. You can set up most of their vendors and customers through Online Bill Pay, and then have payments issued by the bank without getting signatures. Furthermore, since the Bill Pay amounts are deducted from the account immediately, it will be easier for you to know what that client's bank balance is at any one time.

Remember, what works for the checking account will also work for the credit card accounts. The more you can access those accounts online, the easier your job is going to be and the more you will be able to get done for them for a fraction of the cost and your time. So get the credit cards setup for remote access at the same time you set up the checking account access.

Step 3 – FILING AND ORGANIZATION

When you start working with a client, the first thing you're going to want to do is bring along a big fat storage box. Most likely, your client will be behind and you'll need to catch them up. You aren't going to want to do that in their office; you'll want to do it in your office. That means, you're going to need to haul a whole bunch of stuff from their office to your car and then from

your car to your house. More than likely, they won't have a decent storage box hanging around their office that you can use. Thus, it helps to bring your own.   I like a simple basic cardboard storage box (with lid) from

Office Depot, which costs about $3 a box. Or, you could spend a little more and get something fancier. Either way, you basically want to find something with handles for carrying, and a space for writing the client's name on the side of the box.

Once you've brought your box in and are ready to get going, simply gather up all of the loose paperwork tossed around their office, plop the papers into the box, and drag that box back to your office for sorting and data entry. Then, when you bring those papers back, they will be presorted into manila file folders and ready to be dropped back into your client's filing cabinet. By doing this – by taking the paperwork with you – you are instantly giving your new client a visual picture of how much you're helping them right off the bat. It can be a huge relief to a lot of your clients to know that someone has taken over that mess and that they won't have to deal with it.

Quick Warning: Some of your clients may NOT be okay with you taking their paperwork home. Some clients have this neurotic need to keep everything near – i.e. "in their office." Those are the clients that will be most resistant to you doing their bookkeeping remotely. So after you gather up their paperwork, check to make sure that they're okay with you taking it home for sorting and data entry. Reassure them of when exactly you will be bringing all of that paperwork back, and then follow through. This will help ease their compulsive need to keep everything near.

If they still aren't okay with you taking the paperwork home, then tuck the box into an area of their office that is out of the way for the next time you come to do data entry. This will help them keep their "feeling of control," while still allowing you to visually show them how valuable you are going to be.

Creating a Filing System That Works for You AND Your Client

Digital Filing

I don't know about you, but I HATE filing...hate it, hate it, hate. Filing wastes a HUGE amount of a bookkeeper's time. It's menial, boring, and often results in painful paper cuts that worker's compensation refuses to cover. Having said as much, I fully believe that Small Businesses should ditch their office filing cabinets and save all their paperwork digitally.

At this point, you're probably thinking, *"But filing is a necessary evil. After all, the IRS can demand that a small business produce seven years of previous tax documents. We have to use filing cabinets to organize all of the office paperwork that the IRS will require."* My answer to that is, the IRS never said that your paperwork had to be in order! They just said you had to produce it.

(No good? Okay...let's try that again.)

I am not saying that businesses should no longer keep their receipts, invoices, bills, etc, etc, etc. What I am saying is that small business owners and bookkeepers should consider electronic filing in lieu of paper filing. Paper filing – or filing paperwork – is a time consuming process. On the other hand, hitting "Save" on a computer is much faster, as is faxing paperwork to an eFax. By saving a company's paperwork digitally, you can free up all the hassle that comes with shoving paperwork into alphabetized manila folders. Instead, they can do a search on their computer to find any digital receipt instantly, especially with the search methods that newer computers offer. With older computers, where indexing the contents of digital files is not done automatically, you can still use QuickBooks as an index and do a search for the month that digital file would have been entered, and thus saved. As a result, you save time filing, your client saves time searching for documents, and they also save money on paying to have items filed.

How to do Digital Filing Quickly, Easily and Cheaply:

1. **Scanning Paperwork.** Remember how in Chapter 1, I told you to get an eFax? This is where your eFax will come in handy. You can fax paperwork from any fax machine to your eFax number and those files will automatically be scanned and saved as PDF files. If you

refuse to get an eFax, you can use your Multi-Function Printer to also scan files directly to your computer. If you do this method, you would have to tell the computer to "Scan it to a File" (and not an image or picture), and then save it as a PDF file. If you save it as anything else, each paper will be individually saved and you would have to go into each file to see what it is before renaming it. So – use your eFax or your Scanner.

a. If you use the eFax, the images will not be as clear as with a scanner, but then you don't have to sit and babysit your computer as it scans. You can put the paperwork in your fax machine's feed, hit send, and walk away.

b. If you use a Scanner, you will have to check that file periodically and make sure nothing is going wrong. Computers and printers can have a "glitch" occur, and you could lose that file. (Believe me, it's frustrating.) However, scanning does produce better copies, and you can also avoid any "Overage Charges" from your eFax if you find yourself close to your eFax limit at the end of the month.

2. **How to File Easily and Digitally.** Technically, there are three ways to save digital files to a digital filing cabinet (by data entry date, by month, or alphabetically). Each one comes with its own procedure and has its own level of ease or difficulty. You need to figure out which one will work best for your client. Here's a recap:

a. **Saved by Data Entry Date:** As I stated earlier, you can actually use your computer's Search Feature as an Index for the digital files you are saving. With newer computers, the contents of files are usually indexed automatically, so "Searching" for a name can often produce results where the name is not in the file name, but inside the document itself. This is a great feature to have and usually comes standard with computers that have Microsoft Office 2007 or newer. But even if a client has an older computer without this feature, you can still use QuickBooks as your digital filing cabinet's index. Simply open QuickBooks and search under the vendor or customer name, and you will see what date that transaction was entered and possibly saved.

i. To save by Date-Entry: When you do your data entry, you would enter all of your transactions' dates as the date you are posting them, and then save the main PDF file by that date also. Then, when your client asks you for a receipt, you would search the file on QuickBooks, see what date it was entered, and then pull the digital file. You could also do a "Search" on the computer (without QuickBooks) and newer versions will show you a list of all the files with that name in the file and on the file.

b. **Saved by Month:** This is another very easy way to save all of your files. When you receive one master file from your eFax or Scanner, you would save it by the month that is listed on those transactions. Then, when a client says, "I want the file for Vendor A from March," either one of you could go to the March digital folder and do a quick search through the one or two main files that will be listed there. In the same way, this makes paper filing easy because after a stack of paperwork has been digitized, the hard copies can be tossed into a folder in a filing cabinet by month also. Thus your client's physical filing cabinet would match their digital filing cabinet.

   i. To do this quickly and easily: Whenever you send documents to your eFax or scan them, simply sort them by month first, and then scan one month's documents at a time. This way, all you have to do is drop the main incoming file into the digital filing cabinet and you're done.

c. **Saved Alphabetically by Company Name:** This is the most time-consuming method of the three because it involves opening and saving each file by name and possibly date. Then, you have to "Drag and Drop" that file into the filing cabinet by name. It is the most thorough, but it can take a while.

   i. If you Scan your files, you can save time by saving those scanned files as ANYTHING OTHER THAN A PDF. Saving it as a jpeg or a tiff file will create individual files. Then, you don't have to take anything apart (like when you receive an eFax). You simply open each file, then "Save (it) As" whatever name you want in whichever folder you want. It's that easy.

   ii. If you receive your files on your eFax, then you have to take those files apart. You would do that by "Extracting" the pages from the main file, and then "Saving (it) As" whatever file you want to save it as and wherever you want it saved. It's that easy.

iii. For both scanning and filing: If you're using the "Save As" feature from the original files, once you've saved the new files by name, don't forget to delete the original files to keep your hard drive clean and clear.

For all three methods of digital filing, the majority of work will be done while your seated at your computer. The rest of the paperwork can then be put into a file folder by month and dropped into a filing cabinet. This way, you can save the largest amount of time, and save your client money.

Physical Filing

While it is absolutely 100% possible to ditch your filing cabinet and index every receipt, invoice, bill, eBill and statement that ever crosses a bookkeeper's desk, I am not so foolish as to actually believe that everyone will embrace this advice wholeheartedly. In fact, I fully acknowledge that ditching the filing cabinet is the one piece of advice that a large majority of small business owners will hate. They would rather do things "the old fashioned way" and have a paper copy of everything they have ever touched crammed into cabinets and boxes in their offices and storage areas. The ever present fear that the IRS will come knocking is the biggest factor behind this choice, and it backs up the whole "not fixing what isn't broken" belief. So if you want to ignore that last tip, it's fine...because I still have an opinion on Filing Paperwork. (After all, it is one of my pet peeves.)

One of the most irksome things I see on a daily basis as an Independent Bookkeeper is another bookkeeper's "Filing System." I put "Filing System" in quotes because – quite frankly – I'm being hugely sarcastic. What some bookkeepers cook up as "Filing Systems" is just short of nightmarish to the professionals that have to come in behind them and clean things up – and it's a nightmare for the business owners. Trying to find a receipt or a bill that a virtual bookkeeper has filed into their fancy-shmancy filing system can turn into a huge waste of time for everyone but the bookkeeper.

So here's my philosophy: **Bookkeepers should be completely dispensable at all times.**

The best bookkeepers will do their jobs so well, another bookkeeper can step into their shoes at any time and take over. Bookkeepers that are on top of everything don't need people to come in and "clean up after them" because their systems are completely accessible for every single employee in the office all the way down to the janitor who empties the trash. In my opinion, that one single quality makes a bookkeeper more trustworthy than anything else they could possibly do in an office. It says, "Come in – feel free to look around. You're not going to find anything you shouldn't because I'm awesome!"

Now, having said that, your "Filing System" can be done by month that the transaction is entered – as stated in the Digital Files subsection above – and you can still use QuickBooks as your index. But, if your business owner is really against that idea, then you need to keep your filing system as simple as possible. It should not take a degree to know where things are. Instead, here is what your filing system should be (if it isn't already):

1. **Ditch the "Categories."** While it may seem important to have IRS-related paperwork in one section, bank-related paperwork in another section, credit-card information in another system, SBO Identity information in another section (etc, etc, etc) the truth is, this helps no one but you. If your SBO doesn't know your system, they are going to waste countless hours trying to figure it out, and then they'll come to hate you. So instead...

2. **Alphabetize.** The simplest "Filing System" is the good old fashioned A-through-Z system. Anyone can find paperwork when it's in alphabetical order, and they can find it quickly. The faster an SBO can find something, the happier they will be with you and the cooler they'll think you are. (They might even hire you an assistant, should you ask, and then your assistant can do all the filing for you...and they won't even need to be smart to do it). Once you start alphabetizing, the next step is to...

3. **Condense, Condense, Condense.** Again, under the guise of simplifying the filing cabinet, you should now be thinking of bringing everything into one place. That means, STOP putting some folders in your desk while others go in this filing cabinet or that one. Some are with your SBO while others are with other employees. Instead, put all of your Income Folders (or Customer-Related Files) into one drawer (two max), and all of your Expense Folders (or Vendor Folders) into another, and Employee Info into a third. The only files that should be in your desk are the ones that you have to access every day – like private credit card information, social security information, or things that you work with but no one else does.

Your desk should be for you alone...I know what you're thinking: But what about security? My answer to that is...

4. **Keep Receipts from Different Years Separated.** By this, I mean transactions that all happen in one year should be kept together. This is so much easier when it comes to setting them on fire later – after the 7 year "mandatory hold" the IRS demands. Make it simple by creating new folders every year before January 1st so that you're ready to go and don't have to sort anything else out later. You can then put that Old Year's Files in another drawer or storage boxes and get them out of your way. (My general rule is to keep the past year in the cabinets – because you will be accessing those in the following year – and packing away folders that are more than two years old.) Once that is done, then you'll want to...

5. **Simplify Your Labeling System.** While it may be tempting to recreate a folder for every single Vendor or Customer you have, the truth is, it's not always necessary. In fact, it's wasteful. You'll waste boxes of filing folders, as well as cabinet space, if you have a folder for everything. So instead, copy the previous year's folder names only if they had more than 5 items in them, or you know you're going to be getting a lot more paperwork from them in the future. For everything else, create a "Miscellaneous" Folder which can be by Letter or a single folder at the front or back of the cabinet, and store all the items that have less than 5 pieces of paperwork in those folders. The General Rule is: More than 5 gets a Folder; Less than 5 is just "Miscellaneous."

Now, if you implement all these strategies into your filing cabinet, you will begin to save tons of time searching for documents, and anyone can step in and do the filing for you – including your college assistant. And that really is the goal: to make yourself replaceable at all times, and thus make yourself indispensable. (It's a bizarre philosophy, but it works.)

Step 4 - YOUR CLIENT'S CHECKLIST

Once you've got the bank and filing systems agreed upon, the next issue to tackle is when you're going to be doing that client's books. You want to set a specific day so that they will know when to check up on your work, and so that they won't be sitting in their office wondering,

"When am I going to get an update on my bookkeeping?" Furthermore, by agreeing on a date ahead of time, that client will know when they need to send you their receipts and paperwork so that you won't have to chase them down during the time slot you have available to work for them. So here are the things you need to agree on (you can find a sample checklist in the Appendix):

1. **Time Slot:** Will you be doing that client's books weekly, every other week, monthly or bi-monthly? Will you be doing the data entry every other Monday, Tuesday, etc? What time of the day will you need to access their computer, and will it be at night? Whatever time slot you agree on, the client is going to need to leave their computer on so you can access it.

2. **Your Client's Checklist:** Basically, your client needs to know when they need to get information to you so that it can be entered in a timely manner. The busier you get with other client's, the more often you will need them to stay on top of things. Therefore, give them a mini-checklist that includes the day that you will be doing the data entry, and thus the time that they will need to get you their paperwork. Also, list the ways they can send you that paperwork – via fax, email, pickup/deliver, snail mail, or overnight mail. Then, email them a reminder one or two days before you do your data entry work so that they will get you that paperwork on time.

3. **Give Them a Clear List of What to Expect From You:** When you're done with your data entry, you want to let them know it. You never want them to wonder if you actually are doing what you say you're doing. As such, one of the easiest ways to prove your working is to turn over reports that they can understand. These reports include: Accounts Receivable / Accounts Payable Summary Reports, Checking Account Registers, P&L's for the month-to-date and/or Year-to-Date, and even Budgets vs. P&L-to-Date. Then, those reports will either be printed on their printers when you're done (which is easy to do remotely), or you will email / fax those reports to them. The two of you need to agree on this ahead of time.
    a. Things to include for your client to do: Faxing / emailing paperwork; putting paperwork into the pickup / delivery folder, downloading the banking and credit card accounts into QuickBooks files, if you don't have direct access to the online accounts (and I do recommend that you NOT access their online banking accounts for security's sake), and anything else they want you to know about.

4. **A List of How to Handle Daily Bookkeeping Issues:** This is the one thing they will really be interested in – NOT dealing with bookkeeping questions. Your job is to make their job easier, so do that by telling them that they can refer all of their vendor and customer money-related issues to your voicemail line. If you have an internet phone account with free extensions (a benefit that RingCentral.com offers), then you can leave specific messages for incoming Vendor/Customer calls on those extensions. Just make sure that on those messages, you say that you will return their call in 24 hours. You don't want to make your client's Vendors and Customers angrier when you don't return their call in the same day. (And sometimes, you just won't be able to.)

Again, see the Appendix for a Client's Checklist.

HOW TO HANDLE PHONE CALLS, EMAILS, TEXT MESSAGES, AND FAXES

Once you begin running your bookkeeping business –whether it's virtual or not – you are going to be so tempted to answer every phone call, text message and email that comes in as they come in. You need to fight this temptation. (Seriously – *fight it*.) Especially if you are in a client's office. If you don't fight it, it can have negative repercussions later on. Here's some examples:

1. **Answering Phones in a Client's Office is Unprofessional.** Even if you have a monthly package deal agreed upon with your client ahead of time, many clients will feel that you should not be focusing on any other client but them when you are dealing with their bookkeeping. In addition, if they have any employees or ever had employees, they will feel like they are paying you an hourly rate (again, even if it's a monthly package). Therefore, you are wasting their time and money by taking phone calls. It gives the impression that you are unprofessional. You don't want them to think that – ever. So the best thing you can do is turn your ringer off when you go into a client's office and never take a phone call (unless it's from your family because those will be dismissed as "family

emergencies). Instead, wait until you leave the client's office to check voicemail or return phone calls.

  a. **Now if the client leaves the office**, I would still not recommend answering phone calls because the client could walk back in at any time. But answering text messages...go for it.

2. **Answering the Phone at Your Home Office Can Upset Your Groove.** Again, even when you're in your home office, it may be tempting to answer the phone. But, if you are in your home office and doing work, don't stop. These kinds of interruptions will upset your "Groove" and it will take you a decent portion of time to "get back into the swing of things." In other words, every time you allow a phone call, email or text to interrupt you, it could take as much as 20 minutes per occurrence to get back to work. The largest reason this happens is because you are forcing your mind to change directions. That new direction could be upsetting – having to deal with IRS drama or an angry vendor – and then you'll feel an urgency to "Fix Everything" when you need to be focusing on wrapping up your first project. So, if you are working on something at your home office, ignore the phone calls, texts and emails until you've finished the project you're working on.

3. **Changing Your Answering Pattern Can Disappoint Expectations and Lead to a Bad Reputation.** If you answer every phone call as soon as it comes in, you create a reputation among your clients that also comes with expectations. The expectation is that a client and their vendors or customers will be able to get hold of you whenever they wish. But, the busier you get, the harder it will be to take all those phones. If you suddenly change the way you handle these phone calls, then your client will begin to wonder what's going on with you. They'll start to come to their own conclusions, like "my bookkeeper's too busy for me, or is forgetting about me, so maybe I should find someone else." This can also happen if vendors can't get hold of you and they you're your client back to complain. By not answering every phone call straight off the bat, you will get them used to a method that works for them and you, and when you return their call later, it will be "no big deal."

4. **Answering the Phone around Your Family or Friends is "Just Plain Rude."** Have you ever hung out with a very popular friend who was constantly answering their phone

when they were hanging out with you? The two of you are hanging out for the first time in a while, but suddenly they're having a conversation with someone else that can last 20 to 30 minutes. (No? Just me?) I've had it happen many times, and it irritates the heck out of me. It feels like they're wasting my time. If I'm going to take time out of my busy schedule to hang out with family and friends, I want to make that time worthwhile. Having to deal with "emergencies" that are rarely ever emergencies, diminishes the quality of your time and your friend & family time. So if you've set aside time to actually be with your friends or family, turn off your work phone. All of those problems will still be there when your quality time is over.

I can guess what you're thinking at this point. *"If I'm not supposed to answer my phone when people call, then how am I supposed to handle all of my client's bookkeeping issues? Won't they get mad?"*

No, they won't get mad. They won't get mad because you are going to create a system that works for you, your clients, and their vendors or customers. You are going to communicate clearly and on your time. You will do this by:

1. **Choose a Time-Slot Where You Can Return Phone Calls Each and Every Day.** Most vendors and customers won't be irritated if they know *when* you're going to return their call. A good time to return phone calls is the next morning before you start your normal data entry day or between 4-5 PM, before people go home. In the morning, your mind will be fresh, and with coffee in hand, you'll be ready to tackle any problems. It's also a good time because you will never know if you're going to spend too much time working on a client's books, and thus end up missing that time slot. The key here is consistency...you want to return calls during a time that is easy to remember, and that you only have to post to your voicemail once.

2. **Leave a Message on Your Voicemail that Indicates When You Will Call Back.** Once you know when you can call someone back without dipping into someone's data entry time, then you need to communicate that to people calling in. By changing your voicemail message to say something like, "I am with a client right now, but I will return your call by

tomorrow at 10AM," most people leaving a message will be satisfied with that, and will be happy to leave a message.

3. **Ask The Caller to Leave a Detailed Message.** Remember, you will be dealing with multiple clients and all of their contacts. As such, you want to know ahead of time what their issue is. Explain that in your voicemail as well, and ask that they name the client and issue, as well as a return phone number.

4. **Actually Call Back.** Obviously, this won't work if you can't call back. You want to be consistent. If you start dropping the ball, you'll start making people mad, and that could result in you losing clients. Therefore, make sure you call back in your phone-call time slot and then everyone will be more than satisfied with how you handle their issues.

Now all you need to do is do what you do best. Get to work.

Chapter 7

Step 7: Payroll

SPOTLIGHT ON A BOOKKEEPING BUSINESS – AuditMyBooks

Accounting errors and fraud are serious issues for all businesses, but they are especially challenging for small companies where cash is always a top concern. Errors and fraud undermine decision making, lead to financial losses, and in some cases, even force companies to lay off staff or shut their doors. Unfortunately, both accounting errors and fraud are common problems for small businesses.

Research by the Association of Certified Fraud Examiners (ACFE) shows that more than 30% of all fraud occurs in small companies. A startling fact considering that the estimated fraud losses for businesses of all sizes were nearly $2.9 trillion in 2009. Small companies pay a high price when it comes to fraud. The ACFE research found that the median fraud loss for a small business was $150,000. Despite the severity, very little has been done to help small businesses proactively address the problem. As a result, in the majority of cases investigated by the ACFE, the fraud was discovered accidentally or via a tip from someone outside the company.

In some small businesses, the risk of fraud is low or even non-existent. Still, accounting errors can potentially be a big problem. One small mistake in recording a payment from a customer can lead to underpaid sales taxes, ultimately resulting in unnecessary penalties and interest charges. Recent research by Indiana University showed that 60% of accounting errors result from "simple bookkeeping mistakes or misapplication of easily understood accounting standards".

The most common reason for errors and fraud occurring so frequently in small businesses is that they typically have small or even single-person accounting staffs and limited internal controls.   When the bookkeeper is also the office manager and receiving clerk, problems can arise if for no other reason than the fact that no one double checks the work. Besides being more susceptible to errors and fraud, small businesses are also less likely to discover them since financial audits are almost never performed.

Comprehensive analysis of small business accounting data can help to identify errors or possible fraud, much like anti-virus technologies are used to protect your computer from attack. With Intuit QuickBooks, products like AuditMyBooks automatically assess every accounting transaction in a matter of minutes to identify errors and possible fraud.   The sooner these issues are discovered, the sooner corrective action can be taken.

As with protecting computers from viruses, analysis of financial data to detect irregularities should happen on a routine basis. Whether manual or automated with software the added diligence of even a monthly scan of your QuickBooks data reduces the chances that accounting errors or fraud harms your business, ultimately helping you to stay focused on growth and financial success.

CP Morey, CPA
Vice President of Products
AuditMyBooks - Automated Detection of Errors & Fraud for Small Business Accounting Systems
Web: AuditMyBooks.com | Twitter: @AuditMyBooks |
LinkedIn: AuditMyBooks | Facebook: AuditMyBooks

If you are going to be a Virtual Bookkeeper who plans on doing payroll for your clients, then there is a whole passel of information you are going to have to know and share in order to make this particular step happen seamlessly. For starters, you'll need to get your clients to send timecard information to you via email or fax. That means someone else needs to tally up regular hours, overtime hours and vacation time hours. (Of course, there are ways that QuickBooks can do this on a daily basis, but that means the business owner would have to invest several hundred dollars to get a QuickBooks time punch machine. While most business owners will be resistant to investing this kind of money, it may actually save them money in the long run – and you a headache from having to constantly remind them to send things to you – by getting it from the beginning.)

In the meantime, let's assume that the owner is going to want to do the "for now" method (meaning, whatever is cheapest "for now"). That method is going to consist of either you going into their office and physically handling the timecards, someone from their company faxing copies of the timecards to you, or someone at their company tallying the hours and sending those tallies to you. You have to decide which way is going to work best for each company and each business owner. Keep in mind, a business owner has hired you because they don't want to have anything to do with the bookkeeping. That means, if the business owner does not have an office assistant, you are probably going to have to go to their "office" (whether a closet in their house or a physical commercial/retail location) and pull those timecards yourself. Even if the business owner swears they will send you those timecards on time, the facts are, *bookkeeping is only going to be a priority to them when they absolutely have to face it*. In other words, they are going to forget to send you those timecards after a while because their mind will be on the other aspects of the business. Thus, becoming another "problem" in their lives (and thus having them fire you after a while because it's just too much hassle for them), then you are going to want to deal strictly with the office manager, or go get the timecards yourself.

GETTING THE TIMECARDS WITHOUT GOING IN

As stated above, the preferred way for a Virtual Bookkeeper to get the timecards is to have an office manager or office assistant (and *not* the business owner) to send you the timecards (largely because the business owner will get frustrated with such a "menial task"). Here are some of the solutions you can present to your small business owner from the beginning to get them on board:

Having an Office Manager (or Receptionist) Tally the Totals

Let's assume that your client is not going to want to waste their valuable time tallying up timecards for payroll. Having an Office Manager or Receptionist tally the payroll totals and fax or email them to you can be a really effective and inexpensive way for you to receive the payroll totals without extra work for your client. One way to do this is to use a summary time sheet with each Employee's Name and Hours Worked. (The Hours Worked includes the regular hours, overtime hours, sick leave and vacation time.) Another way would be to have the employees tally their own time cards, enter the total hours at the bottom of the card, and then have either the office manager or business owner approve those hours. Then, for both methods, the Office Manager can enter the total hours for each category on the Summary Sheet, and fax you the summary sheet or attach it to an email. Here is a very simple example of what that form would look like (you can find a usable copy in the Appendix):

Name	Regular Hours	Over Time	Sick Pay	Vacation	Totals	Other (i.e. Bonuses/ Reimbursed Expenses)
M. Mouse	72	2.5	0	8	82.5	
D. Duck	64	0	16	0	80	

This is a great method to use because the end result would be one simple page that anyone can fill out by hand, and then fax or email. But, don't expect to receive the above worksheet with hours totaled in the "Totals" column to always be accurate. People make addition problems all the time. Double check the numbers by using a blank Excel worksheet to plug the hours into and then letting Excel calculate the totals for you.

Have Timesheets Faxed and You Do the Work

Deciding how to process a client's payroll will depend on the size of the business and the number of employees. If there are only two employees, faxing timecards is no problem. However, if there are twelve employees, a single page summary sheet works much better. Of course, there is always the possibility that a small business owner will have such a small business, they won't even have an office manager or administrative assistant to help out. In this case, it could be easier and more efficient for them to email or fax the timecards to you and then you would have to total them yourself. This is obviously going to cost your client a little bit more in regards to your hourly wage (unless you worked out a package deal with them from the beginning), as well as cost them more of their own time. Think about it: your small business owner is not going to want to hover over a fax machine waiting and making sure that every time card goes through and doesn't jam. More likely, they will stick the timecards on the fax machine and leave. Then, without a doubt, the fax machine will jam and you will only get half of the timecards. At this point, you will have to call the business owner and tell him to go back to his fax machine and resend those timecards. Once that happens, you are no longer an asset, but a pain in your client's backside. And the more often you have to do this, the more frustrated the client is going to get. So, while this is an entirely feasible option, having the timecards faxed or emailed to you should be the fall back option, after having an office droid do it, and only if you absolutely do not want to go in and do this yourself. Then again, there is always...

A Third Option

I probably should have lead off with this option since it is the best option regarding timecards, but this is one of those options that a lot of business owners will probably be resistant too. For one thing, people (and especially business owners) often like to do things the same old way they've always done it, as I mentioned previously in a chapter. Timecards and timecard machines are the "good old fashioned way" to fix things, and in a business owner's mind – "if it ain't broke..." You get the idea.

However, if you can sell this option to a business owner, not only will it save you time, but it will save them both time and money.

The Third Option, quite simply, is to turn the timecards into a summary sheet right from the beginning. This summary sheet will be filled out on a daily basis by the employees (which is the biggest reason why a business owner may be resistant to this...if a business owner has a timestamp machine, they are going to want to use it). But before I tell you how to sell the business owner on using this feature, here is an example of the timesheet:

Name		Monday	Tuesday	Wednes day	Thurs day	Friday	Satur day	Sunday	Notes
	Time In								
	Time Out								
	Time In								
M. Mouse	*Time Out*								
	Time In								
	Time Out								
	Time In								
D. Duck	*Time Out*								

(A copy of this timesheet is available in the Appendix. You have our permission to print or photocopy it and use it with your business.)

I will say this: I prefer a summary sheet over the "Time In/Out" Method where I have to calculate hours. Leave that task up to the Client. But, if your client is too busy, or doesn't add well, then go ahead and use the Timecard Method.

As you can see, a timestamp machine may not work very well with this type of timecard, and filling this out would be a major nuisance to a business owner who doesn't have OCD tendencies. Thus, selling this to a business owner who doesn't want to deal with bookkeeping, or have to increase their workload, comes down to a few simple sales pitches. Here is how you should pitch it to them (if they aren't 100% on board, of course).

If the business owner (and the employees) works outside of the office, you could suggest the following:

1. This is a compact timesheet that can fit on any clipboard, thus the business owner could keep this timesheet with them at all times. This means that the employees will have to come to the business owner to clock in and clock out, and will keep the business owner apprised of who is still on the job and who isn't. This will also let the business owner know immediately who is taking longer-than-usual lunches, who is clocking in late, and who is working overtime. In other words, it's a great (and easy) way for a business owner to monitor their employees without having to do a lot of extra investigatory work. Instead, the employees will seek the business owner out, thus making the business owner's job easier.

2. Once the week is done, the business owner can see at a glance how busy their employees have been and be able to analyze which employees are reliable and which ones aren't.

3. This worksheet can be attached to outgoing invoices as "backup" for that company's clients, just in case the business has any clients who require proof of work before making a payment.

4.   The business owner can make any notes on the pages for the bookkeeper, and then fax it. It's one simple page to send, which would take only a minute, thus saving the business owner time faxing the timecards to you.

5.   Since this sheet is easier to tally then individual timecards, it's going to save you time, which will save them money in regards to paying you.

For business owners who operate retail locations:

1.   This timesheet can be put up on any bulletin board in the break area.

2.   If the business owner is concerned about employees lying when the business owner isn't around, they can either have another employee on duty initial that the first employee clocked in on-time, or they can have the employee clock in with a timestamp machine and a timecard, but then write their own times on the spreadsheet which matches the timecard. It will take only an extra few seconds on the employee's behalf, while still saving the business owner bookkeeping time and money.

3.   Again, the business owner can see at a glance how busy their employees have been and be able to analyze which employees are reliable and which ones aren't.

4.   Again, the business owner can make any notes on the pages for the bookkeeper, and then fax one simple page instead of many timecard.

5.   And again, this sheet is easier to tally then individual timecards, so it's going to save you time and them money.

So how about it? Do you think you can convince your business owners to switch?

CUTTING CHECKS

This is where things can get tricky if you're going to be a proficient payroll bookkeeper for your clients. You see the simple fact is, most employees don't want to receive their paychecks in the mail. In fact, many employees live paycheck to paycheck, so they will be waiting with bated breath for the minute they can pick those checks up and run down to the bank.

Truth is, they will probably start calling you to see where their checks are if the checks are so much as 10 minutes late (and believe me when I say, the owner *will* have passed your phone number on to the employees so that they can call you about this issue). It would be more beneficial for the employees if the paychecks could be picked up in their office.

On the other hand, you are not going to want to have to run to an office to drop off paychecks. That is a time consuming process that can take a big chunk out of your day, especially if the business is not close to your office. Furthermore, if you are a Virtual Bookkeeper, then your client may not even be in the same state, so dropping checks off may not be an option. And even if you were to write the checks, *you will not be signing them, so you would have to get them to the small business owner anyway.*

What's a Virtual Bookkeeper to do?

Here are two simple solutions you can utilize, and they depend completely on your client's office setup:

For Businesses without Computers or Computers that You Can't Access Remotely

If your client does not have a computer, or does not have remote access to their computer, then you are going to go with a basic off-site routine. This consists of processing the payroll as if you were in their office, but instead of printing paychecks, you are going to print paycheck stubs. Once you have the paycheck stubs in hand, you can either email or fax those paycheck stubs to your business owner *or to the employees directly.* (These paystubs can be password-protected through QuickBooks, thus protecting any personal information should your business owner opt for this service.) The business owner would next handwrite the checks to match the paycheck stubs, then hand the stubs and the checks to each employee individually.

However, keep in mind that this may become irritating to a business owner over time, because the business owner will have to handwrite a lot of checks. As a result, they may eventually decide to "find another way" and stop using this service if they determine it to be too much of a hassle.

For Businesses with Computers that You Can Remotely Access

The ideal client is going to have their own computers *and printers*, and they are going to allow you to remotely access their bookkeeping files from your own office. If this is the case, the next step for you is to make sure they have the right kind of checks – checks that can be printed-on versus hand-written. If the client does not have checks that can be ran through their computers (and preferably checks with the stubs that can be torn off), you are going to want to sell them on buying this type of checks. For one thing, a set of 500 is usually only $50 and it means the difference between wasting paper and saving the business owner tons of time in having to write all the checks themselves. When most business owners realize that for only $50, they can save hours of their own time, they'll opt for the printable checks instead of the handwritten ones – especially since they are usually the same price as the handwritten checks.

So once you know the business owner has the right checks, you are going to process the payroll in QuickBooks (whether from your computer or theirs), and then call in and have the printable checks put on their printer. You can hit print remotely, and then they will sign the checks once the checks are done. They can also distribute the checks, and then, all you have to do is issue all the payroll taxes.

(If you don't know how to do payroll tax processing, then keep an eye out on our blog. We will be posting a mini-payroll tax processing guide before the end of the year.)

Just FYI: QuickBooks offers DIRECT DEPOSIT for a fee of $1.05 per paycheck. No monthly fees. No minimum number of checks.

Chapter 8

Step 8: Taxes – Don't Do 'Em

Utilize an Accountant

FINAL ADVICE FROM ROSS P. ALLAN CHAPMAN ON DEALING WITH ACCOUNTANTS

"I already have an accountant, why should I hire a bookkeeper?" Let's start off with the definitions:

<u>Accountant</u>: a professional person who performs accounting functions; <u>Accounting</u>: the theory and system of setting up, maintaining, and auditing the books of a firm; art of analyzing the financial position and operating results of a business house from a study of its sales, purchases, overhead, etc.

<u>Bookkeeper</u>: a professional person who performs bookkeeping functions; <u>Bookkeeping</u>: the work or skill of keeping account books or systematic records of monetary transactions.

Similar… yes, the same… no.

Accountants and bookkeepers both perform a necessary service to businesses and business professionals so why hire one over the other. Well in actuality you honestly should be looking at both. Much like a nurse compliments a doctor a bookkeeper compliments an accountant. The Doctor/Nurse/Patient relationship works to protect your health. The Accountant/Bookkeeper/Client relationship works to protect your business's health, further also minimizing your tax liability. We, bookkeepers, are here to look after the day to day health of your small business enterprise. In doing so you are proactively preventing issues that may arise. Issues such as non-compliance with governmental filings; frauds; business decisions that should be made in a timely manner; timely payment of all accounts payable as well as receipt of accounts receivable and a host of other issues.

Having a professional bookkeeper deal with the bookkeeping for your business saves you time as well as money. We save you money as we perform services at a fraction of the cost of an accountant. Time is saved as you are not spending hours a month dealing with the administration of the books of accounts of your business, time that could be better served investing in your business and/or your family. Look at it this way, as a nurse deals with the day to day issues of his/her patients so does a bookkeeper. The accountant/doctors are the big picture people, the diagnosticians for your life or the life of your business. .

Bookkeepers are professionals just as much as accountants are. A good bookkeeper is as much a necessary member of your professional advisor's team as is your accountant, lawyer and marketing specialist. Properly trained bookkeepers will have a similar knowledge base as your accountant in GAAP as well as tax issues, or they should. GAAP is generally accepted accounting principles, and it is the standard by which a bookkeeper and an accountant use to compile prepare and present financial data for small business enterprises.

In conclusion a good bookkeeper will partner with your CA/CGA/CPA to assist you in managing the financial affairs of your business. This mutually beneficial symbiotic relationship is just one of the keys to success of your business, a success that all parties are engaged and encouraged to facilitate.

When you begin doing a company's taxes, it is going to incredibly tempting to do everything for that business, including what an accountant does. Doing all of the Accountant-Type work as well as the bookkeeping work could be a big mistake, especially if you've never done it before or taken any classes required to become a CPA. There are a whole lot of issues that CPA's can deal with that bookkeepers aren't necessarily equipped to deal with. My recommendation when it comes to doing the filing the Tax Paperwork – whether monthly, quarterly, or annually – is to let an accountant do it. They have the licensing and the experience. They also know where the extra write-offs are and are not.

Additionally, if you're working with an accountant who referred you to their clients, you don't want to piss that accountant off by taking work from them...especially since that accountant will have other clients they can refer to you. If you recommend your clients to the accountant you're working with, and you openly encourage the accountant's existing clients to go back to the accountant, the accountant will most likely reward you by referring you to other future clients. So, if you want what's best for your business, let accountants do the accountant work, and you stick to the bookkeeping work.

Not to mention – if you mess up, you are the one who will have to suffer the consequences. You will be the one that has to deal with the IRS, and an angry business owner. Truly, if you want to keep your clients happy, don't do the accounting. Stick to the bookkeeping.

Still, there are going to be clients who are going to push you to do everything for them. If that is the case, and you really believe you can handle dealing with the IRS for that client, then feel free to do so. However, it will always be our recommendation that you let an accountant do it simply because your client is not only client. Your accountant can be your client too.

What an Accountant will Expect From You Before Doing a Company's Taxes:

Here's a list of items Accountants commonly ask for from business owners:

Personal Income Tax Returns:

- A copy of your prior year tax return (if using a new tax preparer or CPA)

Income:

- 1099's (Interest, Retirement, IRA distributions, Pensions, Social Security, Unemployment, Dividends, Stock/Bond Sales, State Income Tax Refund, etc.)
- W-2 forms (wages)

Expenses:

- Educator expenses
- Tuition
- Health savings account deposits
- Child care expenses, including name and Tax ID # of Child Care Provider
- Moving expenses
- Student loan interest
- Schedule A - 1098-Mortgage Interest Statement, property taxes, medical & dental expenses, motor vehicle taxes (copy of DMV bills), both cash and non-cash donations (include name of charity and amount or value of donation), un-reimbursed employee expenses, and tax preparation fees (for 2008 returns).
- If you purchased a home in 2009, provide a copy of your HUD-1 or closing statement.

Business Income Tax Returns/Schedule C:

- A copy of your prior year business tax return (if using a new tax preparer or CPA)
- All 1099-Misc's received as an Independent Contractor, Partnership or LLC
- Copies of all 1099s/1096 distributed to independent contractors you PAID
- W-2 & W-3 forms and Quarterly Payroll reports for wages PAID by your business
- Payroll Summary for the year
- Any other Quarterly Tax reports (Sales & Use tax, etc.)
- December's Yearend and January's current bank statements & reconciliation reports
- The Petty Cash or Cash on Hand balance and reconciliation report
- Credit Card statements and total finance charges for the year
- List of Inventory and Assets, including any NEWLY purchased assets

- Mileage records

- Home business office information (Total Sq. footage of home & of the home office, mortgage payments or rent, annual insurance and utility costs)

- A detailed printout of any draws, investments or payroll information on partners or shareholders

- Health insurance paid by the company for the owners/partners

- Year End financial statements: Balance Sheet, Profit and Loss Statement & Trial Balance

- A copy or backup of the company's automated accounting data file if you use one (QuickBooks, Peach Tree, MYOB, etc.)

- If you haven't recorded your business transactions throughout the year, provide copies of the entire year's bank and credit card statements.

This list is not intended to be "all inclusive", but rather a guide or quick reference to the forms and documents most commonly requested by a tax preparer or CPA. Many tax preparers and CPA's will provide you with a checklist of the documents needed to prepare your tax return. In addition, many use a questionnaire to obtain information and/or determine any changes that may have occurred over the prior year (your filing status [got married, divorced], dependents [had or adopted a child], if sold or purchased property [primary or secondary residence, rental property, stocks or bonds, etc.]).

Just a Thought: You may want to consider hiring an independent bookkeeper to record your accounting transactions, and reconcile your bank and credit card statements for the year. Accountants and CPA's often employ bookkeepers to handle this task for them and charge a much higher rate for the service than you'll pay an independent bookkeeper directly.

Chapter 9

Step 9: Getting Paid

FINAL ADVICE FROM LINDA A. HUNT:

Here is the step-by-step to creating your very own Client Planning System:

By Linda A. Hunt

(This excerpt is from Linda's blog entitled, "5 Steps to Create a Client Planning System that will let you Manage Your Clients on Autopilot")

"STEP 1: Get all important tax compliance dates from the federal and state governments.

STEP 2: Collect a list of Federal holidays – you need to know when banks are closed.

STEP 3: Create profile for each client and update every quarter. (Set aside time to do this. Calendar it or designate a staff member to do this.)

> NOTE: This is the most extensive and involved part of the Client Planning System. There are about 15 items. Once created, it is an IMMENSE timesaver and value provider!

STEP 4: Determine day or days to do client processing.

STEP 5: Create Client Calendars – processing, monthly, quarterly, annual and payroll.

Client Planning Systems give you peace of mind, more time – and definitely more freedom. This is what saved me from closing my doors for good…it allowed me to go from "Fed Up" to "Freedom". It can do the same for you!"

To read more, simply go to her blog at:
SumSolutions.com/Blog

Have you ever read the book "The 4-Hour Workweek" by Timothy Ferris. It is, without a doubt, one of my favorite business books of all times, and I recommend it to nearly everyone I talk business with. But the reason I bring it up today is that this book is creating a phenomenon of lifestyle changes across the country. People are working in offices less, and working from other areas in the world more. In fact, families are now taking year-long sabbaticals from their normal daily grinds in order to live the life of "digital nomads" – i.e. traveling and working from anywhere in the world.

What does that have to do with getting paid, you may wonder. Simple. This is a trend that is growing just as fast as Atkins or the South Beach Diet. Soon, it will be something everyone considers at least once, and possibly even tries (...including this author. Come August, I plan to take my own family on a year-long sabbatical around the world). It is a trend that you can hop on early by catering to these people before they move out of your market area. Here's what I mean...

A common mistake a lot of businesses make is not accepting every form of payment they can possibly accept. Obviously, everyone takes cash, although not everyone wants it. Money orders and checks are common in industries like the property management and rental industries, but not much else. Cash and credit card are common in the restaurant industry, but not checks or money orders. Checks, money orders and "creative financing" are used in the automotive industry, but again, it's rare that they accept anything else. But none of these payment methods are really feasible for someone who lives on the other side of the world. These are all payment options that often require being in a location in person, or having someone sign a slip of paper. To cater to people you never physically see – like virtual bookkeepers and their clients – you need to start accepting payments in other forms. *Because if you are the only person or company accepting the "other forms of payment" while your competition does not, you will dominate your industry in your area.*

Now think about what payment types the bookkeeping accepts. Most bookkeepers happily take cash, check, money order or cashier's check, but little else. The truth is, there are tons of other payment options you can take that will help you get paid when it's time for your clients to pay you.

<u>The truth is, the more types of payments you take, the more useful you'll be to your customers, and the more likely it is that you will get paid in a timely fashion.</u>

Now that I've got you thinking, here are some other payment options you need to consider accepting:

- **<u>PayPal</u>:** PayPal is quickly becoming one of the fastest, easiest, and least expensive ways to pay money for something. With it, you can instantly wire money to anyone anywhere in the world, for a small fee that *the receiver pays*. You can also receive credit card payments or bank debit transactions, and you would pay as little as 1.9% of the transaction, if you chose to allow your customers to pay via PayPal. This is completely an Internet-based payment option, and all you would have to do is put a link on your website that allows your customer to pay you, or send an invoice from PayPal to your client's email that they can pay. But, there are many other benefits to accepting PayPal. For one thing, the account is free to setup, and any payments received can be transferred directly to a preselected bank account. For another thing, you can get a debit card that accesses this account, and thus use PayPal as your second bank account. Honestly, there's no real reason *not* to use this payment option.

- **Credit Card:** There's a saying in Mary Kay that I've always found to be true. If a customer can use a credit card, they will often buy 25% more than if they had to pay cash. Why? Because a credit card can be paid back over time, and thus doesn't feel like real money when a customer uses it. Thus, credit cards create more impulsive purchases. The same goes for your clients. Many of them operate solely on credit to get by with the Day-to-Day expenses. So if you take a credit card, they will be more willing to use you for multiple things. In fact, you may find that they soon will start trying to use you for all of their daily Office Administration jobs, like running errands, going to the bank or post office, or even picking up office supplies. Yet many companies don't accept this form of payment because they usually have to pay a fee of 4-6% of a transaction. But think about it: Would you rather spend 4-6% to increase your sales by 25%, or would you rather not make that money at all? In my opinion, not taking credit cards is foolish. Not only can you increase your profits instantly, but you can also expand your local market area to a *global market area*. Therefore, if you aren't taking credit cards, you should be. I don't care if your industry's standard is not to take credit cards. Credit cards are basically "Creative Financing" for the average business. And since PayPal allows you to take credit cards and pay as little as 1.9% of the transaction, there's no excuse for *not* taking credit cards.

- **Creative Financing / 3 Monthly Payments:** One of the "effective tricks" that I've also seen Mary Kay consultants use is to accept postdated checks – an excellent type of creative financing. They would take one check for a portion of the total that they could cash instantly, and then another check that they would cash at a later date, thus allowing the customer time to earn the money or get it in the bank. By doing this, they are offering their clients credit without actually extending credit. They have the check in hand, and they can call the bank at any time to verify the funds are available before cashing it. And oddly enough, I never heard even one tale of a customer calling the bank to cancel the check ahead of time, especially because a cancelled check fee runs $18 to $30. Even if they close the account and try to run with the product, they would still have to pay the bank the bounced check fee if you went to cash that check.

Legally, anyone can take up to three postdated payments at once for any services or goods rendered – which is why when you settle with creditors, they will try to get you to make three monthly payments. You can have someone postdate those checks to when they would like to have them cashed and then not worry about trying to collect later...you have the money in hand. While I would not always recommend this as the "standard" for a payment, it is an excellent way to make sure you get the money for a product without dealing with credit cards.

- **Cashing a Check like a Debit Card:** Have you ever gone to a business, written a check, watched the check get validated, and then been handed back the check with the word "Void" written all over it. If you have, then you would already be familiar with this payment method. You see, much like a credit card is usually run through a machine to access the customer's funds, a similar machine exists that allows a customer's checking account to be accessed and a payment taken instantly and digitally. The check is validated and cashed right there at the time of the transaction, and the voided check is handed back to the customer as a valid receipt. The money is instantly deposited into your account, and there is no longer any need to worry that that check will bounce. Even if you don't accept this type of payment, you could suggest it to your clients when they accept payments because it acts just like taking a credit card.

- **Check Cashing by Phone:** One of the websites Timothy Ferris suggested in his book for processing payments is www.GreenByPhone.com. This site allows you to process checks over the phone and only pay a $5 transaction fee. While this may not seem like something you want to utilize, think about this. If you accept a payment for $100, then your transaction fee is 5% - less than many merchant services usually charge. For $200, you are paying 2.5% of the transaction. For $1,000, that is only 0.5%. And all you have to do is call in or go on the internet to process that check instantly. No longer will you have to hope that a check is valid or has enough funds. And this means that you can take a check from anyone in the world and instantly receive payment for goods or services. Why not use this service. It makes accepting checks a more secure transaction.

So think about it. Why not utilize these payment methods into your business? They are low cost options that can help you get paid or increase your sales instantly.

PAYMENT UP FRONT

When you start any bookkeeping job, it is always a good idea to get some form of payment up front. I know how difficult it is to ask, but you still need to do it. For one thing, it further cements the agreement that you and the new client made regarding your work for them. It is as effective as an Engagement Letter. For another, you have no idea how that client is going to pay you yet. They may be a flaky client, and you won't know until it's too late. By asking for a payment in advance, or a retainer, you will at least make money for the initial work that you do for them instead of doing a whole lot of work and getting nothing in return. Therefore, don't be afraid to ask for a check up front.

INVOICING YOUR CLIENT

After you receive the initial payment for getting to work, you are going to want to bill that client regularly. Explain to the client that until you establish a payment history with them, you will be billing them weekly, bi-weekly, or every time you reach $100. Then, once they've established that they pay regularly, you will begin billing them monthly. By doing so, you protect your time and your work. You don't want to invest a lot of time and then leave with that client owing you hundreds or even thousands of dollars.

A good rule of thumb for how often you are going to bill them is this: How many hours of work are you willing to do for free for a client? Because basically, if the client turns out to be a deadbeat and refuses to pay you, you're going to walk away with nothing. You could take them to small claims court, but that usually costs around $75 just to file the paperwork. You also have to take time out of your busy schedule to go to court and explain your case – and that often takes several hours. So, you will be out the hours of work you did for the client, the hours you will be doing for another client, and $75 for filing your paperwork. Therefore, I ask again: How many hours of work are you willing to do for free (or walk away from) for any new client? If you're willing to lose two weeks' worth of bookkeeping income, then that's how often you should bill a new client in the beginning. If it's a week, then bill once a week.

WHEN YOU'RE NOT GETTING PAID

One of the benefits of being a bookkeeper is that you cut the checks for a business. Every time you cut a check for a vendor, you should be cutting your own check at the same time. If a business owner says they can't afford to pay right then, then you need to firmly let them know that you are going to have to stop work for them until they can pay you. After all, your work is valuable and you have other clients. Make sure you still give them your invoice, and keep sending them reminders to pay you at least once a month. But, if after 90 days you still haven't received payment, then it's time to get firm. Call and ask them when they plan on making the payment, and if they brush you, you know it's time consider taking them to court.

LETTING CLIENTS GO

If you have clients that aren't paying, or you can't handle your workload and you don't want to hire more help, then the next thing you need to consider is letting some clients go. For a lot of bookkeepers, this will be difficult. Our job requires us to be people pleasers, and it pleases no one when you have to let someone go. But the whole point of this book is that you want to create a lifestyle. You want a life with less stress, less drama, more money, and more free time. The best way to make sure that you happens is to only keep the clients that are easy to work with and that are eager to pay you. Anyone who does not fit that bill needs to be let go. So, never be afraid to fire a client if things aren't going well or if you end up with too many other clients.

What to Give Back

If you have to fire a client, don't give them a reason NOT to pay you. Give them back all their paperwork and files, because it legally belongs to them. You don't want to show up in court against them and then have to defend your business practices.

On the flip side, the work you entered into QuickBooks is legally yours. So, the only file you have to give back in regards to QuickBooks is the last file (i.e. backup) that they paid you for. However, if you give them *everything* back, you then have a right to demand payment for everything in a court of law. Thus, in my opinion, when ending any relationship with a client, give back everything, including backup copies of any of their paperwork.

What to Keep

Even though you're giving back everything that legally belongs to them, there are still things that you should keep long after they're gone. For one thing, you want to keep any correspondence between the two of you. You never know what they're next bookkeeper might accuse you of, which could result in shocking accusations against you and your business, or a nerve-racking court battle. Or maybe you will want to sue them for money they never paid.

Either way, you are going to need copies of the correspondence between you to verify the exact tone of the relationship.

Also, <u>ALWAYS KEEP A COMPANY'S QUICKBOOKS BACKUP FILE</u>...Always!!!   Just because a relationship ends with a client – whether good or bad – at some point, that client just might come back to you and ask you to continue working on their books, or they may ask you to fix their books. Guaranteed, they will hire a bookkeeper after you at some point, and who knows what the next bookkeeper will do. They could totally embezzle or screw up the books, and you may end up with the only un-corrupted copy. Or, a client may not do anything with their books at all, and then a couple years down the road, call you asking for help in catching them up with the IRS. It's time like these were having a backup really comes in handy so that you *can* pick up where you left off.

Lastly, keep a record of their payment history. If you can't remember how they paid, it's handy to be able to look it up. It's also handy if they come back begging and they still owe you money.

Chapter 9

Step 10: When Your Company Gets Too Big

MORE TIPS FROM THE VIRTUAL OFFICE GODDESS AND THE VIRTUAL EVOLUTION MAGAZINE

- Create your own mailing postcards to save money. Set them up in MS Word using a 4x4 table in landscape, and use a light grey dotted outline around the cells for ease of cutting. Design them yourself, photocopy or print them on a standard 8.5"x11" sheet of 110# white or colored cardstock, and cut them apart by hand. Create only enough cards for your current mailing list; create/print 'lead' and 'follow-up' postcards at the same time and then mail them 4 weeks apart. Look for 'color copy' sales at the office supply to make your logo 'pop' on the cards. (You can print your own business cards, too.)

- Marketing and networking are the keys to getting clients. Have you decided what services you want to provide? Once you have done that, the next step is to determine WHO you want have as clients (target market). Then start sending out marketing materials, going to local networking meetings (try meetup.com for groups in your area), join your target market's forums and post answers to questions (this portrays you as an expert in your field). Place business cards and/or postcards in fish bowls and on bulletin boards everywhere you go. Experts say 80% of sales are made on the 5th-12th contact!

- Knowledge is power and eBooks/e-zines represent knowledge! As VAs, we need to 'stay on top' of what is going on that is directly related to the services we provide. Collect eBooks and e-zines on everything from small business information to marketing to trends in your target market(s) to the VA industry. Try reading all eBooks/e-zines one chapter/article at a time (as time allows). As you read each chapter/article, print the pages that have information that you may want to reference later, highlight the info on the printed page, and insert the pages into a notebook, tabbed by subject, for future use.

- Online Forums and Professional Associations can be valuable – BUT – don't pay for anything you don't have to and be choosy about where you spend your time. There are lots of professional associations, VA forums and target-market-specific forums available. Find groups that can help you keep up on industry specific skills and industry trends, as well as providing valuable networking opportunities. Local networking groups can also provide opportunities to 'fine-tune' your face-to-face networking skills, build up comfort with public speaking, and help you to 'brush up' your elevator speech.

HIRING HELP

At some point in your business, depending on aggressive you are in gathering clients, you may find that you want to hire help in running your bookkeeping business – especially during tax season when every client you've ever had calls you begging for help, as will your accountant colleagues. Either you will need to start turning people away, or you're going to need to get help. You can contact other bookkeepers you know to help you, train a local college student that will hopefully be taking accounting to help you, or you could hire a virtual assistant to help you with the extra workload. Additionally, you may want to use what I like to call "Digital Assistants," which are basically programs that will help you keep track of a wide variety of business information – both for your clients and for yourself. Either way, I have detailed out some places where you can find help, both digitally and virtually.

Digital Assistants

- Many people have heard of Virtual Assistants – a human assistant that helps you solely through the internet. They are easy to find and utilize at sites such as Elance.com and ODesk.com, and they cost a fraction of what it would cost you to pay someone to come into your office and physically gather information for you. Digital Assistants, on the other hand, are not people at all, but websites or programs that can track so much information for you, it's ridiculous. The point of these sites is not about making money or having to maintain constant upkeep. Once you have set them up, they will keep doing the work for you over and over.
  Here are some of my favorites:

  - **Pageonce.com** (Financial Information): With Pageonce, you can actually track the balances of just about anything you have a balance on. This includes utilities, mileage, other travel accounts, credit card balances, bank account balances, social networking sites, and even email – all in one place. For a bookkeeper, being able to track all of these items for your client will make you look like a Super

Bookkeeper. Plus, it can help you keep track of all your own balances without having to keep your own books current. (Because let's face it, when our day is done, we don't want to have to do our own bookkeeping as well.)

- **TripIt.com** (Travel Information): If you're still printing out confirmation sheets and putting them together in a folder when you go on a trip, you are *way behind* in technology. With TripIt, you can actually just forward all of your email confirmations to their site, and they will create an itinerary for you with confirmation numbers, maps, walking routes, and even weather conditions. This itinerary can then be forwarded to your email or phone, and you can also access it easily through the web. If you (or your clients) still love to have a paper copy when arriving at the airport counter – that's just fine – you can print it out before you go. Or you can print out an itinerary for your client and again look like an amazing bookkeeper.

- **Ping.fm** (SEO and Social Networking Help): Have you ever spent so much time updating all of your social networking sites that you begin to feel like you're just wasting your time? Well now with Ping.fm, you can update every single one of your social networking sites with just a few clicks of your mouse and a comment or two. In less than one minute, every site you're on can be updated with your current status, ad, recommended website, photos, etc. It's the fastest, easiest website I've found for promoting yourself and/or your business – and especially your business blog/website.

So, there are three of my favorites. Check them out; they're free. It can take a bit of time to set them up, but once you're done, they will save you time day after day and just make your life easier. Best thing is, many of these have free iPod / iPhone or Blackberry and Smartphone Apps as well to make your life even easier.

Hiring Help Locally

If you need an assistant, there are tons of places you can go locally. Here are a few to get you started:

1. **Local Colleges:** I like to post advertisements at the local college because college students always need money, and they have difficulty finding jobs that work around their schedules. Many have cars (at least on the West Coast) and can do a lot of pickup and delivery that you may not want to do. That takes no training at all.

    a. To place an ad at a local college, go to the office first. Most paperwork has to get a college's official stamp of approval, and then they will tell you where to post those ads. Sometimes there is a small fee for posting these ads, but generally, it's less than $20. The best type of college student to advertise for are accounting majors...they will be more than happy to learn whatever they can from you, and they can often turn the work experience into college credit that will help them fill some requirement for graduation or transfer.

2. **Temp Agencies:** It makes sense to hire a Temp Agency because then you don't have to deal with taxes, benefits, worker's comp, etc. The Temp Agency pays for all this and you simply pay them as if they are a subcontractor. The best thing is, you can place an order for exactly the type of help you are looking for, and you can make QuickBooks knowledge a must-have skill.

    a. Accountemps is a great place to go to find bookkeeping help.

3. **Other Bookkeepers:** I've posted ads online for bookkeeping help and been pleasantly surprised at the people that have replied. I've even learned a thing or two from one of the bookkeepers I've hired – namely, shortcuts I had not known about. Thus, you can post an advertisement, or contact your "competition" in the area to see if they want to build a coalition instead. It's a great way to get work when times are slow, and to get help when times are busy.

    a. LinkedIn is another great place to go in order to find bookkeeping help. You can post jobs there for free and get responses from all over the world.

4. **Websites Where Freelancers Look For Work:** There are a multitude of websites where you can go and find bookkeepers who are looking for Freelance work. I like Elance.com because many of the workers are from countries where the dollar is worth so much more money than the local currency. You can pay as little as $3-$5 an hour for data entry, and to someone in another country, that is so much more money than they would make with a local job. So what may be a pittance to you may be a small fortune to them because it will go so much further in that country. However, there is now a $10 charge to set up with Elance (which last time I checked, they said they give you credit for toward paying a contractor in order "to weed out the lookie-lous", but I still love working with this site.)

  a. Some good sites to hire virtual assistants include: Elance.com, ODesk.com, Freelancer.com, BidsCC.com

Rules for Your Employees

When you hire an assistant to do work for you, don't ever trust them completely. After all, embezzlers often become embezzler years after they've worked for the same company. This is your business, your license, and your reputation at stake, so you need to be vigilant when you work with an assistant. Here are a few things you should be doing when you hire help:

1. **Set Clear Deadlines**: If you don't set deadlines of when the work is done, you will get the old "I didn't know when you wanted it" excuse. One of the most stressful experiences you'll have is believing your assistant is working hard for you, only to find that they've done nothing and the project is due the next day. You now have to bust your behind to get the work caught up, and you may already have a full workload. Therefore, give your Assistants clear cut deadlines of when you need something back every times you assign a project...*every time.*

  a. A good deadline to set is to have them turn everything in by Monday, that way they have the weekend to work on it, and you can turn it into your client on the same day or on Tuesday.

2. **Be Specific in Your Instructions:** The more specific you are, the less likely they will be to let something slip through the cracks.

3. **Ask Them to Paraphrase What it is They Believe You Are Assigning to Them.** It's amazing how directions can be misinterpreted, both in person and through email. Have them repeat back what you are asking of them so that you can reduce some of these misunderstandings.

4. **Encourage Them to Ask Questions if They Don't Understand Something.** You'd be amazed at how people interpret things, or how nervous some people get if they believe you're going to get angry with them. They may not bring up a valid point simply because they don't want to upset you. By encouraging them to ask questions, you are keeping the doors of communication open, which can reduce mistakes later on.

5. **Double-check Their Work, and Make It Clear You Will Be Doing So:** Some people are just swindlers. Period. They will tell you they're doing work when they're not simply because you are not there watching everything they do. By making it clear that you will be double checking their work, and by the deadline you've already assigned, they will be sure to do their best work – as long as they think it means you might catch them goofing off. You can keep them in line by saying you will check their work...but then, actually do it, especially in the beginning, because again – this is your company and your reputation on the line.

6. **If You Email Them an Assignment, Make it Standard Procedure for Them to Acknowledge that Assignment.** With Spam filters and other email security, they may not always get the email. Or, they may be out of town for a couple days and have not communicated that to you, which may mean that they won't get the assignment back to you in time. You have to stay on top of everything, and one of the ways to do that is to have them acknowledge that they received the assignment and the deadline. Once you receive that confirmation, that's one less thing you have to worry about until you receive it back.

Now that you have a few ideas on how to work with an assistant – especially a Virtual or Flexible Assistant – remember to "give yourself time." Give yourself time to check their work before you turn it over to the client. It's always best to overestimate when you will have a project back then to underestimate and drive yourself batty over a deadline.

Chapter 10

Protecting Your Own Ass(ets)

SPOTLIGHT ON PROTECTING YOUR BOOKKEEPING BUSINESS

Many years ago I worked for an employer who owed the IRS $90k in unpaid payroll taxes. The debt was incurred for several reasons starting with a bookkeeper who did not know the proper procedures for dealing with payroll. She incorrectly recorded and reported wages and withholding taxes to both the Federal and State agencies for 4 quarters and on the annual payroll returns (Form 941's, California Form DE6's, W-2's/W-3, Form 940, California Form DE7). When she left the company, the next bookkeeper failed to pay the payroll tax deposits. On top of that, the Small Business Owner (SBO) wasn't particularly diligent about paying the company's debts even though he had an installment payment agreement in place with the IRS and was making monthly payments.

As a result, my first goal on the job was to tackle the IRS debt. After correcting the payroll records, I amended all payroll tax returns and wrote a letter of explanation to the IRS. We met with an IRS agent to review the corrections. During the ensuing meeting, the agent noticed my signature on the payroll tax returns*.

"Are you a signer on the company checking account?" the agent asked.

"No I'm not", I replied.

"Well, if you were a signer on the company's checking account, you could have been held liable for this company's payroll tax liability," the agent told me with just a hint of intimidation. **When it comes to payroll taxes, the IRS can** *'pierce the corporate veil'*. They will go after an owner's personal assets regardless of whether the company is organized as a Corporation, LLC, Partnership or sole proprietorship.

Can this be true?

Yes it can!

The <u>Internal Revenue Code Sec. 6672(a)</u> *"imposes a penalty against any person required to collect, truthfully account for, and pay over any tax imposed by the Code who willfully fails to collect, or truthfully account for and pay over the tax."* The code is used to recover payroll taxes from bookkeepers responsible for withholding and paying payroll taxes.

The Lesson

- If the bookkeeper has signature authority on any account – even one not involving payroll tax payments – it can put the bookkeeper in a position of being personally liable when their job includes paying other creditors. This is just one of many reasons that bookkeepers should not be a signer on your employer's or client's bank account.

- Further, the IRS is of the opinion that Payroll Taxes belong to the employees from which the money was withheld. The IRS is as serious as a heart attack about collecting back payroll taxes, and they have the authority to place a lien on and withdraw monies from any bank account with little more than a notice (and without a court order).

- Once an employer has an installment agreement in place with the IRS, it's imperative that each payroll return be filed on time and all payments made on or before the due date. The employer can not be a day late or a $1 short on any payroll taxes until the previous debt is completely paid off. If the tax deposit or payroll report is late, the installment agreement can be voided and the past due taxes become due immediately.

So what's a bookkeeper to do when the owner's out of town and payroll is due? Have another signer available in the owner's absence. Perhaps the company's CPA. If the owner uses a signature stamp *(not recommended)*, the CPA can keep the stamp to use in the owner's absence. This way, you have someone else available to review and approve any checks disbursed in the owner's absence without taking the liability upon yourself.

When a bookkeeper does have signature authority, another excellent option is to require a second signature on all checks. The second signature should belong to a supervisor or corporate officer with the duty of reviewing and signing *after* you've signed checks.

Therefore, whenever possible, choose your employer or your clients carefully. If you end up working for an employer who is far less than diligent about paying the company's debts, keep your resume current and your eyes open for another job.

Normally I sign tax reports and returns as the person who completed the forms. I had no idea the practice could potentially make me liable as an "officer" of the company had I also been a signer on the company's bank account. Another option is to complete the forms, but have an owner or officer sign the final return before submitting to the appropriate tax agency.

WHAT YOU SHOULD NEVER DO – <u>NEVER!!!</u>

When you sign with a client, it's guaranteed that your new client is going to want you to take as many problems as possible off of their hands. Problems in bookkeeping usually include opening mail, having to sign checks when they're not in the office, dealing with the IRS, Vendors' or Customers' communications, and many types of purchasing. They are going to look to you – their new bookkeeper – to help solve these problems they don't want to deal with. However, if you are not careful, or if something goes wrong with that client, you could be blamed and even sued for something you didn't even do. The more difficult you let things get, or the more complicated your systems are, the more a business owner is going to assume that you are hiding something. Trust me – I know what I'm talking about. Business owners often avoid taking responsibility for their actions, and the bookkeeper is the easiest person to blame. I've been blamed for everything from losing a client's passport to "not sending a payment" to a vendor. In many cases, the business owner is using me as a scapegoat so that they can buy more time to make a payment they can't afford. In those instances, I don't mind. But in other instances, where the business owner honestly can't remember if he did or did not do something, I will not take responsibility for his mistakes, and things can turn ugly.

Therefore, in the spirit of keeping your personal and professional reputation spotless, NEVER do the following things:

1. **Never Open the Bank Statements.** If you do open the bank statements and some fraudulent charges show up on the statement, you are going to be the first suspect. After all, you have a unique access to that company's money that other company employees don't. Even though embezzlers find very unique ways to steel, you will still be questioned first. By refusing to never accept sealed bank statements and by always insisting that someone else in the company open them right off the bat, you are protecting your personal and professional reputation from any kind of wild accusations.

2. **Never Sign IRS or Tax Paperwork.** As stated at the beginning of this chapter, anything you sign for the IRS, you can be held responsible for. You don't want to have to be the one that pays for a business owners (or their previous bookkeepers') mistakes. So, save yourself hundreds and even thousands of dollars of future potential fines.

3. **Never Sign Checks – NEVER!!!** I don't care if a small business owner insists that you go ahead and forge their name because they can't make it back to the office in time...don't do it. Just like with opening bank statements, forging checks leaves you open to all kinds of accusations. In some cases, if you were sued for a check you shouldn't have signed, you could be forced to pay that money back. So save your reputation and your pocket book, and don't sign checks. Insist that the owner sign them, and that whoever needs that check asap will just have to wait. (No one ever died from waiting 24 hours for a check.)

4. **Never Become a Second Signer on a Checking Account.** Just like with the IRS paperwork, or with signing checks, you can be held responsible for making sure those checks clear, or are repaid if they bounce. And again, if anything happens with that account, you will be Suspect # 1. You don't want to be held responsible or be blamed, so if you're asked to become a second signer on a bank account, say "No." Period.

5. **Never Pay for Items for Your Small Business Owners with Your Personal or Business Credit Cards.** In many cases, especially the ones where your clients are tight on money, you will be asked to go ahead and buy something from your own cash reserves, and then you will be "reimbursed on your next invoice." As tempting as this may be to do – don't. You don't want to get stuck "holding the bag" so to speak, when that relationship ends. Instead, do the research for them and send them an affiliate link to

the product they want. That way, they can get the product at a discount – with their credit card – and you can get an affiliate commission.

6. **Never Co-Sign Any Financial Documents.** I know – that's obvious, but I'm saying it anyway. Some bookkeepers get suckered into doing it.

There are a lot of other things you probably shouldn't do for your clients, but these are the only ones I can think of at this time. However, if you ever have any questions about whether you should or should not do something for a client, you can email me at ETBarton@OneHourBookkeeper.com, or pop on over to LinkedIn and join one of the many bookkeeping groups there. You can post your questions and have many different bookkeeping professionals answer you within a very short period of time.

Chapter 11

How to Supplement Your Income

SOME FINAL ADVICE FROM OUR OTHER BOOKKEEPING BUSINESS EXPERTS:

From Tina Gosnold: Confidence often comes with the first client. Show your clients the faster and easier ways of data processing, estimate how long it will take you to do their work, and then offer a flat monthly fee for your ongoing services.
And you know what they say..."Just do it!"

From Elena **Oppedisano**: One thing I think all new freelance bookkeepers are guilty of is not being able to say no and to take each and every client because they're just starting out and don't want to turn potential income away.
In the process - clients can wind up taking advantage of that. Once you've established yourself and have a good client base, you can set boundaries.

From CP Morey: "Experts say that while techniques such as surprise audits can be useful in detecting fraud, perhaps their most important benefit is in preventing fraud by creating a "perception of detection". Generally speaking, fraudsters only commit the crime if they believe they will not be caught. Since the threat of surprise audits increases employees' perception that fraud will be detected, they can be a strong deterrent for potential fraudsters."

ADDITIONAL SERVICES YOU CAN OFFER

For a lot of people, only offering bookkeeping services may not feel like you're doing enough work or making enough money. If you feel that way, or you would just like to know how to make even more money without too much work (after all, you're dream goal is to work less and make more, right?), then here are 31 Additional Ways to Supplement Your Bookkeeping Business's Income.

Office Administration / Virtual Assistant Services

Keep this in mind. Many of the services in this subsection can actually be delegated to an assistant (or several assistants) who make minimum wage or less. You can then charge a much higher fee and make extra money without actually doing any work.

1. **Copying...(Possibly with Free Delivery):** If you got the right printer, you are already set up for this. All you would have to do is collect the items that need to be copied from your clients, copy them, and then return them to your client either the next time you see them, or the next day depending on the service you offered. As far as pickup and delivery goes, you can either go yourself to your client's office, send your local college student assistant, or even FedEx / overnight them. Another really great thing to do is have your client email you the file that needs copying, and then deliver them. This will save you even more money and time, and the quality of the copy will be even better then feeding a file into your copy machine. (By this, I mean there will be fewer flaws and crooked columns that can happen with a feeder.)

   a. **Outsourcing Options:** If you want to make extra money but do less work, then you need to outsource whatever you can. You can outsource your copying by: 1) dropping the projects off at Office Depot or some other inexpensive copying service, then pick it up and drop it off for your client. Or 2) you could give it to your assistant to do and charge the higher hourly wage. You would make less money these ways, but you could still charge more per copy then the copy service and the pennies add up very quickly when it comes to copying.

b. To price your copies: Simply look at what the local Kinkos or copy shops are doing, and then price your copies around the same price, or a couple cents per copy cheaper. The more money you save your clients on this item, the more often they'll use your services.

c. If you don't know what type of printer to get, go back to Chapter 2 and read the subsection on stocking your office. We went into extreme detail on the best features for multi-function printers, and we even recommended a couple models.

2. **Scanning:** Again, with the right printer already in place, this would not take much extra to add the service. In fact, your printer could be doing all the work for you while you do other stuff. Simply collect the items that need to be scanned and put them in your MFC Printer's feeder. Then, you can email the file back to your client, and drop off or snail mail the original file (if you don't want to go to their office).

   a. Outsourcing Options: Again, you could 1) find a service that does this cheaply and then charge a higher rate, 2) give it to your assistant to do, or 3) have them send it to your eFax like RingCentral.

   b. To price this service: I would do a test run on your printer to see how fast it scans. *For 10 minutes*, scan as many pages as you can and then count up the final tally. Multiply that number by six to figure out the average number of pages per hour your printer can scan. Then, take your hourly administrative wage and divide it by the number of pages. This would give you a MINIMUM "Per Page" price for your scanning service. Then, you can either offer the service based on a "Per Page" fee, a "Package Cost" for every 10 pages, or a basic hourly administrative wage.

      i. An Example: If your printer ends up scanning 15 pages in 10 minutes, then your scanner would basically scan 90 pages per hour. If your hourly administrative wage was $15 an hour, you would divide $15 by 9 and you could easily charge $0.16 to $0.17 per page to get your hourly wage. That would be $1.60 to $1.70 for every 10 pages, or I could discount the 10 pages and sell the 10-Page Package for $1.50. While this may not seem like a lot of money to add to your service, you'd be amazed at how quickly the money can add up...especially when you scan reports of 100 pages or more.

ii. **Of course, you can always have your clients FAX you the file that needs to be scanned.** When they do that, it will go to your eFax, which creates the document for your automatically, and then you can send the file back to your client as if you spent all kinds of time scanning it. Just be careful if you do it this way because some eFax Packages have a per page or an hourly limit for whichever package you chose. As such, you could end up paying $0.10 a page for every page they sent you. Therefore, make certain you charge extra so that you can still make money on that without having done anything other than emailing it back to the client.

iii. **Notice I said a 10-Minute Test Period!** I did that for a reason. Many printers can scan really quickly for a short period of time, but when they scan for a longer period of time, they have to pause more often to cool down and recalibrate. They also have to send the file to a computer, which also slows down the scanning process. If you scanned for less than 10 minutes, you won't have an accurate scanning timeframe for your calculations. Ten minutes is the perfect timeframe because it forces your computer to go into a recalibration/cool down period, while simultaneously uploading the files to your computer. It will give you a better cost per hour then say a 6-minute test period.

3. **Digital File Backups:** This is basically the same thing as Scanning. You're just marketing the service in a different way. Some people see scanning as "I will have a digital file that I can change and manipulate" while a "Digital File Backup" would be seen as "I will have all my old files put into single PDF files I can store on any computer or hard drive and access digitally at any time." It's a very subtle difference in thought process.

   a. **Outsourcing Options:** Again, you could 1) find a service that does this cheaply and charge a higher rate, 2) give it to your assistant, or 3) have your client fax it to your eFax number.

4. **Off-Site Digital Computer Backups:**   One of my favorite websites is <u>Mozy.com</u> because of the backup service they provide. Quite simply, you can sign up for a free account and then download Mozy's backup program to your computer. Once it's set up, Mozy will create an Off-Site Digital Backup of any and all folders that you choose. You want just the Main C-Drive backed up? Done. Just the "Client" folder? Done. Or maybe you just want a backup of your Network's files. No problem. The only time you pay is if you need to access what's been backup due to faulty files or your computer crashing. The best part about Mozy is that it begins to do a backup any time you walk away from your computer for more than 5 minutes. That means, you can almost always have the most recent backup stored somewhere out of your office. Think about the possibilities. Your office burns down...you have a backup. Someone steals your laptop...you have a backup. Your toddler spills a huge glass of orange juice on your computer, frying the ever-lovin,' stupid-freakin' motherboard...you have a backup. (Can you tell I have some experience in the last one? ☺)

"But how does this make ME money?" you may be wondering. Quite simply – steal the idea. Offer your clients the opportunity to have their computer's hard drive backed up off-site (in your private office) for a small monthly fee of $10 or so. That's $120 a year extra for you. Multiply that by numerous clients and you could easily make a couple grand a year. Then, if something happens to their computers or offices, you can easily and quickly restore their files to any new computer they buy. This is an extremely handy service for your clients any time they "accidentally delete" a file and need to get it back. You just might have the most recent copy on file.

Of course, you will always keep and offer a backup of QuickBooks for free for your clients. This is just in addition to the QuickBooks backup.

a. **Outsourcing Options:** You could find another service to do this, but honestly, it doesn't take much extra time to do, and it would be most profitable if you did it yourself.

b. **How to do this service:** All you will need to do off-site digital backups is have an external hard-drive that can store a ton of information (around $75 for 500 GB at your local Target or Office Depot) and www.GoToMyPC.com which will allow you remote access to their files, hard drive, and possibly their network. Every time you access their computer, simply "copy" the files from their desktop to your hard drive by "dragging and dropping the files" into the different folders, and by the time you're finished with their bookkeeping, their computer will have been backed up and you just made your extra $10 a month for basically doing nothing but dragging and dropping.

5. **Transcription Services:** There are always businesses that need transcription services, and so far, many of them have not caught onto the fact that they can buy program which will take MUCH of the work out of the job – especially because there are still a lot of people that type with two fingers. So instead, those people would rather hire a person to do typing for them. This is something you can totally take advantage of. Whether or not you type fast is actually irrelevant. You see, you can buy a program called Dragon NaturallySpeaking made by Nuance for around $50 at Target, Office Depot and even Best Buy. This program can recognize and transcribe speech for you into all sorts of programs. All you would have to do is get a recording from your client of what they would like typed, and then play it for your computer's microphone.

a. **There is one problem however.** Dragon is not always 100% accurate. It can do all kinds of spelling errors if it doesn't recognize the words you are speaking. So be sure to speak clearly, spell check your document, and then do a thorough proofreading.

b. **Outsourcing Options:** Dragon is basically your outsourcing option. It's worth the one-time investment because it does all the work for you. However, you can give the document to your assistant to do a quick once-over, but I would still check the document myself once they've seen it.

c. **To price this additional service:** The easiest thing to do here is to charge either you're administrative hourly rate, or charge a per page fee. If you charge per page, you could actually offer a package deal and find yourself making a whole lot more than your hourly wage.

6. **Research:** While a lot of business owners may think they don't need you to do research for them, they may rethink this decision if you sell it right. If you point out that you can research what all their clients are doing both by going into their retail or office locations, as well as doing research online – especially at an affordable price – they will quickly rethink this decision. Also, put together a sample research report ahead of time that you can show your client, and they may quickly get excited about you doing work for them. You can also research similar business models in other towns across the country.

- **Outsourcing Options:** This is always something you can give to your assistant to do, but it would be a whole lot cheaper to hire an assistant from Elance.com or ODesk.com to do this. You could pay the assistant as little as $2 an hour, and then charge your client 10 times that amount.

   a. **Research Resources:** There are a ton of places to find research, but here are some of the ones I use the most;

      i. **Customer Demographics:** MapPoint is an excellent program for finding demographics on any location in the United States. The program is expensive to buy (around $250), but it's a one-time fee and you can give your client all kinds of demographic information on their local territory, as well as other areas. The U.S. Census is another good place (Census.gov).

      ii. **Financial Information:** Whenever I want to find out information about a corporation, I go to Yahoo! Finance and then the company's stock profile. From there, I look for the "SEC filing" and Voila. Tons of dollar amounts on various business elements.

      iii. **SurveyMonkey**: Sometimes, all a business really needs is a good survey to grow. With sites like SurveyMonkey, you can poll your Client's customers quickly and easily, and then download the corresponding reports.

      iv. **And of course, competitors websites.**

7. **Business Plans**: This is a perfect service to offer your small business clients. Why? Because a whole lot of businesses today start their companies without business plans. Without business plans in place, they will have problems getting financing because today, banks want a business plan as a standard part of the loan application. They want to know where the business is planning to grow and how they're planning to make money – especially in these risky times. However, by the time business owners really need the money (for expansion purposes), they're usually too busy to take the time to do them.

   a. **Outsourcing Options:** First off, there are tons of books in the market today that can help you make up a standard template business plan for any type of business. Second, this service goes hand in hand with the Research Service. Anytime you add in a chapter on what the Competition is doing, you instantly impress your clients. So in theory, you are offering two services for the price of one. (Really, you are just working more hours and charging a higher price.) Therefore, as far as outsourcing goes, use your college assistant or Elance assistant to do most of the research, MapPoint for demographics, books for a basic business plan template, and then just give it the old "once-over" to make sure it's up to your business's standards.

8. **Policy & Procedure Manuals:** This is basically the same thing as doing a business plan. You can find templates online or in books. Then, just customize them for your client. Once you have a Standard Policy & Procedure Manual typed up on your computer, it would take very little work to update it for the next client, and the next.

   a. **Pricing:** Since you will have this as a standard manual, you can either charge an hourly rate, and then make up an hourly rate, or else just offer a custom price. Price it too high, and you won't get any orders. Price it too low, and they may think it's a generic manual – even if it is. Also, don't forget to offer at least three pricing options for this manual – one for printed copies, one for digital copies, and one for bound copies. Each price has its own cost associated with it that you need to pass onto the client (like printing costs and binding costs).

Personally, when I do a "Package Product" that I sell to my clients (like a Policy & Procedures Manual), I take all the shortcuts I can. I may customize it by changing the header of a Word Document so the client's company name shows up on every page, or I might type it into Excel and link up all of the spaces that need the client's name inserted to the first page of the worksheet. This way, I can type the name once, and it fills in all the appropriate spaces. I don't need to remember where the name needs to go at all. Then I PDF and ship it.

9. **Collection Company:** If you're a bookkeeper, then you already have experience doing collections for companies. You've made phone calls, sent out invoices and statements, and probably even sent out threatening letters. As such, you already have experience in this field, and this is something you can offer to businesses outside of your bookkeeping services. You would offer to take over the collection policies, contact the delinquent customer in place of your client, instruct that the payment should be sent to you, then do all of the steps necessary to try and collect the money owed to the client. If the customer pays, then you could claim a percentage of the amount, which could be hefty. If the client didn't pay, then you could get the small claims paperwork for the client – making sure that all bases have been covered in the small claims process – and then you would collect your fee if the small business owner needed you to appear in court and testify to the steps you took to collect. Either way, it's an additional service you can offer to non-bookkeeping clients as well as your regular bookkeeping clients.

   a. **Outsourcing Options:** There isn't much you'd need to outsource with this step. QuickBooks has all of the standard forms you would need to go through the collection process, including forms of communication that gently and not-so-gently persuade the customer to pay. All you would have to do is enter the invoices into a related QuickBooks account for that client, and then create, print and send the forms. Then, you could use your College Student Assistant to stuff and mail envelopes, run to the courthouse for necessary small claims paperwork, and even run to the post office to send certain items as Certified Mail.

   b. **Just Make Sure** to check up on the laws that govern debt collectors. In many states, you are not allowed to call someone who owes money if they tell you,

"Don't call me." Also, there are often time limits on how long you can take to collect from someone – for example, in some states, you have one year from the last purchase to collect a bad debt. Finally, you can't really sue someone that's located out of state unless you – or your client – have an office address in that same state. Every state has different laws, but these are a few of the biggies that could harm your effectiveness as a debt collector.

10. **Office Organizer:** If you've worked in an office before, then you already have a good idea of what types of office organization systems work and don't work. Since a big part of your job is already clean your clients' messy bookkeeping desks, why not offer the service of organizing the rest of their office as well. Some people would be thrilled if you could get them organized, especially when professional organizers often charge $75 an hour and up. All you would have to do is buy a couple organizing books and read up on what systems truly work best for various environments and which ones don't.

   a. **Outsourcing Options:** You can order organizing products online at Office Depot and have them delivered to the Client's Office for free whenever an order is over $50. Then hire a college student to go in and put everything together and get the office organized. Just make sure to train the college student first so that they don't haphazardly throw away things that shouldn't be thrown away.

   b. **Pricing:** I would charge a minimum of the office administration bookkeeping fee, and an average of your bookkeeping fee if you're going to do it yourself. If you feel brave, try to get more out of it, or give them a "Package Price" for getting their whole office cleaned at once. Most likely, they'll go for the hourly rate in hopes that they'll save the largest amount of money.

11. **Notary Services:** Apparently, as of June 1st, 2010, Kinkos no longer offers notary services in their retail locations. This is bad news for a lot of people looking for notary services, but good news for you. I recently asked a local notary how much it had cost her to get her notary license, and she said "around $300." To get it, she just had to sign up for a very quick class, order some study books, take the test, and then do a few notaries as an intern. She said, in less than two months, she had her notary license and was able to

start promoting her own business. From then on, she was able to charge a minimum of $10 and up to $150 for her notary services. Imagine being able to offer that service to many of your clients.

a. **Outsourcing Options:** Technically, you could make a deal with someone who's already gone through the Notary classes and has started their own Mobile Notary Business and thus ask them to give you a commission on every client you bring to them. This way, you could avoid doing all the work, but still get paid.

b. **Something to Consider:** If you do decide to become a Notary, you could approach local Shipping Companies – like the UPS Store – and offer your notary services. That company would most likely be willing to hire you to come in for a few hours each day so that they could have an on-site notary. You could, in theory, use their office to do your work and potentially gain clients from people that walk into that store. It's a win-win for both of you.

c. **Other Potential Notary Clients:** There are always people who need notary services, but the companies that often use them the most are the companies related to real estate. Real Estate offices and Title Companies have to get paperwork notarized every time a property sells. You could offer your mobile notary services to them and make $150 each time they call you. The time frame usually takes less than an hour, and you do it at their site any time of day or afternoon. It's a very flexible and profitable service to offer.

12. **File Shredding:** I recently saw a Shredding Truck when I was leaving a client's office, and I realized – that is a perfect service to add to a Bookkeeping Business. You are already working with a client's confidential paperwork and information. Why not offer to shred and haul away their unwanted paperwork as well? After all, you wouldn't have to go out of your way, and it would be easy to do from home.

a. **Outsourcing Options:** College Student Assistant

b. **Pricing:** There are two basic packages you can offer. The first is a One-Time Shredding Fee, and the second is a Monthly Shredding Fee. Either way, you could offer them a box to fill, and then charge based on how full that box gets.

13. **Blogging:** One of the fastest growing marketing tools that businesses are using is Internet SEO (Search Engine Optimization). This means that a website needs to be constantly changing for it to come to the attention of Search Engines – like Google. The best way to utilize SEO is to constantly update your website with information. A blog is a perfect tool for that, but a lot of business owners don't have the time. You can offer to update their blog regularly for them with a quick article here and there about some industry standard.

    a. **Autoblogging:** Believe it or not, you don't even need to write anything to have a blog. Nowadays, there are tons of "Autoblogging" programs that will do the work of a blog for you. How it works is that every day, writers all over the world write a blog post which they then submit to "Article Submission" websites with the knowledge that other blogs and websites can and will pick those articles up and publish them on another blog *for free*. In exchange, the writers get a "backlink" from the site where the article is published to their site. By doing this, their own blog rankings and status goes up in the Search Engines' lists for free. A higher status equals more free traffic. Thus, backlinks are good, and you want them too if you want to get free traffic. There are a lot of programs out there that can help you get backlinks, just as there are a lot of programs that can help you Autoblog. Here are three autobloggers I recommend, not only because they will blog for you, but because they will help you make additional "commission" from sites like Clickbank, Amazon, eBay, etc. Not only that, these two products only have a one-time fee while others charge monthly. So, if you want to do a blog, then "Set it and Forget it", check out these three products: CBAutoBlogging (linked with Clickbank Only), AutoPress and Power AutoBlog. (These are all Clickbank items. I like Clickbank because its where all of the "Techno Geeks" go to sell their products and teach others how to "Steal from The Man." In other words, a lot of the products are creative "out of the box" items that can do amazing things for bloggers.)

    b. **Outsourcing Options:** If AutoBlogging is not for you, you can always outsource your blogging, there are many places online you can go. For starters, you can Google industry-related topics and then "Share" them on a blog – being sure to cite the original source and create a link back to that webpage. For another, you can find articles that are free to list on your site or that have a small fee for accessing and posting a particular number of articles per month. Finally, you could also hire someone who blogs regularly to create a certain number of blogs per month for you for really cheap, and then turn around and charge a higher price for them.

      i. Some Outsourcing Sites for Blogging: <u>Elance.com</u>, <u>ODesk.com</u> and <u>Freelance.com</u> (all good places to find jobs as well as hire for jobs), and <u>EzineArticles.com</u>.

14. Business Newsletters: Just like with blogging, creating newsletter can help keep any business fresh in a customer's mind. If you are already blogging for a client, why not offer to put all those blogs into a standard newsletter format once a month and then send then via email to all of your client's customers. It would take much more work then you're already doing, and most of the things you'd have to deal with would be issues relating to formatting.

    a. Outsourcing: Again, you could send these things to an assistant at <u>Elance.com</u>, <u>ODesk.com</u> or give it to your college assistant.

    b. Create a Template: I like to use PowerPoint whenever I do a business newsletter. It's easier to place things where you want them then Word is, and once you've got a template, all you have to do is drop in new articles where the previous ones were. That means less work for you, a branded look for your client, and something that is easy to sell to multiple customers.

15. Photoshop Services: If you know how to use <u>Photoshop</u>, there are a whole list of things you can do for your clients. For one thing, you can create graphic artwork. For another, you can create website backgrounds. You can also use this service to create letterhead, or customized photos for the newsletters you work for. The sky's the limit here. You just need to figure out what your client's need and offer your services. This is a very handy program to have, especially if you ever decide to do your internet marketing campaign or create your own graphic designs. For as little as $20, it's a worthwhile investment.

16. **Website Design:** Website Design has come a long way since the days it was originally created. No longer do you have to know all of the technical programming languages – like HTML and Java – nor do you have to know about the confusing world of website design programs – like Dreamweaver or FrontPage. Instead, you can download User-Friendly website design programs and then put together a website in under an hour. There are thousands of free background templates you can use for new sites, and then all you have to do is basically drag and drop information where you want it. The best part is, you will look like a genius to your clients.

a. **Outsourcing Options:** A couple of really great sources you can use are Yahoo!'s SiteBuilder, which is much like PowerPoint. (In other words, if you can operate PowerPoint or even Word, you can create a great website with Yahoo!) You simply insert text boxes for your "copy," and then drag pictures where you want them until it looks exactly how you want the website to look. The only thing is, the website would have to be hosted by Yahoo! (which is around $12 a month), but there are tons of benefits that come to being a Yahoo! Website. So, recommend to your customers that they pay the monthly fee, and use the handy dandy SiteBuilder to create a custom website fast.

   i. **For Blogging**: I prefer Wordpress (although Blogger is supposed to be good too). Again, there are thousands of free backgrounds (or themes) you can find from all over the internet, and thousands of "Plug-ins" that allow the blog site to do all sorts of automatic stuff – like recommend products from Amazon, advertise affiliate products, promote to Twitter / Facebook / LinkedIn, etc, and even create a store on the site. But keep in mind, if the client wants to make money with their blog, they need to host their blog at a site like JustHost.com (which is about $4 a month). This is to their benefit since they won't have the name of the blog site in their own url.

   ii. **Other Website Designers:** Again, I have to recommend Elance.com. You can find website designers from all over the world.

b. **Pricing:** It's really up to you. Website Designers often charge thousands of dollars for their services, but then they know all the programming lingo that you may not know. I tend to charge my customers a minimum setup fee to create the website (like $75 for setup), and that would include 3 to 5 pages of the website (usually the Home Page, About Page, Contact Page, a Product Page, and possibly a link to a Blog Page). Then, I charge an additional $10 a page. You see, the first few pages are usually the hardest because it takes the most work, but each additional page is usually easy because you "Copy" a page and then simply move things around. It's a great service to offer, especially if you are using a User-Friendly version of the program. (And a blogging site is even easier because all of the main pages are already set up – you just type in the copy for the new page.)

17. **Creating Files in Excel/PowerPoint/Word:** This is one of my most popular services, especially since I'm so dang fast at it. (Although the truth is, I'm not fast at it – I just have the right program, and I know where to find standard templates.) In every business, there is always going to be something that someone wants put into a document that they can customize or claim as their own. Why not offer this service and charge a flat fee for the service. Then, with a program like Nuance's PDF Converter Professional, you could actually scan whatever document(s) they want created and convert them into Word, Excel, PowerPoint, or even a Rich Text format.

    a. **Outsourcing Option:** If you don't want to get Nuance's PDF Converter Professional, which costs about $100 for the latest version, then the next best outsourcing tip would be to give the work to a college student or someone from Elance.com, but the truth is, you'll spend a whole LOT more money in the long run then if you just did it yourself – and the program can do a hundred pages in just a few minutes. It's really worth buying.

    b. **Pricing:** Charge either your basic hourly rate – whether administrative or your bookkeeping fee – or charge a per page fee.

    c. **Just Pay Attention to** the final converted report. Most times, the program transfers a scanned or faxed document without a problem, but there are times where the computer can't recognize the words or images and then it stores it as a mini-jpeg or it can misspell the word. Still, even with the mistakes that often popup, you still get a majority of work done instantly, and a spell check will often catch the mistakes...so read the end product carefully and do a spell check for the best final product.

18. **Defragging / Cleaning Registries / Speeding Up PCs:** A common problem with a lot of computers – and especially computers used for businesses – is that computers often slow down over time. When this happened to my computer, I asked a "Computer Nerd Friend" of mine why this was happening to me, especially since my computer was less than two years old. The way he explained it was this: "Your computer is automatically setup to download updates. Those updates are meant to protect the computer from viruses or program glitches, and they are like little bridges created to lead your computer to where the original programs were originally downloaded. When those updates install themselves onto your computer, they often destroy the bridges that came before them ...at least "*most*" of the bridges. Often, small remnants are left behind. Your computer tries to cross those bridges, but then realizes the bridges don't go the whole way, so they look for a new way. This process slows your computer down." (I think it made more sense when he explained it to me...) His resolution for getting rid of those bridges is to do a thorough cleaning on your computer. You can do this by cleaning the registry, defragging the hard drive, and even using programs that will "tweak" your system and make it run faster. If you can do this for your clients, they will think you are a genius...and most of what you need will already be listed in their Start Menu under "Accessories – System Tools."

   a. **Other Excellent Programs to Use:** CCleaner (with TWO C's) is a free program you can download from www.FileHippo.com or Piriform.com. Once you've installed it on a computer, you can clean both the computer hard drive and the computer's registry from one easy screen. You can also uninstall programs from their screen, and it cleans out the recycle bin. In less than 10 minutes, you're computer can be marginally faster. Another program I LOVE is Uniblue's Power Suite. It can clean your Registry, Speed up your computer by *a lot*, and then update any out-of-date drivers on your computer. When you use these two programs in conjunction, your computer speed increases by a lot. (And yes, I do use BOTH of these programs at the same time. It does no damage and they don't conflict with each other. In fact, they both find items to remove that the other doesn't find.)

b. **Another Quick Note:** For any programs that you do use to clean the registry or hard drive, make sure you run that program several times in a row to make the computer its absolute fastest. (Although, you only have to run PowerSuite once.)

19. **Secret Shopping:** Secret Shopping – for anyone who's never heard of it – is simply going into a retail location, approaching a random sales associate so that sales associate can try to sell to you, and then grading that sales associate on whether or not the experience lived up to company standards and if it was a positive or negative experience. You can either offer these services to your clients – basically spying on their employees – and hire out another college student assistant to secret shop them, or you can sign up with some Secret Shopping services to add an extra income to your business. Then, the secret shopping companies would send YOU out to their customers and clients, and you would fill out a questionnaire about how the people you shopped fared.

a. **A Few Sites I Recommend:** I've done Secret Shops with all of these companies, so I know that they pay well, consistently and are free to join. MarketForce.com, ATHPowerOnline.com, BeyondHello.com, MercSystems.com, and BareInternational.com.

20. **Binding Reports:** A lot of small businesses like to create professional looking reports for marketing. Take advantage of that by offering binding-with-deliver services for the same price as your local Kinkos. The fact that you are personal and have a relationship with your clientele pretty much guarantees that they will use your services, especially because you are already in their office...thus, you're just way more convenient.

a. **Outsourcing Options:** One of the shortcuts I take in binding reports is to take it to the nearest Office Depot copy center. They regularly charge less than $3 to do the binding (that includes all the materials and the labor), and then I charge $8 to my client, which is the standard price at Kinkos for binding. Thus, you are competitive with your competition, but you also deliver the product, so it gives you a leg up for doing nothing but picking up and dropping off.

21. **Travel Plans:** If you enjoy booking travel at all, then finding travel plans should be a great service you can offer. You would simply find the best deals possible for your clients, and then offer to book it for them. To make it even better, you can use your website and your affiliates to find the best deals possible, and make a nice commission every time you book a flight for your clients.

   a. **Outsourcing Options:** One of the best ways to find deals on airlines is to use www.Travelocity.com's Fare Watcher. You simply sign up for the free account, and then list the areas your client is hoping to fly to. Travelocity will instantly show you the cheapest prices, and then email you whenever the price drops an additional $25. Once you have an idea of which airlines are giving the cheapest flights, go to the airline's websites direct and see if they are offering the same price, and if they are offering any free deals when you book an airline – like a free hotel room stay or car rental. If they aren't, also check at CheapOAir.com to check if there are any other great prices.

22. **SEO (Search Engine Optimization):** Remember how in Chapter 3 I said how everyone these days is blogging. Blogging is changing the way that business is done because it's personal and it drives traffic to someone's business website. Well, SEO (or Search Engine Optimization) is one of the most useful tool for bloggers. SEO happens every time someone shares an article or blog on their social networking sites – like Facebook, Twitter and LinkedIn (three social networking sites you should already be on) – and then other people go and read the article. The tool increases website traffic by 1) directing people to the article and website/blog, and 2) the more hits or visits a website/blog receives, the higher Google and other search engines rank them, and the more prominent that site will become in Search results.

Here's another way to put it...You know how when you Google something you're looking for and Google gives you a list of one million websites that could potentially have your answer? The order of those websites is determined by the website's popularity

– or the number of visits that website receives. Every time you share a blog or article, people visit that article, and that website moves up a little higher in the search results. The higher the blog/website goes in the Search Results, the more people will visit that website.

Therefore, anyone who blogs or has a website will most likely be happy to receive SEO help. That means that you will be sharing their information with your "Online Friends" so that more people will start coming to their website. The more you share, the more of an expert you will appear to other clients. Obviously, you can charge an hourly rate for this service, and you probably won't need to work for one client for more than one hour a week, but it's a great service to offer. It only takes a few seconds to share a blog or website, and you can share multiple sites at once.

The key to SEO, however, is adding "online friends" to your social networking sites. Most sites have a fairly simple way to do this, and if you do offer this service, you are going to want to "Friend" as many people as you possibly can. The more "Friends" you have online the better for every client you give SEO services too.

a. **Outsourcing Options:** You can hire either an SEO expert from Elance.com or ODesk.com to do this for you, hire a college assistant, or you can use an Automated Program like or . But I would recommend doing it yourself and using Ping.fm to do the work for your (see below for details).

b. **Pricing:** Generally, you would charge an hourly administrative rate to do something like this since anyone can do it. However, you can also offer monthly package deals.

c. **To be effective at SEO, sign up at the following Social Networking Sites and add as many friends as you possibly can:**

   • Facebook.com: There is a limit of 5,000 friends, and then you have to switch to a Facebook Fan page. One Automated Tool you can use is Facebook Blaster. Another that allows for posting options and setting up fan pages is the FBCreator.

   • Twitter.com: There is a limit of 2,000 friends until you get 2,000 followers. Then, you can add 10% of your followers over and above that number max. Automated Programs that work well include: Twittenator and Twitter Blaster

<u>Pro</u>. They can be a bit confusing to set up, but once they're up, they work better than you could ever imagine.

- YouTube.com: If you or your clients have videos, you absolutely have to have an account with YouTube. This is the number one place for videos, and thus will drive a huge amount of traffic to a blog because of the videos you upload. If you wish to automate this site, try the <u>YouTube Friend Adder Elite</u> (to add friends) and then the <u>YouTube Friend Bomber</u> (to advertise the videos and thus the blog / business).

  - You can get the Friend Blaster Pro, Twitter Blaster Pro, and the YouTube Friend Bomber in a "Package deal" which will actually save you money. So if you are interested in those three, look for the package link.

  - Make Sure you go with the "Unlimited License" options, that way you can run sites for multiple clients for a one-time fee instead of having to buy the programs again and again.

- <u>LinkedIn.com</u>: Adding "Colleagues" on LinkedIn is a very slow pain in the butt, however, you can join as many groups as you want, and sharing with the groups allows you access to hundreds, thousands, and even hundreds of thousands of people (depending on the group) instantly.

- <u>Stumbleupon.com</u>: I have yet to come across a limit on friends yet, BUT, if you only "Submit articles" to Stumbleupon and you don't "Stumble" other articles, they will ban you from using their site. So make sure you "Stumble" articles regularly so you can post articles regularly. (Download the Stumbleupon toolbar in order to make Stumbling super fast and super easy. You'll be amazed at the great articles on there.)

- <u>Digg.com</u>: You can only share with 200 people at a time on Digg before they put you on a time-freeze. It's kind of a pain. But you can post an unlimited number of articles, and as far as I know, there's no limit on friends.

- <u>FriendFeed.com</u>: I have yet to come across a limit on friends yet.

- And any other social sites you can think of...

- **Finally, sign up for <u>www.Ping.fm</u>**, and then give Ping.fm all of those social networking sites' logins and passwords. That way, whenever you want to share someone's blog or article with your "friends" and "followers," you can just to go Ping and put in the web address (also known as "url) of the blog-article, and Ping will instantly put that information on all of the sites that you've given it passwords for. It's that simple and literally takes less than a second, but most people don't know about Ping, so they assume it could take at least an hour.

23. **Snail-Mail-to-Email Processing Services:** In Timothy Ferris's latest edition of "The 4-Hour Workweek," he recommends a website that processes mail for people that are travelling. The website is called GreenByPhone.com and the basic premise behind the website is that they receive and then scan mail for people who don't want to open and scan mail, or who can't because they're out of the country. Generally, what they do is receive the mail, and then scan the outside of the envelopes into a digital file their clients can access. They charge a monthly fee just to scan the outside of the envelopes, and then they charge extra when a client requests that a particular piece of mail be opened and then digitally scanned into their digital filing cabinet. I LOVE the thought behind this service because – quite frankly – I hate getting mail. I hate opening mail; I hate reading mail; I hate junk mail. I am an Email-Girl all the way. I literally open my personal mail once a week so that I can avoid it as much as possible. I would use the GreenByPhone service except that I don't want to have to pay $20 a letter to have them open my mail.

Having said that, you could offer this service and go one step further – open and scan the inside of the mail. The best way to do this would be to rent a P.O. Box at a local post office or a local mail store, and then encourage your clients to send their mail there. You or your assistant would then pick it up once or twice a week and fax it to your eFax, or you could just scan it. From there, you could easily email the files to your client, or access their computers remotely and save the files in various files on their hard drive. You would then take the original paperwork and put it in your "Go-Back" folder that you take to your client, and you would then file away.

    a. **Outsourcing Options:** This could easily be outsourced to a local college assistant to pick up, drop off, open and scan. They can even put the files onto each client's hard drive remotely through GoToMyPC.com.

WITH YOUR WEBSITE

Making money with your website is incredibly easy. You just have to be willing to put in the work. All of the steps for making money with your website were detailed out in Chapter 3. (So, go back to Chapter 3 and re-read it if you don't know how to do the following.) Here are some ways to make money with your virtual bookkeeping business's website:

24. **Place Google Adsense Ads on your Website.** If you blog, pepper the Adsense ads through your articles, and at the top and bottom of your articles. For websites, use Skyscraper ads down one side of your blog. (Finally, most bloggers agree that using Text Link Ads that blend into your website make more income than Image ads. Keep that in mind as you begin creating your custom Adsense ads.)

25. **Place ClickBank Ads on Your Website.** (The same advice that works for Google Adsense also works with ClickBank.)

26. **Market some of ClickBank's Digital products on your website to make up to 75% on various products.** There are tons of great digital files that relate to all kinds of businesses – including bookkeeping – so take some time and see if there are any products you don't mind advertising.

27. **Make Affiliate Income by Joining Sites like <u>Commission Junction</u> or <u>Esellerate</u> and putting Affiliate Links on Your Site.** (You can make money every time you place an order for your clients, and even when you place orders for yourself.)

28. **Create and Sell an EBook or Digital File that Your Customers Need or Should Have and sell it on your website with PayPal.** That Digital file could be anything from a Podcast to a video, or an eBook to an Excel Sheet that relates to a particular niche your bookkeeping company services. You can also do PDF files, PowerPoint files, or even

29. **Sell Any Complimentary Products on your website**, like a Business Starter Kit or a Bookkeeping Starter Kit that people might need. This could be QuickBooks, Word/Excel, a calculator, file folders, etc.

30. **Advertise Your Clients' Services on Your Website.** Since your clients know that you will be working with other clients – although they may not know who – you can offer them the opportunity to advertise their services on your website for a low monthly fee.

31. Guest Blog at Other Websites About Anything: Websites to check out for income include:

  a. Triond.com

  b. Helium.com

  c. Elance.com

  d. ODesk.com

CHAPTER 1

APPENDIX

Planning Your Business

MONEY GOAL WORKSHEET

How Much Money Do You Really Want to Make?

Right now, I am making $_____ per hour, $_____ per week, $_____ per month, and $_____ per year.

(For this next part, calculate a minimum of 30% higher than your current wage.) In order for me to feel comfortable making a living as an independent bookkeeper, I would want to make $_____ per hour, $_____ per week, $_____ per month, and $_____ per year.

Ideally, I would like to make $_____ per hour, $_____ per week, $_____ per month, and $_____ per year.

This would be my DREAM Job if I could make $_____ per Year, which is $_____ per month, $_____ per week, $_____ per day, and $_____ per hour. (Notice how this last one is reversed.)

How Much Time Do You Want to Spend Working?

Right now, I work _____ hours per day, _____ hours per week, _____ hours per month, and _____ hours per year.

To make the same amount of money I make currently, but charge my "new comfortable wage" (i.e. my currently hourly wage + a minimum of 30% or more), I would have to work _____ hours per day, _____ hours per week, _____ hours per month, and _____ hours per year.

To make a Comfortable living (i.e. the wage I would like to make to feel good about this career change), I would have to work _____ hours per day, _____ hours per week, _____ hours per month, and _____ hours per year.

To make my Ideal living, I would have to work a minimum of _____ hours per day, _____ hours per week, _____ hours per month, and _____ hours per year.

If this were my DREAM Job (...now, be outrageous! ☺), I would only have to work _____ hours per week, but I would still make $_____ per week.

MY MONEY PLAN

*"I am going to start this new business by working a minimum of _____ hours a week and <u>charging a minimum of</u> $_____ an hour (*a minimum of 30% more*) in order to make $_____ a week, which was approximately the same as my take home pay after taxes working at my "J.O.B."*

To make a more comfortable living, I will work _____ hours a week and charge $_____ an hour for a total of $_____ a week.

Ideally, I will work _____ hours a week and charge $_____ an hour for a take-home amount of $_____.

Eventually, I would like to build this business up enough to work _____ hours a week, but still earn $_____ per week."

CHAPTER 2
APPENDIX

Switching Offices

COMPARTMENTALIZING YOUR DAY

Various Bookkeeping Tasks	Time It Takes to Complete This Task Each Day:	CCD It – Will you Cut, Combine, or Delegate It?

NEW BOOKKEEPING BUSINESS SHOPPING AND TO-DO LIST
(2 Pages)

— **The DBA (Doing Business As) Name** (Usually less than $100)
  - Go to your local City Hall or Courthouse and fill out the DBA form.
  - File a classified ad in a local newspaper for 30 days announcing your DBA. $50)

— **The Business License** (Usually less than $100)
  - Go to your local City Hall or Courthouse and fill out the Business License Paperwork. (Based on Projected Income)

— **Employer Identification Number (EIN)**
  - Apply online at: IRS.gov/Businesses/Small/Article/0,,id=98350,00.html
  - Or by fax at: IRS.gov/Pub/IRS-PDF/fss4.pdf.

— **Get a Laptop** ($400 - $1,200)
  - CD/DVD Burner
  - SD Card Slot
  - Bluetooth Access
  - Wireless Access
  - Optional Features
    - 10-Key Keyboard ($100-$300 additional cost)
    - Or a 10-Key Keypad ($10-$40)
    - LightScribe Burner ($0-$50)
  - Our Recommendations: Anything HP, Sony or Toshiba
    - REMEMBER: If you get a 10-Key Keyboard laptop, invest in the warranty to cover the hinges. The extra weight on the computer makes the hinges easy to break.
    - We recommend you AVOID: Mini Netbooks, Acers, Compaqs, Gateways, IBMs and possibly Dells.

— **Multi-Function Printer with Printer, Scanner and Fax**
  - Laser Printers have higher printer and toner costs, but print faster and cleaner than inkjets. A Must-Have if you plan on making money selling Copies to your clients.
  - Inkjet's cost less for both the printer and the cartridges, but they print slower. However, it's cheaper for the color options.
  - Also – make sure the ink / toner cartridges aren't too expensive for when you have to replace them.
    - MUST-HAVES: Flatbed scanner, Heavy Duty Feed Scanner (minimum of 30 pages at time, preferably 50 pages or more at a time), and a Fax Machine.
    - Our Recommendations: Brothers with partially upright feeds. (No vertical feeds – they jam too much.)

— **eFax** – We like <u>RingCentral.com</u> ($10-$50 a month depending on account) or <u>eFax.com</u> ($13-$20 a month depending on account)

— **Add a Second Line to Your Cell Phone and Get Text Messaging Added** (if you don't have it already...usually adds about $10 to $20 to your bill per month).

  o **Must-have features for your phone:**
    ▪ High Definition Camera
    ▪ Slot for SD Card / Mini-SD Card or USB port for transferring pictures.
    ▪ Bluetooth Access
    ▪ Text Messaging
  o **Optional Features:** Internet and an MP3 Player
  o **Our Recommendations:** iPhone, Android Phones, or Blackberry

— **Shredder:** (Could potentially add an extra income to your business...$25-$300)

  o **Recommended features:** Should be able to shred CDs, DVDs, credit cards, staples, and paper clips.

— **Internet at Home** ($20-$50 a month)

— **A <u>PayPal</u> Account** (Free)

— **<u>QuickBooks</u>** (You can probably get this for FREE from your clients – although it never hurts to buy the latest version for about $150 on sale.)

— **A Car** (Or you can hire a college student with a car to do all your pickups and deliveries.)

— **A Plastic Box or Two for Hanging File Folders for the Trunk of Your Car** ($10)

— **Microsoft Office (or at least Word and Excel -** $100 if you get a student to buy it for you or you buy just Word and Excel – this is the average sale price, so wait for the price to go down if you wish; $200 if you buy the full non-student version.**)**

CHAPTER 4
APPENDIX

The Email Blast

To Send an Email Blast:

1) You must first begin by creating a email list in Excel.

    a. With Outlook, you simply open the Contacts, then click on File – Import & Export - Export to a File (and Next) – Microsoft Excel (1997-2003) and Next – select Contacts and Next – choose where you want to save it by selecting "Browse", the location (I like the Desktop because it's easy to find later), and rename it then OK to get back to the save screen – Next – then Finish.

    b. Once you have created the list, you will want to open it and remove any names of people and companies that you don't want to get your email blasts. This could be names like United Airlines, any credit card company contacts, people you think are jerks, etc. Also, remove any names that don't have emails.

2) Open up a Word Document and type up your email message exactly how you would like it to look. That means add your signature line.

3) When you're done, go to the Mailings Wizard and click on "Start Mail Merge". For 2007 Office it will look like this:

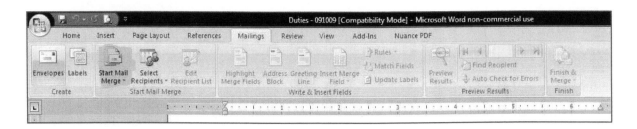

- For older versions, you want to find the Mail Merge Wizard. You may have to search the "Help" topics to know which menu item it's under.

4) From the Start Mail Merge menu, click on "Step by Step Mail Merge Wizard" (usually the last choice in the drop-down menu.

5) A sidebar will pop up that will walk you through the steps. It will look something like this:

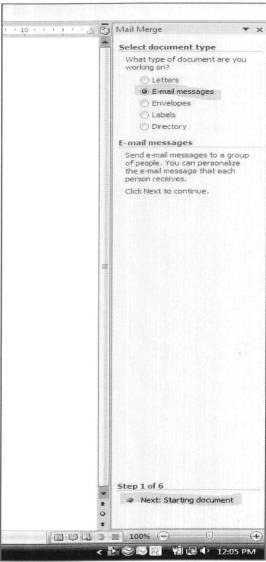

6) From this menu, just click "Email Messages" and click the "Next" step at the bottom. Go through each of the steps until you get to the final screen. As you can see, it's only 6 Steps.

7) At Step 3, you will be prompted to select your Excel Email list. You will "Browse" for it, then find it – hopefully on your Desktop. Once you open it, the Mail Merge Wizard will prompt you to choose a Worksheet Tab – and usually show you two. Pick the worksheet that has your contacts in it.

8) Next, you will be taken to a "Mail Merge Recipients List" where you will match up the headings from your Email List to your Word List. Most of the headings will be filled in correctly already. Just double check that there are actually emails where emails belong and names and companies where they belong before you press OK and continue onto the Next Step.

9) At Step 4, you will be able to add your address blocks and greeting lines. Make sure you choose at least the Greeting Line feature so that each email will be customized to the person receiving the email.

10) After you've completed "Step 6 - Complete the Merge", *the emails will be ready to go, but they will not be sent.* You have to actually click on "Finish and Merge" in the toolbar at the top. It will look like:

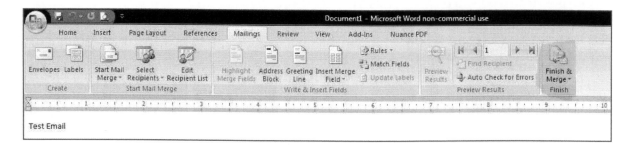

- Then click "Send E-Mail Messages."
- Once you click "Send," your computer will attempt to send it through your Microsoft Outlook Outbox. That means, if you have not set up your Outlook outbox before, you will need to set that up.

That's it – You're Done.

CHAPTER 5
APPENDIX

Bookkeeping Package

INTERVIEW CHECKLIST

1. WHAT TO WEAR: Dress in Casual Business Attire

2. YOUR SALES PITCH: Listen and let them talk. **The key is going to be how you can take all of their bookkeeping stress away, and how affordable you'll be as you're doing it.**

    a. **Remember to keep the interview confidential – no name dropping.**

3. THE TWO-WAY INTERVIEW – Searching for Your Ideal Client

    Remember to pay attention to:

    a. Who was doing their bookkeeping before you? If it was another bookkeeper, why is that bookkeeper no longer there?

    b. Are they going to insist that you be in the office whenever you do your bookkeeping, or will they trust you to do it "out-of-office"?

    c. Is this person an Ego-Maniac who is spending all of his time bragging about themself? Or are they talking about their business?

    d. Do they seem to care about your expertise? Are they letting you get a word in edgewise?

    e. How far behind are they in their bookkeeping?

    f. Where do they feel they need your help most of all?

    g. Are they behind with Vendors or the IRS? And if they are, how far behind?

    h. Do they appear to be someone who spends a lot of money on themselves, while their office is suffering?

    i. What is the condition of their office? Is it run down or shabby? Do you feel comfortable or uncomfortable?

    j. And finally, what is your overall feeling about this person? Do you get a good vibe or bad vibe from them?

YOUR BOOKKEEPING PACKAGE

1. **The Folder / Poly Envelopes with String Ties and Pockets for DVDs:**

2. **Full-Sheet White Labels (Non-Glossy):** On the labels, print your logo, billing address, phone number, fax number, website, and your email. You can also create a space to write the company's name, the owner's name, pickup/delivery dates, and the day(s) and time slots you will be doing work for them.

3. **A Pricing Sheet:** List all the services you offer and the various prices you charge.

4. **TWO New Client Services Checklist:** A checklist listing all the services you provide, and thus, the services they might want to order. Have them sign on a line at the bottom. Take one with you and leave one with the client.

5. **A Time-Saving Checklist:** Give them a list of things they can do to help save both of you time, and thus save them money. For example, switching their bank account to a bank that can download QuickBooks files; using their credit card or debit card as much as possible; using a second checking account instead of the main checking account, etc.

6. **A Mini-Mini Informative Brochure:** Make your brochure have information they actually want to know – like how to protect their bank accounts from embezzlers.

7. **A Letter of Engagement.** QuickBooks actually has a really good Sample Letter of Engagement that they let people use. You can find it at:

8. **Extra Business Cards.** Off the business owner a reward for referring your services to other small business clients. **Offer to refer business to them as well**

WARNING SIGNS THAT A CLIENT IS A BAD CLIENT

If you see any of these signs when meeting with a new client or when doing their book, realize that you are very likely in a bad situation and should get out as soon as you can in order to avoid wasting your time and money.

1. **The Vendors aren't getting paid in a timely manner.**

2. **The Employees' Paychecks are bouncing regularly.**

3. **The Company owes the IRS a large sum of money.**

4. **The Company has high balances on nearly all of their credit accounts.**

5. **Fewer and fewer customers purchasing from their company.**

6. **The business owner cares more about buying toys then buying business necessities.**

7. **The business owner is "just plain weird."**

8. **And finally...They tell you they fired their last bookkeeper for making ONE mistake.**

Sample Engagement Letter

http://accountant.intuit.com/practice_resources/articles/practice_development/downloads/q bservices_engagement_letter.doc

CHAPTER 6
APPENDIX

New Client Setup

THE "SETTING-UP-THE-CLIENT" CHECKLIST

1. SETUP REMOTE ACCESS TO THEIR COMPUTER – GoToMyPC.com

2. DISCUSS THE BANK ACCOUNT

   a. Does their Bank offer downloadable QuickBooks files?

   b. If no, will they be willing to switch to one that does?

   c. Do they have a separate checking account for your bank balance, and are they willing to keep one?

   d. Would they be willing to use a credit card for their purchases instead of a debit card?

   e. Do they have online banking and online bill pay?

3. FILING AND ORGANIZATION – Pack up their extra paperwork.

   a. Double check that they are okay with you taking the paperwork with them, or do they prefer to keep it in the office?

   b. Creating a Filing System That Works for You AND Your Client. Will it be:

      i. Digital Filing

      ii. Physical Filing

      iii. Do they prefer you to alphabetize by data entry date, month, or alphabetically?

4. YOUR CLIENT'S CHECKLIST

   a. When will you be doing their bookkeeping?

   b. When do you need their information emailed or faxed to you by?

   c. What information will you need from them?

CHAPTER 7
APPENDIX

Payroll Worksheets

PAYROLL SUMMARY SHEET

Name	Regular Hours	Over Time	Sick Pay	Vacation	Totals	Other (i.e. Bonuses/ Reimbursed Expenses)

Payroll Approved By: _____

TIME CARD WORKSHEET

Name		Monday	Tuesday	Wednes day	Thursd ay	Friday	Saturday	Sunday	Notes
	Time In								
	Time Out								
	Time In								
	Time Out								
	Time In								
	Time Out								
	Time In								
	Time Out								
	Time In								
	Time Out								
	Time In								
	Time Out								
	Time In								
	Time Out								
	Time In								
	Time Out								

Payroll Approved By: _____

CHAPTER 11

APPENDIX

Supplement Your Income

Checklist

ADDITIONAL SERVICES YOU CAN OFFER

Checklist and Links to Various Sites

Office Administration / Virtual Assistant Services

32. **Copying...(Possibly with Free Delivery):**   Office Depot, another other inexpensive copying service, or an assistant.

33. **Scanning:**   A service that does this cheaply, an assistant, or an eFax service like RingCentral.

34. **Digital File Backups:** A service that does this cheaply, an assistant, or an eFax service like RingCentral.

35. **Off-Site Digital Computer Backups:** Mozy.com, bring your own portable hard drives, or use www.GoToMyPC.com to access the computer.

36. **Transcription Services:** Dragon NaturallySpeaking

- **Research:** Elance.com or ODesk.com

    i. **Customer Demographics:** MapPoint and The U.S. Census (Census.gov).

    ii. **Financial Information:** Yahoo! Finance "SEC filings"

    iii. **Surveys:** SurveyMonkey.com

    iv. **And of course, competitors websites.** (Compete.com is a good place to start.)

- **Business Plans**: A college assistant, Elance.com or ODesk.com for research, MapPoint for demographics, and a basic business plan template.

37. **Policy & Procedure Manuals:** Templates online or in books.

38. **Collection Company:** QuickBooks

39. **Office Organizer:** Office Depot and a college student for installation.

40. **Notary Services:** National Notary Association (You could then approach local Shipping Companies, Real Estate offices, and Title Companies with your new service.

41. **File Shredding:** College Student Assistant

42. **Blogging:**

    a. **Autoblogging:** CBAutoBlogging, AutoPress and Power AutoBlog.

    b. **Outsourcing Options:**   Elance.com, ODesk.com, Freelance.com and EzineArticles.com.

43. **Business Newsletters:** Elance.com, ODesk.com or give it to your college assistant.

    a. **Create a Template:** PowerPoint

44. **Photoshop Services:** Photoshop

45. **Website Design:** Yahoo!'s SiteBuilder,

    a. **For Blogging**: JustHost.com (which is about $4 a month) and Wordpress. Blogger is also good, but I believe Wordpress is the best.

    b. **Other Website Designers:** Elance.com.

46. **Creating Files in Excel/PowerPoint/Word:** Nuance's PDF Converter Professional, a college student, Elance.com or ODesk.com

47. **Defragging / Cleaning Registries / Speeding Up PCs:** CCleaner and Uniblue's Power Suite.

48. **Secret Shopping:** MarketForce.com, ATHPowerOnline.com, BeyondHello.com, MercSystems.com, and BareInternational.com.

49. **Binding Reports:** Kinkos, Office Depot copy center, or another copy shop.

50. **Travel Plans:** www.Travelocity.com's Fare Watcher and CheapOAir.com.

51. **SEO (Search Engine Optimization):**

    a. **Outsourcing Options:** Elance.com or ODesk.com, and Ping.fm.

- Facebook.com: Facebook Blaster and FBCreator.
- Twitter.com: Twittenator and Twitter Blaster Pro.
- YouTube.com: YouTube Friend Adder Elite and YouTube Friend Bomber
- LinkedIn.com: Join the Groups to promote to more people instantly.
- Stumbleupon.com: Download the Stumbleupon toolbar.
- Digg.com:
- FriendFeed.com:
- And any other social sites you can think of...
- **Finally, sign up for www.Ping.fm,** for blasting promotional information.

52. **Snail-Mail-to-Email Processing Services:** GreenByPhone.com or a local college assistant, and GoToMyPC.com.

WITH YOUR WEBSITE

53. **Place Google Adsense Ads on your Website:** Google Adsense

54. **Place ClickBank Ads on Your Website:** Clickbank.com

55. **Market some of ClickBank's Digital products on your website to make up to 75% on various products.**

56. **Make Affiliate Income:** Commission Junction or Esellerate

57. **Create and Sell an EBook or Digital File that Your Customers Need or Should Have and sell it on your website with PayPal.**

58. **Sell Any Complimentary Products on your website**, like a Business Starter Kit or a Bookkeeping Starter Kit that people might need. This could be QuickBooks, Word/Excel, a calculator, file folders, etc.

59. **Advertise Your Clients' Services on Your Website for a low monthly fee.**

60. **Guest Blog at Other Websites About Anything:** Triond.com, Helium.com, Elance.com, ODesk.com

If you liked this book, please consider reviewing it.
Every review helps the author.

Plus, if you review the book, I will send you a free PDF Copy of "How to Save Money on Bookkeeping and Accounting." Simply go to one of the following sites to do the review:

http://OneHourBookkeeper.com/VBBookOnAmazon
http://OneHourBookkeeper.com/VBBookOnBN
http://OneHourBookkeeper.com/Smashwords
http://OneHourBookkeeper.com/Goodreads

Then email me at IReviewedTheVBBook@OneHourBookkeeper.com
and I will send you the PDF for free.

To Get Your Free Copy of
**"The One Hour Bookkeeper's
Top 10 Strategies for Getting Bookkeeping Clients"**
Go to:

http://onehourbookkeeper.com/wp-content/uploads/2010/06/Top-10-Strategies-for-Attracting-Bookkeeping-Clients.pdf

Also, for your free Printable Bonuses (or to print/see this Book in Color) go to:

http://onehourbookkeeper.com/our-ebooks/thank-you-for-your-preorder/
and enter the password: bookkeepersrule.

Other Products by E.T. Barton, Robin E. Davis or the OneHourBookkeeper.com website:

THE ONE HOUR BOOKKEEPING METHOD:
How To Do Your Books In One Hour Or Less

HOW TO START A LUCRATIVE VIRTUAL BOOKKEEPING BUSINESS:
A Step-by-Step Guide to Working Less and Making More
in the Bookkeeping Industry

HOW TO DO A YEAR'S WORTH OF BOOKKEEPING IN ONE DAY
A Step-by-Step Guide for Small Businesses

10 WAYS TO SAVE MONEY ON BOOKKEEPING & ACCOUNTING

DIARY OF A BAD, BAD BOOKKEEPER
A Cautionary Embezzlement Tale
for Small Business Owners Everywhere

Printed in Great Britain
by Amazon.co.uk, Ltd.,
Marston Gate.